MUSLIM AMERICAN YOUTH

QUALITATIVE STUDIES IN PSYCHOLOGY

This series showcases the power and possibility of qualitative work in psychology. Books feature detailed and vivid accounts of qualitative psychology research using a variety of methods, including participant observation and fieldwork, discursive and textual analyses, and critical cultural history. They probe vital issues of theory, implementation, interpretation, representation, and ethics that qualitative workers confront. The series mission is to enlarge and refine the repertoire of qualitative approaches to psychology.

GENERAL EDITORS

Michelle Fine and Jeanne Marecek

Everyday Courage: The Lives and Stories of Urban Teenagers
Niobe Way

Negotiating Consent in Psychotherapy
Patrick O'Neill

Flirting with Danger: Young Women's Reflections on Sexuality and Domination
Lynn M. Phillips

Voted Out: The Psychological Consequences of Anti-Gay Politics
Glenda M. Russell

Inner-City Kids: Adolescents Confront Life and Violence in an Urban Community
Alice McIntyre

From Subjects to Subjectivities: A Handbook of Interpretive and Participatory Methods
Edited by Deborah L. Tolman and Mary Brydon-Miller

Growing Up Girl: Psychosocial Explorations of Gender and Class
Valerie Walkerdine, Helen Lucey, and June Melody

Voicing Chicana Feminisms: Young Women Speak Out on Sexuality and Identity
Aida Hurtado

Situating Sadness: Women and Depression in Social Context
Edited by Janet M. Stoppard and Linda M. McMullen

Living Outside Mental Illness: Qualitative Studies of Recovery in Schizophrenia
Larry Davidson

Autism and the Myth of the Person Alone
Douglas Biklen, with Sue Rubin, Tito Rajarshi Mukhopadhyay, Lucy Blackman,
Larry Bissonnette, Alberto Frugone, Richard Attfield, and Jamie Burke

American Karma: Race, Culture, and Identity in the Indian Diaspora
Sunil Bhatia

Muslim American Youth: Understanding Hyphenated Identities through Multiple Methods
Selcuk R. Sirin and Michelle Fine

MUSLIM AMERICAN YOUTH

Understanding Hyphenated Identities
through Multiple Methods

**SELCUK R. SIRIN AND
MICHELLE FINE**

NEW YORK UNIVERSITY PRESS
New York and London

NEW YORK UNIVERSITY PRESS
New York and London
www.nyupress.org

Library of Congress Cataloging-in-Publication Data
Sirin, Selcuk R.
Muslim American youth : understanding hyphenated identities
through multiple methods / Selcuk R. Sirin and Michelle Fine.
p.   cm. — (Qualitative studies in psychology)
Include bibliographical references and index.
ISBN-13: 978-0-8147-4039-2 (cl : alk. paper)
ISBN-10: 0-8147-4039-1 (cl : alk. paper)
ISBN-13: 978-0-8147-4040-8 (pb : alk. paper)
ISBN-10: 0-8147-4040-5 (pb : alk. paper)
1. Muslims—United States—Ethnic identity. 2. Muslims—United
States—Psychology. 3. Muslims—United States—Social conditions.
4. Muslims—United States—Interviews. 5. Youth—United States—
Psychology. 6. Youth—United States—Social conditions. 7. Youth—
United States—Interviews. 8. Ethnicity—Research—United States
—Methodology. 9. Social psychology—Research—United States
—Methodology. 10. United States—Ethnic relations—Research—
Methodology.   I. Fine, Michelle. II. Title.
E184.M88S57 2008
305.6'97073—dc22   2008003616

New York University Press books are printed on acid-free paper,
and their binding materials are chosen for strength and durability.

Manufactured in the United States of America

c   10 9 8 7 6 5 4 3 2 1
p   10 9 8 7 6 5 4 3 2 1

■　　■　　■　　■　　■　　■　　■　　■　　■

For my love, Lauren Roger-Sirin, for challenging me to
follow my passion.　　　　　　　　　—Selcuk R. Sirin

To my guys, David, Sam, and Caleb, and my mother,
Rose, who surround me with love and laughter.
　　　　　　　　　　　　　　　—Michelle Fine

Contents

■ ■   ■   ■

Color maps appear as a group following p. 80.

Acknowledgments

First we thank the Muslim teens and young adults and their families who have been gracious and generous in giving us their time and trusting us with their experiences because they believe, as we do, that another story had to be told about Muslim youth in the United States after the attacks on September 11, 2001. We also specifically thank the young people who formed our advisory group who gave us their time and "expertise" and helped us frame the research questions in ways that "make sense" to their peers. All the names of young people in this book are pseudonyms.

When we think about the beginnings of our collaboration, we remember that Rhoda Unger was the first to insist that we meet. She knew well before either one of us did that important work could emerge at the intersection of our interests in youth, identity, global injustice, and research methodology. Without Rhoda's emails and phone calls, we would not even have realized we were neighbors and certainly would not have begun this collaboration and friendship.

This book simply would not have been possible without the assistance of our students, friends, and colleagues at New York University and the Graduate Center at City University of New York. The Mixed Methods Team at NYU, led by Madeeha Mir, deserves our gratitude. They recruited participants, ran focus groups, conducted interviews, and, more important, provided critical feedback for various versions of the manuscript. Madeeha has been an incredibly resourceful project director supervising a "fluid" team of undergraduate and graduate students at NYU. We are equally indebted to Mayida Zaal and Nida Bikmen from the Graduate Center. Mayida led one of our qualitative studies and made sure that we always clearly described Islam and the Muslims in our book. Nida helped us recruit respondents for our surveys, and she made sure that we understood the immigrant experience in the United States. Dalal Katciaficas, who joined our team as an undergraduate student, provided critical assistance with data collection and manuscript preparation. Madeeha, Mayida, and Dalal also deserve special credit for conducting the interviews that you will read in the following pages. We thank Kyung-hyun Kwon for entering the survey data and Donna Zanjanian for her time and enthusiasm for the project. We also thank our NYU students Christine Cheng, Natalie Zuckerman, Yana Kurchiko, and Kiren Shingadia, as well Selcuk's Montclair State University research assistants Mairaj Ahmed, Sabah Lodhi, and Sibyl Arbelo for their assistance at different phases of the project. We also thank Karen Jenkins and Susan Luke at NYU and Jared Becker at the Graduate Center for their assistance with our never-ending budgetary and office requests.

Several people reviewed our research materials and read our manuscript. In particular we would like to thank Kay Deaux, Shaun Wiley, and Nida Bikmen and all the members of the Immigration Study Group at the CUNY Graduate Center for giving us an excellent place to share our ideas and receive feedback. We also realize that we have learned much about methods, youth, politics, social identity theory, and mapping, and in that spirit we thank Aida Balsano, Thea Abu El-Haj, Valerie Futch, Jennifer Gieseking, Nilufer Gole, Maram Hallak, Rachel Hertz-Lazarowitz, Peter Hopkins, Cigdem Kagitcibasi, Michal Krumer-Nevo, Ethel Tobach, Maria Elena Torre, Eve Tuck, and the award-winning spoken-word artist Tahani Salah. We both are grateful that Carola read the manuscript and agreed to write the preface, as she inspired us throughout the project with her work. We also are very happy to have Jennifer Hammer as our editor at NYU Press. She had a clear idea about the book from the start and made sure that we wrote for both the scholarly community and the general public.

Selcuk would like to thank his graduate school mentors Mary Brabeck, Penny Hauser-Cram, Janet E. Helms, Jacqueline V. Lerner, and David Blustein. Because of their mentorship and support, I was able to take up the challenge to launch this project at a time when many others suggested that I simply shouldn't touch this subject until I was granted tenure. I also am grateful for my wonderful and caring colleagues at NYU's Department of Applied Psychology. I am particularly grateful to Joshua Aronson, Perry Halkitis, Bruce Homer, Gigliana Melzi, and of course, Carola Suárez-Orozco. They all heard a great deal about the project and did not hesitate to share their wisdom. I would also like to thank my friends Kathleen Ting, Ebru Erberber, and especially Derya Sirin, for their care and support as well as for their genuine interest in the work presented in this book. Finally, I would like to thank my parents, Ali and Yıldız Sirin. My father, a secular progressive intellectual in Turkey, continues to amaze me with his critical mind, and my mother, a devout Muslim herself, continues to show me that there is nothing special about being Muslim and to demand justice for all everywhere.

Financial support for the work came from New York University and the Foundation for Child Development, which awarded Selcuk the Young Scholar Award in 2006. Their support made it possible for Selcuk to focus fully on the research projects presented in this book over the past two years.

Finally, we both are grateful for our partners, Drs. Lauren Rogers-Sirin and David Surrey. They read the manuscript numerous times, provided specific feedback about our writing styles, and gave us specific suggestions (Lauren: make sure that chapter 2 is less didactic in tone; David: make sure you place these young people in a history of government-sponsored exclusion in the United States). Of course, beyond this specific help, we are grateful for their patience and support during the past several years while we were working on this project and the manuscript.

Foreword

Designated "Others": Young, Muslim, and American

Carola Suárez-Orozco

Today, there are well over a billion Muslims in the world. Many live in the diaspora in the West; an estimated 15 million live in Europe; and another 3 million to 6 million (depending on the source) live in North America, as well as the millions of others in other OECD (Organization for Economic Co-operation and Development) nations. As a fast-growing population in a precarious moment in history, there is an urgent need to understand the realities of the diasporic and highly diverse Muslim population.

When Americans think about Muslims after the attacks on September 11, 2001, all too often their associations are negative, blurring the enormous variations in the Muslim community regarding their countries of origin, language, class, phenotype, religious practices, and political views. More than ever before, there are substantial misrepresentations, misunderstandings, and misperceptions about Muslims. Today throughout most of the Western world, Muslims are "designated Others" serving as the targets of reflexive hatred. This response has been fueled and rationalized by, among other things, the wars in Iraq and Afghanistan, the post 9/11 attacks, the train bombings in Madrid and London, and the ongoing tensions created by the Israeli/Palestinian conflicts. As a result, daily representations in the news media depict the actions of a few, albeit with enormous repercussions for many.

While much has been written about the adult experience of Muslims in Western settings, very little systematic research has been conducted among Muslims of immigrant origin in the United States. Even less is known about the experiences of adolescents and young adults of this population. *Muslim American Youth: Understanding Hyphenated Identities through Multiple Methods* brings the reader into the worlds of Muslim American youth: a diverse group from many countries of origin, with varying levels of affluence, education, and adherence to religious and cultural practices. While on the surface they have little in common, these young Muslim Americans share the profound formative experience of coming of age in the United States at a time of tremendous tension and hypersurveillance.

This book tackles a number of complex issues: How do Muslim American youth contend with growing up under the shadow of suspicion in a climate of surveillance by federal authorities? How do they walk the tightrope of scrutiny by both their own communities of origin and the American populace they encounter in a variety of "contact zones?" How do young people respond and make sense of these tensions? How do they forge fragile collective identities that honor both their parents' culture of origin as well as their home in the United States? How can they develop a sense of belonging while coping with the dissonance of "excluded citizenship"? In what ways do young men and young women perceive similar forces at play but respond in different ways? In short, how do Muslim American immigrant origin youth respond to the "weight of the margin"?

Selcuk Sirin and Michelle Fine prove to be exceptionally adept at capturing the voices of these young people who develop in the context of the "toxicity of living amid feuding identities." They use innovative methodological strategies drawing on the strengths of a quantitative survey approach as well as extensive qualitative approaches. Their mixed-methods strategy includes survey scales of American identity and Muslim identity, social and cultural preferences, coping strategies, frequency of perceived discrimination, discrimination-related stress, psychological well-being, and collective self-esteem. In addition, they use the novel strategy of asking the youth to draw "identity maps" to illustrate the inner turmoil of many participants as well as the admirable coping strategies of others. Their focus groups and in-depth interviews capture the themes and convey the perceptions and experiences of these youth. Taken together, these triangulated strategies provide insight into the psychosocial experience of Muslim American youth as never before captured in such depth or with such acuity.

This superb, beautifully written, deeply insightful, and highly empathic book is a tremendous contribution to the fields of immigration studies, developmental psychology, and identity research. Furthermore, it will no doubt be a model for the essential future work that must be done with Muslim origin youth as well as other disparaged and marginalized youth growing up in the Diaspora in all too many settings in our conflict-ridden world.

1

■　■　■　■　■　■　■　■　■

Growing Up in the Shadow of Moral Exclusion

I guess you could say I live on the hyphen.

—Hadice, Syrian American, age seventeen

After the terrorist attacks of September 11, 2001, the identity negotiation of immigrant Muslim youth living in the United States became decidedly more challenging. Although their nation was under attack, *they* were suddenly perceived as a potential threat to U.S. safety. The number of hate crimes against Muslims increased seventeenfold in a single year (FBI 2002). Overnight, "they," Muslims, became the designated "others" who had to be watched, detained, and sometimes deported, in order to save "us." Although many were already well integrated into the fabric of mainstream U.S. society, they came to be regarded as a potential security risk. While learning to navigate through this historical period has been daunting for everyone, young Muslims confronted particular psychological challenges. Hadice, a high school student in one of our studies, explained that Muslim American youth found themselves living then on a very precarious "hyphen" (Fine 1994).

The contentious nature of living on the hyphen did not dissipate after the initial attacks; to the contrary, the moral exclusion continues today (Opotow 1990, 2005), heightened with every local or global terror news story and intensifying the surveillance on Muslims (Bryan 2005; Cainkar 2004). While a full 80 percent of Americans thought racial profiling was wrong before 9/11, nearly 60 percent now favor racial profiling "at least as long as it was directed at Arabs and Muslims" (Maira 2004, 219). Even more alarming for Muslims is the finding that after 9/11, 30 percent of their fellow Americans thought that Arab Americans should be interned (Gallup 2006; Swiney 2006). At this moment in this country, Muslim young people are both culturally grounded and nationally uprooted, transnational and homeless, and swirling psychologically in a contentious diaspora (Bhabha 2005; Levitt 2000). In the last half decade, they have learned that their standing in the United States is provisional, as Sarah Gualtieri would argue, "not-quite-white . . . not-quite-free . . . subject to 'the hyphen that never ends'" (2004, 65; from Suad 1999, 268).

At the same time, the experiences of Muslims in the United States after September 11 are not simply about alienation and struggle but also about their engagement with mainstream U.S. culture. Contrary to what many have predicted, Muslims in this country have not "given up" their American identity for the sake of their Muslim identity, despite the many pressures from Muslim fundamentalists and some Western intellectuals, who claim that one cannot be a good American and a good Muslim at the same time. As our data show in greater detail in chapter 5, the Muslim American youth that we studied for this book maintain in no uncertain terms that they experience no "clash" between their American and Muslim heritage. Unlike their counterparts in western Europe, Muslims in the United States are, in fact, well integrated into the mainstream culture. Integration does not require the erasure of culture but, rather, an engagement with a pluralistic society. According to the Pew Research Center's national polls on Muslims living in the Western world, although 81 percent of Muslims in Britain chose to identify themselves as "Muslim first," only 47 percent of U.S. Muslims felt the same way, which is similar to the percentage of U.S. Christians who identified themselves as "Christian first" (Pew Research Center 2007).[1] Furthermore, the majority of Muslims in the

United States, especially women, have a more positive outlook on their lives than do women in Muslim countries and are very concerned about Islamic extremism. Based on polls like these, the Pew report concluded that "the views of Muslim Americans resemble those of the general public in the United States" and depart from Muslims in Europe and elsewhere (Pew Research Center 2007, 4).

Perhaps because of these differences in integration policies, Muslims in the United States have one of the highest rates of citizenship, whereas most Muslims in Europe are still struggling to gain full citizenship, even when they have been legal employees for more than four decades. After France banned head scarves, Joan Wallach Scott made the obvious comparison: "If America permits the coexistence of many cultures and grants the legitimacy (and political influence) of hyphenated identities (Italian-American, Irish-American, African-American, etc.), France insists on assimilation to a singular culture, the embrace of a shared language, history and political ideology" (2007, B11) (see map 3). Thus in this book, in addition to describing many painful consequences of moral exclusion, we also offer many stories of sustained social integration to illustrate the U.S. context for Muslim immigrants (see color map 28). We indeed have much to learn from the experiences of young Muslims in the United States, about how we can start a new dialogue across the hyphens regarding culture, religion, and gender.

This book lays out a theoretical and empirical analysis of how first- and second-generation immigrant Muslim adolescents and young adults living in the United States have carved out *hyphenated selves* in the contemporary diaspora with creativity, resilience, and hope. Here *hyphenated selves* refers to their many identities, including their standings as Muslims and Americans, that are at once joined and separated by history, politics, geography, biography, longings, and losses. We explore here how these boys and girls, young men and women, make meaning of who they are amid the global conflict. Based on the attacks of 9/11, the global "war on terror," and the domestic passage of the Patriot Act, we consider what happens socially and psychologically when young people suddenly become "designated others" in their own nation.

Although we provide a broad perspective on Muslim American youth in this book, our specific focus is on those who are either first-generation immigrants who were born abroad or second-generation immigrants who were born in the United States to immigrant parents. Currently, they constitute more than two-thirds of Muslims in the United States. As chapter 2 explains, these Muslim youth are distinct from other immigrants in that most have grown up comfortably in working-, middle-, or upper-middle-class families. They also are different from the native-born, African American Muslims in the United States because they are immigrants, and moreover, many "appear" to be white (Deaux 2000). As their stories in this book reveal, most of these young people were born and raised in the United States by immigrant parents with a relatively stable sense of the United States as home.

The accelerated emergence of the "Muslim American" label as a new social identity during the past decade presents a unique example of identity as a socially constructed and historically bound phenomenon (Ashmore, Deaux, & McLaughlin-Volpe 2004; Cushman 1995; Gergen 1994). The popular media, government agencies, and, more important, Americans of Muslim origin have increasingly adopted the label "Muslim American" to refer to Americans of specific religious or Middle Eastern geographical origins (Grewal 2003). Since the 9/11 attacks, a growing number of Americans have joined both national and local organizations under the label of "Muslim American" (Leonard 2003). For example, the Council on American-Islamic Relations, a small organization with eight chapters in 2001, is now the largest Muslim organization in the country, with more than thirty-two chapters. Most college campuses have Muslim student organizations instead of ethnic (e.g., Arab Student clubs) or home country–based organizations (e.g., Pakistani Student Organization).

Immigrants from Muslim countries who previously were identified by their ethnicity and home culture have now come to be identified by their religion. Jamar, a nineteen-year-old man in our focus group, summarized this historical transition:

> Since 9/11, even more recent stuff . . . wars in Afghanistan, Iraq, and Lebanon strengthened the bond of a lot of Muslims and I think that's brought us more to the idea of being unified. It's not worth us being individuals right now because we need each other and we all get support from each other.

Another young man in our focus-group discussions observed how current social contexts shape the overarching "Muslim" identity:

> We really have to dislodge ourselves from the cultures that we came from and we should really become more Muslim as opposed to becoming, "I'm a Muslim Pakistani American" or "I'm a Muslim Syrian American." There are more intermarriages between different cultures. A lot of African American brothers, Muslims, marrying Arab women, Pakistani men marrying Arab women or Arab men marrying Pakistani women. That's one of the things happening nowadays and it's a positive thing.

Thus despite wide variations in race, ethnicity, social class, and country of origin, a fragile collective identity of "Muslim American" has emerged in a relatively short period of time. We set out to study this social and historical construction and the effects of this "marking off" on youth.

In this book we challenge ourselves and our readers to stay with the label "Muslim American," which we use only reluctantly. We constantly remind ourselves and our readers that we are not talking about a single, unitary, fixed identity; rather, we are proposing a fluid, and therefore a figuratively hyphenated, identity that is open to variation at both the group (e.g., racial, ethnic, linguistic, and religious diversity) and the individual levels. One of our participants, a young Pakistani woman, illustrated the problem with fixed, or "boxed" notions of identity in her map (map 1). She is delighted to be out of the box.

Beyond their shared background and experience of exclusion and surveillance, however, Muslims in the United States are extremely diverse. As we demonstrate in the next chapter, they come from more than one hundred different countries, belong to array of religious sects, and while some practice Islam, a majority consider themselves "just Muslims," using the label as a cultural, not a religious, category (Genesis Research Associates, 2006). The young Muslims discussed in this book attend public schools and religious schools (sometimes Islamic, sometimes not), wear religious garb and baseball caps, enjoy the riches of the upper middle class and know the life of the working poor, drink beer with their parents and stay away from proms. In many ways they are unique individuals like any other young group of young people living in this country. Despite their

Map 1. Noor, Female, Pakistani, Age 25

enormous variation, however, they are brought together by the fact they all come from Muslim immigrant households and they all are experiencing something very unusual in post-9/11 United States. As map 1 reveals, these young people do not want to be stereotyped in a box.

Our study of "Muslim American" identity, therefore, is not necessarily a study of ethnicity or religiosity but a study of an emerging collective identity influenced by not only ethnic and religious background but also the unique social and historic aftermath of September 11, 2001, in the United States. Accordingly, this book is a study of the psychological dynamics of working the hyphen by which young men and women negotiate their Muslim and American identities. Whereas we examine the role of religiosity and ethnicity as important background characteristics (Markstrom 1999), we concentrate on how a group of young people negotiates their Muslim and American identifications across contexts at a time when their group is under siege.

September 11: The Dawning of Moral Exclusion for Muslim Americans

In early September 2001, Muslims in the United States already were unusual immigrants. Relatively comfortable in the middle and upper middle classes of urban and suburban life, they spoke English, and many had enough social capital to feel as they belonged to U.S. society (see Deaux 2006; Suárez-Orozco & Suárez-Orozco 2001). They and their families were woven, albeit provisionally, into the fabric of American culture. As social theorists Sunil Bhatia and Anjail Ram (2001) argue, they implicitly rejected a notion of "national culture" and instead embraced identities that were "hybridized, diasporized and heterogeneous" (Bhatia & Ram 2001, 11). As the young artist Dorah wrote on her identity map, "America pre 9/11: integration while maintaining identity; building a community; human rights. . . . Much was still wrong with the world and America had its problems but there was still some semblance of sanity." And yet within a few years, national opinion polls indicated that 46 percent of adults in the United States agreed that "It is OK to detain Muslims indefinitely to protect 'us'" (Deane & Fears 2006). In the fall of 2001, these young people and their families were ejected from the national "we." Quoting Dorah, a twenty-year-old woman (see map 2), "American Post-9/11: fear, hysteria, bias, ignorance . . . goodbye Geneva conventions, hello war crimes, Abu-Ghraib. . . . The U.S. Muslim community cowers in fear." Their hyphenated identities were being perforated or, as one Muslim comedian put it, "We went to bed white on 9/10 and got up 'Muslim' on 9/11."

For the young people of this book and their families, 9/11 indeed marked a rupture in their identity negotiation process. They underwent two kinds of cultural disruption. First they were placed under suspicion, socially and psychologically, within the nation they considered "home." Suddenly cast "amongst those whose very presence is both 'over-looked' —in the double sense of social surveillance and psychic disavowal—and, at the same time, over-determined—psychically projected, made stereotypical and symptomatic" (Bhabha 2005, 13). Varied forms of discrimination and surveillance now penetrated their communities, social relationships, and self-consciousness. As one participant, Aisha, noted:

I remember that day [9/11/01] my father drove home a number of children from school, a religious school. As he dropped them at the elementary school, where they would meet their parents, the police were there, taking names, phone numbers, and licenses. That was frightening enough, but as we drove off we found ourselves in a big traffic jam and some woman screamed out of her car, "Why don't you just go home?" I knew then that everything was going to be different.

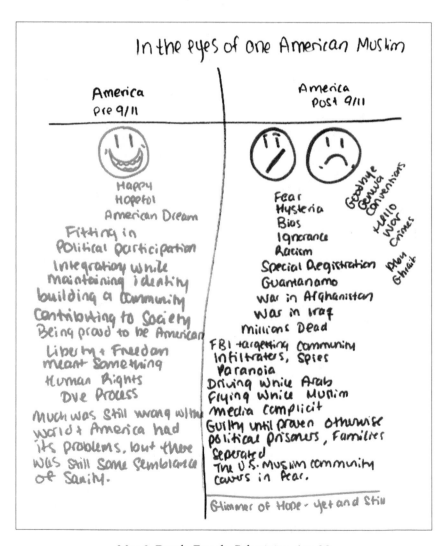

Map 2. Dorah, Female, Palestinian, Age 20

Second, their *other* community, the Islamic diaspora, was shaken as well. Their geographic imaginary, as Edward Said wrote (1979), was shattered. Despite their personal, often quite resilient, responses, these two geographic imaginaries of belonging had become destabilized. Saleed, age twenty-one, a U.S. citizen with family roots in Palestine, explained how throughout his life he had rejected the label of "American" and then found himself considered "American" on his first visit to Palestine.

> I realized that when I would walk into a room, they would all get up to shake my hand, and tell each other in Arabic "this is the American" and I'm like, wait a minute, what's going on here, and I realized that I don't really fit in there, or here, and *I guess to them, I'm American, over here I may choose not to be.*

Sociologist Rabab Abdulhadi, a Palestinian in New York, tells a similar story about looking for "home" on 9/11, running down the street.

> I am already bracing myself for the battle between "us" and "them." My hand instinctively goes to my neck to hide the chain with the Qu'ranic inscription my students . . . gave me before I left Cairo. Luckily I had forgotten to put it on today. My split lives are on a collision course again: I feel like such a traitor for passing. But wouldn't it be better to pass today? Do I want to identify with "them," though? Do I want to escape the collective guilt by association, the fate of my fellow Arabs, Palestinians and Muslims? Should I renege on my roots. There is this nagging feeling that I need some sort of a symbol to shout to the world who I am. I want so much to defy this monolithic image. (2003, 92)

She concludes her essay with questions of home.

> When 1,000 are detained and 5,000 are not so voluntarily interviewed, New York and indeed the United States, feels suspiciously like the occupied West Bank. But this is not the West Bank, where most Palestinians are subject to the same misery and terror and, as my mother would say, "Illi waqe 'ala nass waqe' aleina" [We are very alone here: our diasporic lives are fragmented]. *Our souls are split open. It is perhaps time to go home, but back home exists no more.* (2003, 100, italics added)

In this book we present a developmental story about this splitting: the story of immigrant Muslim youth living in the United States responding and resisting with Dorah's (see the previous map) "glimmer of hope—yet and still." We try to learn what happens when young people find their "souls split open" and "home exists no more."

Designating the "Other"

What is currently happening to Muslim people in general, and to young Muslims of this generation in the United States, is not historically unique in this country. These rhythms of ethnic marking and exclusion resonate with the story of our nation. As children exiled from a place they called home, these Muslim American youth walk in the historic psychological footprints of Native American youth plucked from their communities from the late 1800s through a substantial part of the 1900s; the confusion and rage of Japanese and Aleutian children and adolescents as they were forcibly removed from their homes and sent to internment camps, many in the desert; and youth displaced from homes and communities by "natural disasters" like Hurricane Katrina, who saw firsthand that their nation refused to heed their needs, allowing them to become internal refugees in their own country. Children, teens, and young adults displaced by government-sponsored or -enabled neglect, fear and/or hatred, can teach us much about the experience of and response to being an internal exile. We consider the acute and the cumulative psychological effects of government, media, and social exclusion, and the resultant internal exile on the psychology of immigrant adolescents in the diaspora (Deaux 2000; Deaux & Philogone 2001; Solis 2003).

For Muslims in the United States, the lines of "us" and "them" were drawn well before 9/11/2001. Edward Said first published *Orientalism* in 1978, and in his preface to the twenty-fifth-anniversary edition stated:

> Neither the term Orient nor the concept of the West has any ontological stability; each is made up of human effort, partly affirmation, partly identification of the Other. That these supreme fictions lend themselves easily to manipulation and the organization of collective passion has never been [more] evident than in our time, when the mobilizations of fear, hatred, disgust and resurgent self-pride and arrogance—much of it having to do

with Islam and the Arabs on one side, "we" Westerns on the other—are
very large-scale enterprises. (2003, xvii)

Before 9/11, life for Muslim Americans in the United States was already
marked by toxic social representations. However, when the World Trade
Center towers in New York fell, two cultural identities, "Muslim" and
"American," were reinvented. A vast, incredibly diverse amalgam of spontaneously suspect "Others" were thrust together under the categorical
umbrella "Muslim," abruptly evicted from the moral community of psychological citizenship in the United States (Nguyen 2005; Opotow 2004).
From that point forward, a series of legal, cultural, social, and psychological threats challenged Muslim Americans' status as citizens, their personal
security, psychological well-being, social relations, and public life (Nguyen
2005). Placed under watch in school, on the streets, at the mall, in the
library, and on the bus, young Muslim American men and women "suddenly found themselves the objects of intensified suspicion and surveillance" (Maira 2004, 219; also Foucault 1995). While the demonization
of Arabs and Muslims is no stranger to U.S. history, this "political racism"
following the attacks was intensified (Gualtieri 2004; Maira 2004), a moment captured by the mainstream media and in teen comics. In a Boon-
docks cartoon the teenager Huey announces: "African-Americans are now
only the third most hated group in America . . . right after Muslims and
the French." This is how Samira, an eighteen-year-old high school student
in one of our focus groups, recalled the immediate aftermath of September 11:

> My mom would tell me . . . just right after September 11th—if anybody
> asks you what you are, don't tell them. Lie. I was like, no, I'm not going
> to lie, you can't do that. . . . There was a lot of anxiety. It was really hard
> in the beginning, in the very, very beginning, because people were scared
> and they kind of wanted to point fingers at people and, you know, it was
> just such a shocking event, and they wanted somebody to blame. And
> there we were.

At the same time, an equally diverse group was congealed as "Americans." Huddling together under their flags, African Americans, Latinos,
Irish Americans, Asian Americans, Jewish Americans, firefighters, gays,

artists, police, investment bankers, and bodega workers joined as "Americans," brothers and sisters under attack. Beyond suspicion and wrapped in solidarity, patriotism and exclusion were conflated.

Each of these culturally defined, historically situated identities of "Muslim" and "American" represents a sharp reduction of political and social identities. Each identity was falsely represented as coherent within and sharply distinguished from the "Other" group. Identities were indeed frozen in place (Wimmer & Glick-Schiller 2003).

Muslim youth coming of age in the United States found themselves to be cast simultaneously as citizen and alien, terrorized and terrorist. Perched at the developmental doorway of adolescence and young adulthood, domestic and international lines separating and distinguishing "us" and "them." (see Gualtieri 2004; Maira 2004; Said 1979; Volpp 2002).

As boys and girls, young women and men, and Muslims, these young people became the canvas on which divergent political anxieties and fantasies about "Others" were projected (Levitt & Waters 2002; Rose 1996; Rumbaut 2002). In the very sinews of their adolescent and young adult lives, we document how cultural and gendered politics enter the body and soul of U.S. youth (see Rao & Walton 2004) and how they resist.

Shifting Grounds for Cultural Identities

In this book we try to understand how young people engage these shifting grounds of cultural identities (see Bhatia 2007; Bhatia & Ram 2001; Glick-Schiller & Fouron 1999; Sen 2004). For this analysis we assume that *cultural* identities are extremely fluid and not fixed, particularly when understood through a diaspora and particularly when embodied in youth (Hall 1997). That is, cultural identities are a changing aspect of young selves, flowing in interaction with other complex dimensions of selfhood, including gender, skin color, religiosity, community, passions, fears, material wealth, fantasies, and dreams (see map 26). As Amatrya Sen argued, "Culture *absolutely* does not sit still" (2004, 43, italics added).

So what happens to youth from cultures that are thrust into contestation? To investigate this question, our studies of Muslim Americans after 9/11 looked at how young people negotiate their multiple identities across contexts at a time of heightened visibility and surveillance by police, immigration authorities, media, peers, educators, strangers, families, and friends. Informed by the literature on critical race theory, the criminalization of youth of color, Islamophobia, and surveillance (Bell 1973; Bhatia 2007; Crenshaw 1995; Du Bois 1982; Nguyen 2005; Rizvi 2005; Ruck, Smith, & Fine 2004; Williams 1991), we designed a series of empirical studies to determine how young Muslim American boys and girls, young women and men, confront surveillance, fight these stereotypes, discover allies, and lead meaningful lives in a politically contentious moment. That is, we sought to uncover the individual and collective strategies by which young people embody and practice cultural identities in the face of explicit suspicion.

The Research Projects That Ground Us

To date, there are fewer than one hundred empirical studies published in English that focus on Muslim children or adolescents. The majority of these studies focus on Muslim children in Europe and Arabs in the Middle East, and only a handful of them were published after 2001 (e.g., Abu El-Haj 2005; Ajrouch 2004; Amer & Hovey 2005; Hallak & Quina 2004; Maira 2004; Peek 2003; Sarroub 2005). Moreover, these studies usually concentrate on gender-related issues in general and veiling in particular. When we reviewed the literature on immigrant youth, we found that the field of psychology had generally neglected immigrant child and youth experiences and almost never touched the dynamics of moral exclusion for youth development (Deaux 2006; Suárez-Orozco & Suárez-Orozco 2001). This is quite puzzling, since currently one in every five children growing up in the United States is a child of immigrants, a proportion that is projected to increase to one in three during the next three decades (Suárez-Orozco & Qin 2006). The 2000 U.S. Census reveals the diversity of immigrant youth. The population of foreign-born children under eighteen is 51 percent Latino and 26 percent Asian, and the U.S.-born cohort with at least one immigrant parent is 48 percent Latino and 24 percent Asian (U.S. Bureau of the Census, *March 2000 Current Population Survey*, published in 2002).

Given the lack of research on Muslim youth in general and on their global and historical contexts, we began our project as a research exploration. In addition to our broad critical understanding of culture, gender, and identity, our thinking about adolescent and young adult identities also was informed by theories of youth development in context (e.g., Lerner 2002), immigrant identity in general (e.g., Deaux 2006; Suarez-Orozco & Suarez-Orozco 2001), and moral exclusion and social justice (e.g., Lykes 2001; Lykes & Coquillon 2006; Opotow 2004).

Drawing from Bronfenbrenner's ecological perspective (1979) and Lerner's (2002) contextual approach to development, our research took a comprehensive view of identity negotiation processes within changing psychological, social, and historical contexts (Lerner 1991). As a result of these dynamic interactions among history, individuals, and their contexts, we were able to examine the inextricable connectedness between individuals and their cultural and historical contexts, studying identities-in-context rather than comparing identities across different contexts.

Drawing from Deaux's (2006) social identity approach, we tried to document how youth describe themselves and how they embody and perform their many identities when political or social conditions shift. This is particularly important for young people, who are embedded in times and places where their social identity is redefined by ongoing peer, familial, local, or global conflicts. Our empirical research also followed Lykes and others (Lykes 2002; Lykes & Coquillon 2006) as we documented how young people engage with political and psychological struggles of power and injustice. Thus, using a variety of methods, we describe the conditions under which young people under surveillance turn to despair and when young people mobilize a sense of possibility in difficult times.

With these conceptual approaches in mind, we gathered an advisory group of U.S.-based Muslim youth aged twelve to eighteen to help us craft the research. The group members were boys and girls who were both secular and religious, heads covered by *hijāb* and baseball caps, full-body black robes and facial coverings, attending public and Islamic schools, from the first or second generation, and from various nations and communities (see Fine, Tuck, & Zeller-Berkman 2007). We also told them who we are—a Turkish scholar who grew up Muslim (Selcuk) and the youngest daughter of immigrant Jewish parents from Poland (Michelle)—and that they, the members of our advisory group, were the experts on how Muslim American youth make sense of living in the United States (see Fine et al. 2004).

These girls and boys and young women and men helped us frame the research in ways that would answer our questions about culture and identity, surveillance and discrimination, coping and resilience, community and individual, gender roles and family roles, local and global politics. They described the "many bat mitzvahs I've been invited to since 9/11," and their often heated conversations with peers, strangers, police, airport attendants, family members, and educators. They told us to ask questions that would differentiate "Muslim" ways from "mainstream U.S." ways, even though they all were U.S. citizens and we knew these categories to be extremely problematic.

They asked us *not* to ask respondents about typical "risk" behaviors (drugs, smoking, sex, alcohol, disrespecting parents) because there would be no cultural validity for such items for this community; that is, of the group we surveyed there simply was nobody who used (or admitted using) illegal drugs and only a handful who drank alcohol. (Of course there were exceptions; see map 19.) We were instructed to "really find out what Muslim American teens want [non-Muslims] American kids to know about 'Muslims' in general and 'Muslim Americans' in particular." Following their suggestion, we added a set of open-ended questions to our survey (see appendix A). Our advisory group also suggested that at the end of the research, we collectively produce a video entitled *Islam for Dummies* to be shown in public schools throughout the nation. We were told both informally in focus groups and formally in pilot survey studies that typical research measures of ethnic identification, gender roles, and psychological well-being would probably not be the best tools to use with this population because they failed to account for important cultural differences between the mainstream U.S. population and the Muslim culture.

We knew that young people caught in political cross fires could help us shape the research in ways that would not reproduce common misrepresentations and could challenge the Orientalism that Said described so well. Indeed, we understood them to be the experts on the complexity of their experience (for work on youth participatory action research, see Fine et al. 2004).

With a lively advisory group; feminist, critical race, and postcolonial studies; and the developmental and social psychology literatures, we began to gather qualitative and quantitative material from both individuals and groups and young and older cohorts of varied ethnic and national origins.

We describe the details of our design and methods fully in appendix A, so here we only outline the various methods we used to study these cultural negotiations. Our project covered three areas of inquiry: the negotiation of hyphenated identities, experiences with discrimination and surveillance, and the way that Muslim American youth engage with the broader society. To investigate these areas, we used a multitude of research methods, including psychometrically validated paper-pencil surveys, open-ended questions, focus groups, individual interviews, and a novel technique known as *identity maps.*

A total of 204 respondents in two age groups completed our basic survey instruments. The younger group, ages twelve to eighteen, had seventy adolescents, thirty-two girls and thirty-eight boys. The majority of the younger cohort was born in the United States (84.1%), spoke English as a first language (77%), went to a public school (76.8%), and wore traditional dress, such as head scarves for women and skull caps for men (51.7%).

The older group, ages eighteen to twenty-five, was made up of seventy-seven young women and sixty young men. More than half the older group were born in the United States (58%); the majority were going or had gone to college; about half wore religious dress; and a majority of the women did not cover their hair (57%). The participants' most common native languages were English and Urdu, with Arabic, Farsi, Bengali, Turkish, and other languages also represented.

Both groups were similar in ethnic distribution and parental education to that of the larger U.S. Muslim immigrant population. In regard to ethnicity, they represented the general U.S. Muslim immigrant population, with a third from South Asian countries (e.g., Pakistan, India, and Bangladesh), another third from Arab countries, and the rest from predominantly Muslim countries, including Iran, Turkey, Bosnia, Kosovo, Central Asian countries such as Azerbaijan, and West Indian nations such as Trinidad, Colombia, and Puerto Rico. This ethnic distribution represents the general trends observed in the general U.S. Muslim population (Leonard 2003). The same is true for the education levels of these young people's parents. About two-thirds of their fathers (58% for the younger group and 62% for the older group) and more than one-third of their mothers (39% for the younger cohort and 40% for the older cohort) had a bachelor's or an advanced degree.

Our survey items and scales were designed to measure the *frequency of perceived discrimination* (Krieger & Sidney 1996), *discrimination-related stress* (SAFE-Short by Mena, Padilla, & Maldonado 1987), *"Muslim identity"* and *"mainstream U.S. identity"* (modified versions of the Collective Self-Esteem by Luhtanen & Crocker 1992), *social and cultural preferences* (AHIMSA by Unger et al. 2002), *psychological well-being* (taken from Achenbach, 1991), and *coping strategies* (COPE scale developed by Carver, Scheier, & Weintraub 1989). In addition, we gathered demographic information such as age, gender, and religious practice. All the measures presented in this book were pilot tested and modified in order to meet psychometric qualifications for both item reliability and construct validity. For more information about each of these measures and their psychometric qualifications, please see the following publications: for younger group surveys, Sirin & Fine 2007; for older group surveys, Sirin et al. in press; and for focus groups, Zaal, Salah, & Fine 2007.

In addition to surveys, we also gathered individual-level qualitative data using a novel technique we call "identity maps." Through these maps we tried to capture how young people creatively present their identities through drawings. The maps offered an additional opportunity to learn what goes on below the radar, that is, how identities are embedded in memory, fears, and emotions that might not be voiced in a focus group or survey.

Specifically, we gave the participants a blank sheet of paper and drawing materials (ink pens and colored markers), and the following instructions:

> Using the materials provided with this survey, please draw a map of your many ethnic, religious, and social identities. This should be an illustration of how you see yourself as a Muslim American person. You are free to design the map as you wish. You can use drawings, colors, symbols, words . . . whatever you need to reflect your multiple selves.

We gathered 137 maps, each matched to the survey data and, when possible, to the focus-group data. These maps are distributed throughout the book to illustrate key theoretical issues and to portray the ways in which youth embody their multiple identities.

A random subsample of the survey respondents, nineteen from the younger cohort and thirty from the older cohort, were asked to participate in one of eleven focus-group conversations about culture, politics, and gender for Muslim American youth today. Our objective with the focus groups was to research thoroughly how Muslim American youth speak with one another about being "American" and Muslim and about their relations with public authorities, schools, peers, families, and countries of origin (see Kitzinger & Wilkinson 2003; Wilkinson 1999). These sessions were an opportunity to gather group-level data on these discourses. These semistructured discussions were designed to encourage the participants' conversation about their multiple identities, their negotiation of the heightened surveillance since 9/11, and their relationships in the community and with family and friends. The focus groups were facilitated by Michelle and Selcuk or one of our research assistants, Mayida Zaal and Madeeha Mir. There was always at least one Muslim-identified focus-group facilitator. Most of the focus groups were either male or female, with one exception in which we had boys and girls together. Appendix C provides the focus-group protocols for each gender.

Finally, we also conducted six individual life history interviews with young people aged twelve to eighteen, selecting three girls or young women and three boys or young men from diverse family backgrounds in regard to ethnicity (including Palestinians, Pakistanis, and Turks) social class, and life experiences. In these sessions, presented in detail throughout the book, we listened for how culture, politics, and the stresses of adolescence, layered with suspicion and surveillance, played out in their lives. These interviews were full of variety, humor, worry, and resilience as these young people moved through their everyday lives in schools, families, with friends and educators, in the mall, the subway, and at home; listening to music; eating junk food; worrying about relatives and immigration and about tests, sports, and pressures; praying; balancing; trying to explain to their friends "why I don't date"; writing rap and hip-hop, playing soccer in *ḥijāb*; and pursuing a career as a "Muslim NBA player."

We used the same inclusion criteria for recruitment in each method. The participant had to identify himself or herself as "Muslim," currently had to live in the United States, had to speak English fluently, and either had to have moved to the United States before the age of ten (i.e., first-generation immigrant) or had to have been born in the United States to an immigrant family with at least one parent who was born outside the United States (i.e., second-generation immigrant).

Throughout this book, we draw on findings from these multiple studies in order to illustrate both theoretical and methodological points. In our discussions, we use "girls/boys" for the younger participants and "young men/women" for the older participants. For more detailed descriptions of the sample and research methodology as well as specific statistical findings, please refer to the original journal publications (Sirin et al. in press; Sirin & Fine 2007; Zaal, Salah, & Fine 2007), and for more information, consult appendices A through D.

Why This Book? Why Now?

By introducing the lives and concerns of Muslim Americans to the scholarship on immigrant minority youth, we hope to contribute to the developmental and social-psychological literature on identity negotiation. Muslim American youth usually are not included in the social science literature on adolescence. Furthermore, those studies that have been undertaken disproportionately investigate questions of presumed gendered oppression and *hijāb*. Muslim American youth's own complex and gendered negotiations of identities have not been studied.

We hope this book will map out, for immigrant studies and critical youth studies, a postcolonial and feminist interrogation of the process of youth developing hyphenated identities. That is, we are particularly interested in the practices and consequences of Muslim American adolescent identity negotiations at what we call the *hyphen* of multiple selves and cultures and at an acute moment of global conflict. We offer here a *gendered analysis* to understand not so much how gender is lived within Muslim communities but to reflect on how young women and men live at the hyphen as they embody, resist, and challenge the surveillance of the larger U.S. society and their more immediate community.

We hope this book will forecast the psychological, social, and health consequences and the innovative forms of resilience and resistance that young people generate in the face of *moral exclusion* (Opotow 1990) embedded in government policy, media representations, and social relations among intimates and strangers.

We also introduce here the delights and complexities of a *mixed-method design*—survey, interview, focus groups, identity maps, and history—for our understanding of the lives, identities, experiences of discrimination, and performances of resilience of Muslim American youth. We hope to model and advance our disciplinary thinking about how (not if) to work across the methodological hyphen.

Finally, and most ambitiously, we write with a political hope. In the tradition of W. E. B. Du Bois, Kurt Lewin, Carolyn Sherif, and Carolyn Payton, we join a legacy of psychologists who have stood with youth and communities under siege. The United States has historically shaped itself in relation to targeted ethnic groups for social isolation, misrepresentation, hypersurveillance, and oppression. Psychologists have a responsibility— and we have tools—that can be brought to bear witness and to speak the shameful consequences of social policies of exclusion.

Organizing the Evidence and the Argument

We organize our argument, and this volume, using an interdisciplinary theoretical framework that stitches together history, contemporary politics, and media studies with a deep social psychological and developmental consideration of life today for Muslim American youth. Chapter 2 begins by sketching the demographic and historical background of Muslims in the world in general and in the United States in particular. Here you will find both a brief history and the current demographic realities of Muslims and Muslim Americans. You also will find in this chapter empirical evidence for why we insist throughout this book that the label of "Muslim American" as an identity category should be applied cautiously owing to the diversity of the group.

Chapter 3 applies Susan Opotow's (2001) moral exclusion theory to the case of Muslim Americans and critically reviews U.S. history by focusing on legal decisions and media representations that have constructed and vilified "Others" marked as dangerous and in need of containment in the United States. We concentrate on the ways in which youth of these marginalized communities come to be the canvas on which moral panics and anxieties are projected.

Chapter 4 begins our journey through the data. Here we review how young Muslim Americans have experienced surveillance and discrimination in the United States since 9/11. In this chapter we describe how young Muslim Americans experience such moral exclusion from the perspective of adolescents coming of age, who embody and bear witness to varied forms of state, institutional, social, community, and interpersonal discriminations, including moral panics and negative social mirroring of themselves, their families, and their communities (for a detailed discussion of social mirroring, see Suárez-Orozco 2000).

Chapter 5 looks more closely at how young Muslim Americans negotiate hyphenated identities as we present empirical evidence for our hyphenated-selves approach. By means of surveys, maps, and focus-group materials, we show how these youth craft identities at the intersection of mainstream U.S. society and Muslim community, inventing integrated, parallel, and conflicting identities as Muslim Americans.

Chapter 6 moves from the intrasubjective work of hyphenated selves to an intersubjective analysis of how young people actually engage social relations at the hyphen. Here we focus on conversations held in focus groups about discrimination, to discern how and where self, others and the "differences" in between are negotiated. Through the focus-group materials, we connect our understanding of hyphenated selves as a psychological rendering of self-in-relation with an analysis of how Muslim American youth experience and perform in relation to other young people who report similar and different experiences with discrimination and respond with varied strategies ranging from silence to confrontation.

Chapter 7, the final chapter, shows how the notion of hyphenated selves can be applied to a broad swath of youth. Although we reflect on historic, theoretical, and methodological discussions throughout the text, in this chapter we consider how these theories and methods can be applied to a broader psychological project for studying any youth under siege. We also offer suggestions for future research on Muslim Americans and other groups of hyphenated youth using the materials presented in the book.

Throughout this book, we discuss our interviews with six Muslim teens so that readers can see them as actual young people and not simply as victims or survivors of surveillance but as teens developing in a tense, contradictory, and thrilling world of adolescence in the United States. Our hope is that after getting to know Aisha, Sahar, Yeliz, Ayyad, Taliya, and Masood, our readers will appreciate the diversity of Muslim youth in the United States—eating fast foods, praying, wearing iPods and *hijāb*, laughing, dreaming, getting involved in and avoiding social protest, keeping diaries, watching the news, growing sullen, crying, confiding in friends, studying for tests, thinking about fashion, and, like most youth, simply trying to create lives of meaning.

Our Hyphens: Who Are We?

We write as researchers and friends committed to positive youth development, critical theory, and a psychology for justice. To this work we bring very different biographies. Selcuk is a young developmental psychologist who was raised by Muslim parents in Turkey and moved to the United States as a young adult. Although my (Selcuk's) research and training is in identity development and quantitative psychology, I decided to focus my scholarly work on Muslim youth partly because of my own experience. While teaching undergraduates in Boston on the day of the 9/11 attacks, I felt for the first time the need to disclose my religious upbringing in a Muslim household in a faraway land. Before 9/11, nobody really cared that I grew up Muslim or that I am originally from a Muslim country. However, in class on 9/11, in Boston, I had to "come out." I had to answer questions about Islam and Muslims in general and my own history in particular in a way that I never had to do before. This was indeed the first time I realized that it was also my identity that was being renegotiated from that day forward. Now I am asked about Islam and Muslims all the time, and I no longer can keep that part of my identity to myself. Indeed, the attacks launched the process that culminated in a recent invitation to an international conference to present the "Muslim perspective." Of course, I do not know or claim to represent such a "perspective," which is a point I am compelled to disclaim in many things I say now, including in this book.

A new immigrant is always ready for shifting identity parameters for finding where he or she stands in relation, and in reaction, to the cultural and historical context. In that sense, 9/11 created yet another historical parameter for me, a new immigrant at the time. I found a way to begin to see more clearly than ever before how the meaning of one's identity is indeed a socially constructed phenomenon that changes dramatically with events that have nothing to do with one's own sense of self, events that force one to reckon with and/or embrace an often dormant identity. For me, studying Muslim American youth is therefore also a historical and cultural survey of the times in which we are living. In that sense, I see the study of Muslim youth, and this book, as an extension of that effort, not much different from the study of any other group of individuals whose identity is contested because of historical or cultural circumstances.

Michelle is a fiftysomething social psychologist, raised by Jewish immigrant working-class parents at the moment in U.S. history that Karen Brodkin Sacks (1994) recognized as when "Jews became white." I (Michelle) was a child in the post–World War II era when social policy, GI benefits, funds for suburbanization, and small business ownership opened doors to that generation of (white) immigrants. While they may have appeared a bit too bedraggled and tattered to be fully American when they landed on Ellis Island, they were the raw material the Statue of Liberty was talking about. These were the immigrants who could prove the American dream to be true. After my parents and their cohort came through, the doors were shut again, and as immigrants came from the South, who were darker and poor, the policy context shriveled like an old flower.

My research projects are situated in schools and communities, in prisons and activist youth organizations. My methods range from large-scale surveys to ethnography, but almost all these projects are designed as participatory projects for studying social injustice. Collaborating with Selcuk has meant immersion in new ways of thinking about research, theory, practice, and the politics of youth development. At our hyphen lies this book and all that we have learned from each other and from the young people willing to trust us with their stories.

We both, then, are first- and second-generation immigrants who bring very different histories to the question of Muslim Americans in the post-9/11 United States and very distinct biographies to the question of feeling like an internal exile. In addition to biography and theoretical interests, we also bring together a curiosity about the interdisciplinary theorizing of youth and a commitment to multiple methods. That is, we work hard to understand how survey, focus groups, individual interviews, identity maps fit (and do not fit) together. In this volume you will see the bricolage of our lives, our thinking, our methods, our writings, and our hopes for future work.

We also must note one other area of our backgrounds that culminated in this collaboration, the fact that both of us are methodologists. Neither of us believes in "qualitative and quantitative camps" that have unnecessarily captured too much time and energy in psychology and other behavioral sciences. Both of us are interested in the methodological vitality of mixed methods. And yet, in our working together, we cannot help but recognize that our approaches to social inquiry are indeed shaped by methodological training and "tastes." Selcuk is a methodologist teaching statistics classes who before this project worked primarily with survey data using sophisticated statistical procedures (e.g., Sirin 2005b; Sirin & Rogers-Sirin 2004). Michelle, trained as a laboratory-based experimental social psychologist, is a methodologist teaching qualitative methods classes who has published books on qualitative data analysis and coedits a book series entitled Qualitative Studies in Psychology.

Yet, working across methods, as we have over the past five years, has enabled us to produce research we consider empirically valid and historically and culturally meaningful. More than ever, we believe that there is indeed no methodological justification to limit ourselves to a single, "fixed" methodology. We certainly could not have uncovered the themes, stories, and theoretical links presented in this book without working at the methodological hyphen.

With this book we hope to participate in conversations within cultural studies, youth studies, developmental and social psychology, and education about development and activism among youth under siege. We offer theoretical and research tools to document, and also stand with, these boys and girls, young women and men, as they tremble and thrive, split and integrate, laugh and despair, on the many hyphens of their lives.

Meet Aisha

Challenging and Laughing Her Way
through Suspicion, Surveillance,
and Low Expectations

At age fourteen, Aisha attends public school in Brooklyn, New York, taking Advanced Placement and honors courses, and averaging 90s in all her areas of study. "My goal is to get into an Ivy League school and study biology. I try to do a lot of community service as well." With head covered with *ḥijāb* and religiously appropriate American clothes, she prays five times a day, studies more than ten hours a week for school, and identifies herself as Palestinian. Both her parents are college educated; her father is from Jordan and her mother is from Palestine. Aisha's friends and social life involve youth from various ethnic groups in the United States, including some from Palestine. She explains that "at home I try to balance out being a good Muslim. Many things are prohibited for us but some things I don't follow the rules. I want to be more religious but still feel free to live a fun and stressless life." Her food is a blend of cultures; her holidays are exclusively Islamic, but her music is fundamentally "American." She says, "I'm one of those girls that you see who has like the huge book bag, and it has like eight books in it."

Aisha represents her identity map through the "daily routines" of her life. As she travels across home, school, and clubs, she's always aware of the ways in which "Americans" and even her own community and family do and do not really see her:

> I am usually at home and I go to school and I go to the library a lot. I go to the Arab American Association and help out here. And I go to Muslim youth center and that's where I do most of my religious activities and everything. And, yeah, I do community service a lot. That's what I love to do. . . . I've worked with the Arab American, my Muslim Youth Center, I have also worked with JCRC, they are like a Jewish Community Center, and, yeah, I work with them and I also work at school. And I always study. . . . I want to just show people that like I am a good Muslim, I'm a good person. And show that like Muslim people can do things around. Because people like never expect that.

At the Jewish cultural centers, she explains: "OK, when I go to the JCRC I like it a lot because a lot of them are like Jewish there. Well, it is kids with different ethnicities a lot, but people who are in there are Jewish. So when we come and are likely doing really good and everything, that makes me feel good."

While she relishes these sites of diversity, Aisha also tells a poignant story of friendships fractured when she put on the veil during junior high in a striking similarity to what Tatum (1997) calls the "birthday party effect" to signify the transition from elementary school to junior high school when the friendships become less and less racially diverse.

> So right when I started wearing it, I started wearing it right before sixth grade. And I just did it during the summer to get used to it because if you can wear it in hot weather, then you're good. So when I first went to junior high school, I had a lot of friends that I went to elementary school with, and I would say that half of them stopped talking to me. . . . I don't know if it was just us growing apart and we were getting older. And a lot of them we kept in touch, but it felt more awkward or whatever, and then eventually we just stopped talking completely. So that was just so weird—and I was like OK—why does everybody stop talking to me and I just made new friends with whoever just accepted me better.

Aisha struggles to integrate with her friends at school, and she also struggles with not feeling as connected to Muslims as she could be. Aisha is very clear that it was strictly her decision to start wearing ḥijāb. She wants a more religious and cultural grounding than she is receiving from her family:

> Well, like when I was like a little kid, my parents never really taught me a lot about Islam, so like I eventually had to like learn it all on my own. And I just wish that I had like gone to school and learned all the religious stuff just so that it would be part of me. Because I started learning about Islam during my crazy, mixed-up teenager years, so like, you know, that is like the worst time if you don't know about stuff to learn it. 'Cause you are just always seeing other people doing other things. So like I always wanted to know about like, umm, like more about my religion and my culture, just because I never got to experience that stuff so and I really want to learn it. And I also want to learn about like the Muslim people out in the world that I never met and don't ever see.

And just like all the struggles that they are going through and I want to help them out somehow. I want somehow, whatever career I have that I can have with my family and that I can help people. It is very hard to figure out what that is.

Within her Arab peer group, "like my best friend she doesn't wear the *ḥijāb*, so it's nothing weird between us, but people are always asking like how come you wear it and you don't."

Aisha relies on her different peer groups for different kinds of support. Referring to her Arab friends,

I can talk to them about, like if I have things with my religion or like I am struggling with that. My other friends are just still asking me like, "Oh, you still pray?" like "you still pray like five times a day?" and like they get it my other friends. . . . I have to explain things to them, and like my Arab friends, they get it and everything!

Dalal, the interviewer, who had introduced herself as Greek and Palestinian, followed up: "So how do you feel explaining stuff to them? Is it—what kind of position do you feel that puts you in?" Aisha replied,

Oh, I love it! OK, at first, it was a little awkward to me because like you know they kept on asking me like weird questions, like "is it stuck to your head?" or things like that, and I was just like, OK, but then now there are people just always asking me and I am just so used to it. And . . . like if you just sit there and explain something to somebody and you can bore them. . . . Well I always joke around about it, like "Oh, no I have to cover myself up because I am so hot, so none of the guys can look at me!"

Committed to educating the broader culture of her peers, Aisha imports into the conversation humor and the ironies of sexuality behind the veil. Perhaps, then, it is no surprise that "my favorite book is *Pride and Prejudice*. I just love that book. I read it in like in the seventh grade and fell in love with it. And right now I am reading *Heart of Darkness* and the *Metamorphosis*." Themes of social struggle, change, stigma, transformation, and speaking back to social misrepresentations permeate both her mind and her bookshelves.

Despite all her good humor, at the intersection of gender and the U.S. war on terror, Aisha struggles. For instance, like many immigrant girls, she is distressed by the gender politics in her home. In contrast to her brother, who is supported extensively in his studies, Aisha feels that she is "on my own," trying to get a rigorous education.

My mom has like never told me, like you have to study harder or anything, you know. . . . I have to push myself and I have to force myself to go find all these things . . . if I was a boy, oh yeah, my mom is like dying for my brother. She is like, "Oh, you are going to be a doctor!" My mom will get him tutors if he wants and everything. But like with me, I was talking to my mom the other day and I was like, "you know I want to study like genetics . . . and go to Stanford" . . . she's like, "Aisha, just go to Brooklyn College" . . . because you are going to get married anyway. So you know they don't push me as hard if I was a boy—oh my god!!

So most of my stress comes from studying really hard, and nobody ever helps me to study—so I pretty much do everything by myself. I actually go and I took my sister's SAT book and I'm in ninth grade. So I am looking at her SAT book, and I stole my brother's college book and I am studying out of those. So I just do that stuff by myself. And then like everyday because my mom she like works really late and then I have to come home and I have to clean the house before I do anything. So I start my homework like at about 5 o'clock and my school is pretty far away from my house so I have to go home and clean the house and so all that stuff. And my mom gets mad if I don't, but sometimes I just really can't because I have so much other stuff. And then sometimes I just don't want to because even if I don't have studying. I am just so tired and I just want to veg out and watch TV. And then there's the other thing.

To this point, Aisha sounds like most teenaged girls, particularly an immigrant girl. But the microphone is turned off for a few minutes for reasons of confidentiality, and then she continues:

So like my father, he's been incarcerated because of immigration. So now he is going to get deported. So that's just because we have to find money—like he has to send us money now. And we have to like find a way to try to get him back. My mom wanted us to move to Jordan and my dad is like No Way [laughing]. So just because we have to go visit him now and we are trying to get him back, that is a lot of stress on me.

Later she elaborated,

He's getting deported like right now because they like just closed the case. . . . He asked to leave or he is just going to be sitting there in jail doing nothing. And that is pretty much it so like after September 11, because they went down like really hard on all the immigration stuff so my parents were like, OK, we have to go get our papers like really fast. You know, they are just going to deport like everybody. And you know like when it first happened like all the Arabs were like going crazy did you hear about this? And like they'd be like, "Oh, they are going to deport us all!" and blah blah blah. Which really did not happen. It happened a lot. Like a lot of like they cracked down and everything and they looked at the cases more so that just what happened.

As we saw with many of the Muslim American youths whom we interviewed, Aisha chose not to complain to her parents about these stresses:

I just don't talk to them because they are just like in their own little world. I did share it with my friends—I don't tell a lot of people—I went through junior high school and my friends never knew . . . like if I am feeling stressed out, I will just tell them like "oh my god" [laughing], and then you get it all out and it's just like cool. I like to keep positive. As you have noticed, I am a very giggly person because you just like have to keep your head up. Like you know if you —like in my situation I could make myself so depressed like if I wanted to, but like, why would I? [laughing]

Profoundly aware of the suspicion from the broader culture and gendered expectations she confronts at home, Aisha has developed a style that uses humor and narrates a life, and future, of passion and dedication. She enters what could be tense social confrontations, always laughing, always direct.

Most of the time people make judgments but like that's the reason that you have to be like . . . make yourself open to people and . . . if you keep to yourself, no one is ever going to know anything about you [laughing]. Like I am a very like extroverted person so like I can just go up to people . . . I like to use the big words [laughing], but I never get them right.

Aisha offered an example of how she defuses potentially tense situations with a clever style. She recalled going to a largely Jewish school:

Oh, I joke around with them about it. 'Cause if I just say that I am Palestinian, they will be weirded out by it. So like my friend she was telling me, I was just sitting with this girl in art class and she was talking about where she was from and she goes, "Oh I am from Israel," and I go "Oh! I am from there too! I am Palestinian!" and she goes, "Really?" and I go, "Yeah, we are like neighbors" [laughing]. So I don't make them feel weird about it and I don't like judge people. Like I don't care if you are Jewish or anything, unless maybe I was in Israel and there was an Israeli soldier with a gun pointed up to my head. That would be different situation. I don't ever judge people so I don't feel that they have a reason to judge me.

Speaking with a wisdom much older than her age, Aisha has decided that it is her job to alter the misperceptions of Muslims in her community work.

You just can't leave people ignorant . . . you have to go up to somebody. You just have to tell people, you know, really I look different but I'm not different in my personality or whatever. So that's just the way it is and now it's not that much—there's not a lot of discrimination as much as it was back then—it's not that bad. There are still spats of people who are discriminating against some people, I mean, it's just the way it is, in like American culture. And I am not saying anything bad about America but it is. They discriminated against African Americans and Chinese people and it's always going to be somebody new. So if it's not us, it's somebody else.

With an understanding of history and psychology tucked firmly under her young belt and laughter in her soul, Aisha steps over the pain and sets forth to educate those around her.

I do feel like it is my responsibility as a Muslim person to make sure that they are not getting the wrong kind of message because if that would happen that would, like people would never understand you and people would never understand Islam. . . . I am not trying to get people to convert to Islam. . . . But . . . I don't like when people disrespect me because I am Muslim or Arab.

In her interview, Aisha offered worldly examples of anti-Muslim bias:

Aisha: Remember when they did the pictures of the Prophet in Denmark and that whole thing? People asked me my opinion and it and I was like, you know I think people went too crazy because they started like burning buildings . . . you can't do that. If we were to actually like have a conference or something to explain to them, oh well, this is why we didn't like this, this is like our prophet —you have to be very respectful to him and stuff. It would have worked better than burning buildings.

Dalal: How do you feel about that role, then feeling like you have to educate people?

Aisha: I find it just a responsibility with life. It's part of being a Muslim, you have to make "dawah" you have to teach people. It's just a part of me.

In her commitment to educate others, she also educates herself:

I watch Al-Jazeera, like it is really weird if you watch Al-Jazeera and you watch American news. It's completely different . . . in Al-Jazeera, they always put the stuff, like remember a couple of years ago when the soldiers were captured and they wouldn't show it on American news, but I got to see it and I watched it. . . . So somebody really has to figure out how to show both things.

For Aisha, life at the hyphen contains challenges, confrontations, and opportunities to critique and resist social injustice. Gifted with social analysis and humor, she thrives on the fissures of hyphenated life that defeat others. She knows she is a talented writer and orator and concluded, "Maybe if I become a journalist one day, then I can just write about this."

2

■   ■   ■   ■   ■   ■   ■   ■   ■

Muslim Americans

History, Demography, and Diversity

"You don't look like a Muslim."
"How do you look Muslim? It's a religion."
　　　　　—A dialogue between two teenagers in a middle school

There are many routes, both figurative and historical, to being a Muslim in the United States. Although there is a tendency to assume that there is a single Muslim American identity because there is so much diversity within the group, the label of "Muslim American" is misleading. A majority of Muslims migrated to the United States from all over the world, predominantly from African, Middle Eastern, and South Asian countries as well as from central and eastern Europe. They came here first as slaves, merchants, and peasants, and most recently as professionals, scholars, and students. They also brought with them their own versions of Islam which, despite contrary perceptions, is practiced quite differently across the world, and these differences have sometimes violent historical roots. To complicate things further, we must add to this long list of Muslim Americans, those—mostly African American, along with some white, and, most recently, Latinos—who have converted to Islam from other religions.

Our goal in this chapter is twofold: (1) to present the most common characteristics of this diverse group in the hope of dispelling some of the misconceptions about Muslim Americans as a group and (2) to underline the many variations within the group in the hope of avoiding stereotypes and oversimplifications. In order to reach our goal, we first present general demographic information about the Muslim American population. Next, we offer a brief historical account of immigrants to the United States from primarily Muslim countries. Finally, we review the available data to illustrate how Muslims have been perceived in the United States both before and particularly after 9/11.

Muslims in the World

Muslim Americans are part of a larger global community. According to the *World Almanac* (2001) and the *CIA Factbook*, there are now about 1.4 billion Muslims in the world. Despite the misconception in the West that most Muslims are Arab, the majority, about 80 percent, of Muslims are not Arab, as most live in South Asia (30%), Sub-Saharan Africa (20%), and Central Asia. In addition to those in predominantly Muslim countries, the number of Muslims is growing in non-Muslim countries, mostly in Europe, North America, and Australia. For example, about 10 percent of France's population is Muslim, representing the largest group of Muslims in the Western world. Although not as high, the number of Muslims in the United Kingdom, Germany, and other European countries also represents a major minority group in each country (Rath & Buijs 2002).

Muslim is the word given to those who belong to Islam, which in Arabic means "one who submits to God." Muslims, like the believers of the other two Abrahamic religions, Christianity and Judaism, believe in a single god, or Allah, but they recognize Muhammad as the last prophet. They believe that their book, the Qur'an, is the word of God as told to Muhammad between 610 and 632 CE. Every Muslim adult is required to follow the five principles of faith in God and his messenger, pray five times a day, donate a portion of his or her income to the needy, fast during the holy month of Ramadan, and make a pilgrimage once in his or her lifetime to see the birthplace of Islam in Mekke (or Mecca). Muslims visit mosques for both daily prayers and Jum'ah, or Friday prayers, but this is not one of the five main principles, meaning that Muslims need not pray in a mosque. Besides these five principles, Islam also sets quite detailed standards for social life, dictating how Muslims should behave in both their private lives and in society. These instructions cover all aspects of life, ranging from how to take a shower and how to invest money to what to wear. More relevant to our topic, Islam also sets very different standards for girls and boys, including the way they should dress, socialize, and interact with the other sex. Most devout Muslims try to follow these religious obligations, but as in every religion, their practices vary, even among the most devout.

Another important aspect of Islam is how one becomes Muslim. Unlike many other religions, Islam does not require any ceremony for conversion; becoming Muslim is a very simple and private act. A person is considered Muslim when he or she, regardless of race, ethnicity or gender, recites in Arabic, "Allah is the only god, and Prophet Muhammad is his messenger." When a person recites these words, he or she becomes a Muslim. Other than the general avenues by which culture is transformed from generation to generation, devout Muslims all over the world attend mosques or *masjids* (i.e., an Islamic prayer area or chapel), and some also attend a variety of religious schools designed to teach the principles of Islam, which are available for all age groups from prekindergarten to post–high school. Although there is no uniform curriculum for Islamic schools, there are some commonalities. Such schools are unisex, offer a religious education, and, in most cases, use the Arabic language for instruction. Their attendance at any such formal, religious school undoubtedly affects young Muslims' identity development. For example, their attendance may limit their ability to socialize with the other sex and with people from other religions and ethnic backgrounds. In the only available study of the effect of school type on Muslim American high school students, Alghorani (2004) found that as the number of years attending public schools increased, participants reported lower levels of engagement with Islamic culture and higher levels of engagement with the broader U.S. culture.

Not only is the ethnicity of Muslims diverse; their religious practices differ as well. The vast majority of Muslims belong to one of four Sunni sects (Maliki, Shafi'i, Hanafi, Hanbali), and a much smaller group (about 17%) belong to Shi'a sects (Jaffari, Ismailliyah, Alawite). The relations between Sunni Islam and Shi'a Islam (or Shi'ite Islam, Shi'ism) have been hostile since the prophet Muhammad died and various Muslim groups fought for power, ending in the bloody murder of Muhammad's two grandchildren. Unlike the Sunnis, who are much more traditionalist in following the word of the Qur'an, Shi'as give more weight to the role of imams, or religious scholars, who can interpret the Qur'an for current needs. In the United States, although Sunnis and Shi'as are not engaged in open hostility, in their countries of origin, their hostility often leads to violence, as in Iraq. These differences and the historical roots of animosity between the two groups are difficult for Americans to understand, partly because they tend to assume that all Muslims are the same. One of the participants in our focus group explained the difficulty of collapsing many different cultures under a single banner:

Islam starts from Africa and goes all the way to China, and you see such different representations. In Senegal, women don't wear *hijāb*. In Saudi Arabia you don't see a woman [who is not] fully covered . . . Egypt is so much different from Saudi Arabia, which is different from Jordan, which is, I mean, they're different people, you know. They have this commonness which is their being Arab, but they're really different people culturewise, historywise. I mean, they're all Muslims and you see so many different representations so that the idea that there should be something homogenous, it's just not going to be like that because it's such a vast geographical area. So many different histories, so many different cultures.

Muslims Coming to the United States

Like most other Americans, the history of Muslim Americans is also a history of immigration that can be traced back to the early European expeditions and the African slave trade, which included some Muslim tribes from Sub-Saharan Africa. The slaves' identity as Muslim is not recorded in their papers, but there are accounts of slaves who spoke a language similar to Arabic and who believed in a god called Allah. Other than the slaves, a few others came to the New World for a better life, and probably the first public person who embraced a Muslim identity in the United States was Alexander Russell Webb. Webb was a European American diplomat who converted to Islam and became the face of Islam in U.S. academic and intellectual circuits until his death in 1916. Aside from individual migrants and some converts, the large-scale migration of Muslims did not begin until the late nineteenth century and took place in two waves, one from the late nineteenth century to early the twentieth century and the other that began around the mid-1960s and continued through the 1990s. These two waves brought about two-thirds of today's Muslims to the United States.

The first major wave of Muslim immigration began between 1870 and 1890 and lasted until the 1924 Johnson-Reed Immigration Act, which prohibited all Asians from coming to the United States, including those from most of the Muslim and Arab countries that were also classified as Asian. During this first wave, the majority of Muslim immigrants came from the Middle East, Albania, and South Asia. Most were illiterate peasants and, as a result, had more difficulty adapting to the life in the United States than did the Christian Arabs who migrated around the same time from Jordan, Syria, and Palestine. These Muslims moved to places like North Dakota, Indiana, Iowa, and Michigan. Around 1915, the first mosques in the United States began to appear in places like Cedar Rapids, Iowa, and Biddeford, Maine. Around the same time, Muslim Arabs joined Christian Arabs in search of work at the Ford Motor Company around Detroit and in Dearborn, Michigan, which became the home of a large Muslim and Arab community in the United States.

The second wave began with the immigration reforms of 1965, which among other things, made it possible for Muslims from the Middle East and South Asia to immigrate to the United States. This wave was essentially ended by the restrictions put in place through the Patriot Act after the terrorist attacks of 9/11. The Muslim immigrants of this era arrived with much stronger religious and national identities than the previous generations of Muslim immigrants, owing to popular movements that had shifted the Muslim and Arab world onto a more Islamic and nationalistic path. As in the previous era, these immigrants came from Palestine, Egypt, Syria, and Iraq, but unlike the previous wave, they also came from the South Asian countries of India, Pakistan, and Bangladesh in much larger numbers. Another difference was the composition of Arab immigrants. Unlike the first wave of immigrants, in which an overwhelming majority of Arabs were Christians, the second wave was composed mostly of Muslim Arabs. Perhaps the most striking difference between the two waves of immigrants was that compared with the earlier immigrants, most of these migrants either had a college degree or came here to pursue one, a change likely reflecting shifts in U.S. immigration policy. Given these differences, both immigration status and the number of generations living in the United States are two critical factors to consider regarding Muslim American identity formation.

In addition to immigrants, there is also a growing Muslim population in the United States which has grown out of those who converted to Islam from other religions. The majority of this group is African American. Although since the arrival of slaves, there always have been some African Americans who were Muslim, the presence of Islam among this population became more prominent with the movements headed by Muslims during the last century. Specifically, the followers of the Nation of Islam, which was first headed by Elijah Muhammad and was popularized by the charismatic leadership of Malcolm X, became a major force in the African American community.

Within both immigrant and U.S.-born groups, Muslim Americans differ in their race, ethnicity, religious practices, immigration status, and historical roots in the United States. Given this diversity, it is reasonable to question the very category "Muslim American." Even so, we rely on this grouping because of recent historical events such as the Iraq War and the 9/11 attacks, combined with the strong belief of most Muslims that their religious ties cut across racial, ethnic, and national boundaries. Thus, even though we use the term "Muslim American" in this book to illustrate a phenomenon of emerging identity, we also must remind both ourselves and our readers that there is no singular, monolithic, category of people called "Muslim Americans." Rather, there are many groups of people who can be labeled as Muslim American.

Like many issues that involve Muslim Americans, their numbers are a matter of political debate (for a methodological discussion, see Smith 2002). There really are no "hard" numbers, partly because by law, the U.S. Bureau of the Census does not gather any information about religious affiliation and also because unlike other religious groups, mosques do not have membership rolls that can be used as a proxy and even if there were such data, many Muslims do not attend mosques. What makes the count of Muslims in the United States even more challenging is the fact that even large-scale surveys fail to count the number of new immigrant populations, which represent a large number of Muslims in the United States. Hence, the number of Muslims in the United States has been estimated to be anywhere between two million to seven million.

In this variation in estimation, we can see how political interests tend to take precedence over methodological rigor. Those groups who would like to minimize and perhaps marginalize Muslims in the United States claim that the number is close to one million, whereas the groups who want to maximize the political clout of Muslims claim that the numbers are as high as eight million. Thus, while an American Jewish Community survey put the number at 2.8 million or 0.8 percent of the U.S. population, the Council on American Islamic Relations survey estimated the number to be 7 million, or 2.3 percent of the U.S. population.

Another way of assessing the number of Muslims is to look at the FACT survey, the religious practice survey conducted by the Hartford Institute for Religious Research in 2000 (Faith Communities Today 2006). Gathering data from the heads of religious sites in the United States, including mosques, this survey found about 2.5 million Muslims in the United States who are associated with mosques. Of course, this survey fails to account for those who are not associated with a mosque. This is a potentially large number because belonging to a mosque is not as central to religious practice in Islam as it is for other religions for which church membership is important to religious practice. According to a more recent study by the Pew Research Center (2007), there are about 2.5 million Muslims in the United States. Given the difficulty of sorting out these numbers, we shall assume that the Muslim American population is a sizable community that accounts for nearly 1 percent of the U.S. population.

The majority of Muslims, both African American and immigrant Muslims, live in metropolitan areas like New York, Los Angeles, Detroit, and Chicago, and four-fifths of U.S. mosques are located in metropolitan areas. The majority of Muslims live in just a few states, including almost 20 percent in California, another 15 percent in New York, and the rest in Illinois, New Jersey, Indiana, Michigan, Virginia, Texas, Ohio, and Maryland. However, Muslims are spreading across the rest of the country as well. Like other immigrants before them, as they settle in the United States, younger generations move to places where their parents could not have imagined living when they first arrived.

Emergence of the "Muslim American" Identity as a Category

As noted previously, the use of Muslim American identity as a social category is a relatively new phenomenon which emerged during the past few decades and was highlighted in the post-9/11 sociopolitical context. But who exactly are we referring to when we use the term "Muslim American"? Young men with beards? Taxi drivers with heavy foreign accents? Oil millionaires with greasy hair? The Nation of Islam led by Farrakhan? Girls in head scarves? Palestinians? Based on media images and popular literature, Americans seem to think of Muslims mostly as Arabs clustered in places like Brooklyn, New York; Dearborn, Michigan; or Paterson, New Jersey. We think of a group of people who are not sophisticated and certainly not well educated, and lately, we have tended to think of them as dangerous. But just how accurate are these stereotypes? Without a clear idea about the makeup of the Muslim American community, we cannot accurately explore the issue of Muslim American identity.

As we have seen, the label of "Muslim American" resists simplistic definitions because there are many routes to being Muslim in America. There is always a danger in making broad, albeit statistical, generalizations about a large group of individuals on the basis of "averages." This attempt can be even more problematic when it is used with minorities, since there is a greater tendency to overlook within-group variation when we have limited knowledge about it. As a result, any general demographic "average" may be inaccurately construed as applying to every individual in the group. Therefore, in order to avoid this overgeneralization, we provide both data-based commonalities that make Muslim Americans a unique group and data that illustrate the great diversity within the community.

First, as a group, Muslim Americans are one of the fastest-growing segments of the U.S. population. According to the American Religious Identification Survey (ARIS) conducted in 1990 and 2001, the number of Muslims in the United States grew by more than 108 percent in a single decade (Kosmin, Mayer, & Keysar 2001). Although not exactly reflecting the trends for all Muslims, an evaluation of the U.S. Census's ancestry data for those with birthplaces in Islamic countries confirms the same trend, that the number of U.S. citizens from predominantly Muslim countries has grown dramatically since the 1970s. A third source of evidence for this huge gain comes from the 2000 FACT survey, which shows that the number of mosques in the United States is rising faster than any other type of religious center in the United States. At the time of the FACT survey, there were more than twelve hundred mosques in the United States, a 25 percent increase from an earlier survey conducted in 1994. Not only is the number of mosques growing rapidly, but the average attendance in each mosque also has more than tripled during the same period, from an average of 485 in 1994 to an average of 1,625 in 2000.

These huge population gains in the Muslim community in the United States may be explained by the ongoing immigration from Muslim countries, higher birthrates, and religious conversions. Although we would expect the number of immigrants from Muslim countries to drop from its historical peak, the high birthrates and growing number of converts are likely to keep the numbers up over the next few decades. Indeed, it is projected that Islam will become the second largest religion in the United States, second only to Christianity.

Second, Muslim Americans are much younger than the general U.S. population. Table 1 shows two large-scale surveys that break down the age groups within Muslim populations. Despite the variations between the two surveys, the general conclusions are the same: The proportion of young adults (18 to 29) is larger than the U.S. average. Likewise, among those aged fifty-five and older, the percentage of Muslim Americans in the United States drops to the single digits, whereas that in the general population rises to 30 percent. These numbers parallel those of other immigrant populations like Latinos and some Asian groups, whose populations also are much younger than the national average.

Table 1

Muslim Americans by Age Categories (%)

	Muslim Americans		
Adult Age	Zogby Survey (2004)	Pew Research Survey (2007)	U.S. Bureau of the Census (2003)
18–29	26	30	21
30–39	52	26	19
40–54	17	31	30
55+	5	13	30

Third, Muslim Americans are highly educated. Partly due to the immigration of professionals and the influx of international students who came to the United States during the past four decades, Muslim Americans today are one of the best-educated groups in the United States (Zogby 2004). In fact, the percentage of Muslims with professional degrees is much larger than that of the U.S. average (Pew Research Center 2007). According to the Zogby survey, almost two-thirds of Muslim Americans have at least a college degree, compared with the U.S. average of 28 percent. Higher educational attainment also shapes parental expectations. In our survey of young immigrants aged twelve to eighteen, 94 percent of their parents believed that college was important, and there were no differences in terms of gender, indicating that they have equally high expectations for daughters and sons. Despite the substantial numbers of professional degrees and low numbers of college dropouts, Muslims are on a par with the national average in the number of those having no high school degree, both around 5 percent, indicating the possibility of a segment of immigrants who came here with no formal education.

Fourth, Muslim Americans are wealthier than most other identifiable social groups in the United States. According to the Zogby survey (2004) a third of respondents reported incomes of $75,000 or more, and an additional 20 percent reported incomes of between $50,000 and $75,000. While half of Muslim Americans make more than $50,000 a year, their median income for the same year was $44,389, compared with the U.S. average of $42,158 (Zogby 2004). The Pew Research Center's survey (2007), however, shows that Muslim Americans' family income is comparable to that of the U.S. population, with a slight advantage for foreign-born Muslims. Muslim Americans' occupations also reflect the middle-class status of the majority of Muslims. About 23 percent of adults work in professional/technical jobs, with an additional 10 percent in managerial positions and 9 percent in medical fields. Furthermore, a majority of Muslim Americans own stock, either personally or through 401(k)s or retirement plans, and own their own homes.

Despite these statistics, it is important to note that not all Muslim groups fare equally well. According to the 2000 U.S. Census data on the official poverty rate among children, 29 percent of Afghan American children, 26 percent of Iraqi American children, and 22 percent of Pakistani American and Bangladeshi American children of immigrant families were living in official poverty, compared with 8 percent of white children living in poverty. However, the children from these same three groups were among the most likely to live in two-family households and to live with an employed father, compared with other immigrant groups in the United States.

Fifth, unlike other immigrant groups, an overwhelming number of Muslims in the United States are legal residents. According to the American Muslim survey conducted by Zogby International, nearly 90 percent of Muslim adults in the United States are U.S. citizens (Zogby 2004). This is surprisingly high, considering the same survey's finding that two-thirds of U.S. Muslim adults were not born in the United States. Conversely, the higher percentage of citizenship is a result of the 1965 Immigration Act, which encouraged highly educated professionals to enter the United States. Given the large numbers of deportations after the 9/11 attacks, suspicious attitudes toward Muslims in general and international Muslim students in particular, as well as the stricter visa screening by consulates in Muslim and Middle Eastern countries, it is likely that in the near future, the undocumented immigration of Muslims will continue to be much lower than that of other groups.

Sixth, Muslims in the United States, as a group, are well integrated into mainstream U.S. society. Given the relatively new immigration history of Muslims in the United States, intermarrying, that is, marrying members of other religions, is more common than would be expected. According to one survey, about one in five Muslim Americans intermarries (Kosmin, Mayer, & Keysar 2001), and it is quite likely that the rate of intermarriage will go up dramatically with each successive generation in the United States, as is commonly observed in other immigrant groups. Another indicator of integration is the use of the English language at home. According to the 2000 census data on language use at home by the fourteen largest immigrant groups in the United States, families from Pakistan, Bangladesh, Iraq, and Afghanistan were the most likely to be bilingual, around 80 percent, which was lower only than that for immigrants from Africa, at 88 percent, and much higher than that for all the other groups, including 61 percent of Vietnamese Americans and 63 percent of Mexican Americans.

Finally, compared with European Muslims, Muslims in America are distinctly integrated into the mainstream society, due to the United States' selective migration, different policies of integration, and less stark forms of social discrimination. American Muslims are better educated and wealthier and, as a result, migrate with more social capital, which gives them more opportunities to engage with mainstream U.S. society, compared with their counterparts in Europe (Rath & Buijs 2002). For example, unlike the underclass status of South Asian immigrants in the United Kingdom (Sirin & Fahy 2006), whose unemployment rate is several times higher than the UK average, South Asian immigrants to the United States have one of the lowest unemployment rates in the country. Similarly, as a result of differences in Europe's and the United States' integration policies, Muslim immigrants have a high rate of citizenship in the United States, whereas most Muslims in Europe still struggle to gain access to civic life in their newly adopted countries. For example, after more than forty years of legal employment in Germany, the majority of Muslim immigrants (mostly of Turkish origin) still have not been granted full citizenship. A similar comparison could also be made between American Muslims and French Muslims, the latter of whom struggle with a national discourse that denies them any right to "Frenchness." These distinctions illustrate a point we will examine further in chapters 4, 5, and 6, that cultural identity is socially embedded and that hyphenated identities develop in specific national and historic contexts.

Diversity within the Group

> You can't just split up Muslims in the cookie cutter fashion. Everyone has their different identities, their different beliefs and whatnot, and we have the one central belief that is our faith, but after that there is just so much difference that I don't think you can have these large labels to just apply to people.   —Hamid, a twenty-one-year-old Palestinian man

As we have seen, making broad, albeit statistical, generalizations about minority groups is problematic because important variations among their members often are overlooked. Generalizations are even riskier for a loosely identified group like "Muslim" or "Muslim Americans." That is, by providing general demographic parameters, we may end up reproducing the discourse that puts a large group of fairly disparate people in the category of "Muslim American." There are indeed deep distinctions and variations among Muslim Americans. Any attempt to study a cultural group, we contend, bears an obligation to interrogate within-group variations in gender, race, class, generation, geography, and sexual orientation.

Muslims in the United States represent the most diverse racial and ethnic community of Muslims in the world, with racial, ethnic, and religious groups from more than one hundred countries. They are not simply Arabs or African Americans. As one of our participants explained,

> America is unique because we have such a diverse group of people and the only other place I have seen this in is in Mecca. All of us went last year, and there were people from Africa, Asia, and Europe. The only place elsewhere where you see it is here [the United States]. And because of that I think we can relate to each other. In a way we share a certain bond, and whatever problems we are facing at least we face them together.

According to a survey by Zogby International (2004), the three major groups of Muslim communities in the United States are of South Asian, African American, and Arab origin. South Asians represent about 30 percent of the Muslim American population, coming from Pakistan, Bangladesh, and India. This group is quite well educated, and they are a relatively new immigrant group compared with other groups of Muslims in the United States. Most African American Muslims are converts to the religion, representing the largest indigenous Muslim group in the United States, around 25 percent of the Muslim American population. One-third of the new converts to Islam in the United States are African American. The third major group is Arab Americans, who represent an additional 25 percent of the U.S. Muslim population. Although the majority of Arabs in the United States are Christian, about a quarter of them, mostly recent immigrants, are Muslim and relatively newer immigrants than their Christian counterparts. The rest of the Muslim American population belong to diverse ethnic groups, including a very large Iranian population (despite the popular belief, Iran is not an Arab nation and, until very recently, was one of the most progressive Muslim countries in regard to women's roles and liberal social practices) and much smaller immigrant representation from Malaysia, Indonesia, Turkey, Afghanistan, Sub-Saharan Africa, and central and eastern Europe, as well as white and Latino converts.

In the United States, where racial and ethnic distinctions play a large role in identity formation processes (see Helms 1994), such variations further complicate the notion of a "Muslim American" identity. For example, some African American Muslims may view their racial identity as more salient than their religious affiliation, owing to the unique history of Blacks in the United States. Similarly, given the significance of physical visibility (Helms 1994), most members of certain ethnic groups, such as Arabs and Pakistanis, are more easily identified as Muslims and therefore may have a much different route to Muslim identity than do Muslims from central and eastern Europe or white converts who are not easily identifiable as Muslims.

Second, American Muslims differ in their religious participation. According to a nationwide poll of Muslim voters conducted by Genesis Research Associates (2006), only 31 percent reported going to a mosque each week, whereas 27 percent reported that they seldom or never attend mosque. A majority, 54 percent said they were seldom or never involved in mosque activities, an important indicator of their religiosity. With respect to denominational affiliation, more than 40 percent of the participants identified themselves as "just a Muslim," rejecting any affiliation with Sunni or Shi'a sects, Islam's largest two sects. These findings are not surprising. Despite popular misconceptions, Islam is not a monolithic religion with a single authority that dictates certain religious practices. In fact, other than Shi'a, which has some institutional authority, every Muslim is free to draw his or her individual conclusions directly from the Qur'an. This structural freedom in interpreting the religious texts results in multiple, sometimes conflicting, interpretations of Islam across the Muslim world. Some of these interpretations reflect centuries-old conflicts between groups like Sunnis and Shi'as, as most recently evidenced in Iraq. Within the Shi'a and Sunni sects, there is further fragmentation in interpretation and practice. Because Islam has no recognized authority to interpret the religious texts, somebody like Osama Bin Laden was easily able to declare *jihad* on behalf of all Muslims, which led to the deadly terrorist attacks of 9/11 and the Madrid and London bombings. Unfortunately, many non-Muslim Westerners are familiar only with such extremist interpretations of *jihad*, meaning waging war against all non-Muslims. The majority of Muslims, however, are as horrified by the violence committed in the name of Islam as their non-Muslim counterparts are. According to most Muslims, *jihad* refers either to defending Muslims when Muslims are attacked (self-defense) or a personal spiritual struggle to be a better, more moral, and more just person.

Beyond the differences between Sunni and Shi'a Muslims, there also are many cultural differences in the way that Islam is practiced in different parts of the world. Each culture seems to adopt the version of Islam that best fits its previous religious practices. Because of these denominational and cultural differences, Muslims do not always agree on even the most important aspects of life, including religious practice and the role of women. For example, the number of days that one needs to fast during the holy month of Ramadan varies widely across the Muslim world, from as few as ten days for Shi'as (e.g., Alawites) to as many as ninety days for some Sunnis. Similarly, whereas Sufis throughout the Islamic world, from Morocco to Pakistan, use music in their religious practice and urge their members to adopt a more personal, spiritual view of Islam, the Taliban version of Sunni Islam prohibits any type of musical sound in religious practice or personal life, and Wahhabis preach a more doctrinal, literal interpretation of Islam.

There also is much variation in women's status. In Arabic, *hijāb* literally means "cover" or "modesty." Accordingly, some Muslim women wear burqas that cover the entire body; some wear a head scarf that covers only the hair; and some dress in low-rise jeans and belly shirts. Even though Saudi Arabian women cannot even vote, Turkey, Pakistan, and Bangladesh —all predominantly Muslim countries—are among an elite group of nations, Muslim or otherwise, that have elected women as national political leaders through general, democratic elections. Because of these differences, many Muslims in the United States find it quite difficult to find common ground on most religious and social issues. These differences also explain why there are large numbers of mosques and religious schools in certain areas in the United States, even though a single mosque or a school could, in terms of numbers, easily serve the whole community.

Third, like all immigrant groups, Muslims have imported their internal conflicts to the United States. Many Muslim immigrants fled their country because of civil conflicts and wars among various Muslim groups. Despite the common view that the only historical disagreement between Muslims is that between the Sunni and the Shi'a, Muslims, like members of other major religions, have a long history of conflicts. For example, Iranians, one of the largest ethnic groups in the Muslim American population, migrated to the United States because of the Iranian revolution of 1979. With the Iran-Iraq war that followed the revolution, many middle-class, well-educated Iranians sought refuge in the West and settled in Europe and the

United States in large numbers. Although the estimates vary, the number of Iranians in the United States is considered to be somewhere around half a million, with a considerable percentage of the population representing non-Muslim Iranians. Similarly, many Afghans left their country because of the civil war there among various ethnic groups that continues even today. Likewise, Kurds and Iraqi Shi'as fled Saddam's regime because they supported the U.S.-led forces during the first Gulf War. In fact, Kurds were massacred by fellow Muslims during this conflict. Similarly, during the conflict in the Balkans, many Muslim refugees from former Yugoslavian states, especially from Bosnia, moved to the United States during late 1990s. Finally, the current conflicts in Somalia and Sudan also are likely to increase the number of Muslim immigrants from these countries.

The struggles left behind undoubtedly shape how individuals determine their identity of "Muslim American." Just imagine the differences in the practice of Islam by an Iranian immigrant who fled from Iran because of a civil war that ended with a Muslim fundamentalist government and the practice of a Bosnian immigrant who fled from Bosnia because of a genocide against Muslims. Similarly, think of Turkish women, including an elected official, who fled their country because of the ban on head scarves in schools and parliament and Egyptian Muslim gays who fled their country for fear of imprisonment. Some Turkish women came to the United States so that they could practice a stricter version of Islam, and whereas Egyptian gays came so they could practice a more flexible version. While all these individuals are at times grouped together as "Muslim American," their identification with this term varies enormously.

Finally, there is diversity in Muslim Americans' civic participation. Unlike Muslim Americans of the past, who sometimes changed their names or hid their religion to escape mistreatment, the Muslim Americans of the present are more willing to publicly assert their Muslim identity. According to the 2004 Zogby poll, 82 percent of Muslim Americans are registered to vote, which reflects their willingness to assert their political rights. With the growing diversity of race, ethnicity, and country of origin, there is also a push for civic participation under "umbrella" Muslim organizations that address the needs of Muslim Americans beyond religious, ethnic, or national lines. In addition to previously established organizations that served only one section of Muslims (e.g., Sunni versus Shi'a or Iranian versus Arab), the new organizations attempt to represent all Muslims in professional, political, and cultural forums. Two such organizations are the Council on American Islamic Relations (CAIR) and the Islamic Society of North America (ISNA). The CAIR is the best known and most politically active Muslim lobbying organization in the United States, and the ISNA deals with mostly Islamic issues facing Muslim Americans and Muslim students today. In addition to these national organizations are student organizations formed around the "Muslim identity" at most major U.S. universities. This type of group represents a move away from similar student organizations in the past that were formed along ethnic and national lines (e.g., Pakistani Student Organization) rather than the broader identity of Muslim American.

Another factor complicating these distinctions is a person's generational status or the number of years that he or she has spent in the United States. Muslim immigrants' racial, ethnic, or denominational differences may disappear or become stronger in successive generations, depending on the political and social pressures from outside the group and inside the community. The question then is what will happen if the negative perceptions of Muslims in the United States continue and problematic global events, such as the Iraqi war, the Palestinian struggle, or the Kashmir crisis, are not resolved? Although we do not yet have enough data on Muslim youth to answer this, we can make some predictions based on data from other immigrant groups. For example, according to the segmented assimilation model proposed by Portes and Rimbaud (2001), "persistence of discrimination" is one of the major challenges for second-generation immigrants' degree of assimilation. What this means is that those who experience persistent discrimination are more likely to gain an underclass status instead of the middle-class status of those immigrants who do not have to struggle with such discrimination. Similarly, Mary Waters (1990, 1999) found that racism against African Americans in the United States encouraged young West Indian immigrants in New York City to identify with U.S. Black culture, even though their parents continued to hold onto their West Indian roots. Hence, *if* the current "us versus them" discourse, based on religious issues, persists in the United States and global conflicts continue in the Middle East and beyond, future generations of Muslims may be more likely to develop a strong "Muslim American" identity rather than a strong racial, ethnic (e.g., Pakistani American), national (e.g., Lebanese American), or denominational (e.g., Sunni Muslim) identity.

Table 2

Number and Percentage of Those with
Muslim Country Heritage

Heritage	Number	Percentage
Afghan	4,448	1.93
Albanian	26,260	11.39
Arab	14,766	6.41
Bangladeshi	32,335	14.03
Bosnian	2,838	1.23
Croatian	11,971	5.19
Egyptian	16,346	7.09
Eritrean	323	0.14
Indonesian	3,601	1.56
Iranian	7,937	3.44
Iraqi	1,006	0.44
Jordanian	956	0.41
Lebanese	11,332	4.92
Malaysian	2,695	1.17
Middle Eastern	1,075	0.47
Moroccan	4,982	2.16
Nigerian	16,904	7.33
Pakistani	40,051	17.37
Palestinian	3,334	1.45
Sierra Leonean	795	0.34
Somalian	17	0.01
Sudanese	943	0.41
Syrian	11,685	5.07
Turkish	12,357	5.36
Yemeni	1,578	0.68
Total	230,535	

Source: Beveridge 2005.

To illustrate how these variations work, we next take a closer look at one Muslim community in the United States, Muslims living in New York City. New York is considered one of the major entry points for Muslim immigrants, and the New York Metropolitan Area is considered to have one of the largest immigrant Muslim populations in the United States. The data from Beveridge (2005), presented in greater detail in table 2, reveal the enormous heterogeneity in this particular Muslim population.

In table 3, Beveridge further breaks down the data by race, education,

Table 3

Characteristics of Those with Muslim Country
Heritage and All Others

	Ancestry from Muslim Country	All Others
Male	55.8%	45.6%
Black	9.2%	28.9%
White	56.8%	47.3%
Asian	35.6%	10.1%
Other	14.6%	17.3%
Four years or more college	37.3%	27.3%
Married with spouse	61.3%	44.3%
Noncitizen	43.7%	19.9%
Working	58.5%	52.9%
Owns house	25.7%	30.4%
Median household income	$40,000	$37,000

Source: Beveridge 2005.

marital, citizenship, employment, and house-ownership status, and annual income compared with others in the city. As he explained, "Some are black, some are Asian; more than 50 percent are white. . . . When compared with other New Yorkers those whose heritage is a Muslim-majority country are richer, better educated and more likely to be married than other New Yorkers. Most are citizens" (2005).

Because of this diversity and current dynamics both in the United States and abroad, Muslim Americans now must define and, at times, defend their newly acquired "Muslim" identity to the world. At the same time, many desire an ongoing connection with their social, cultural, and economic backgrounds as well as their racial, ethnic, and denominational histories, which may conflict with those of other Muslims.

Speaking Back to America: Let Us Tell You Who We Are

In order to allow Muslim youth to speak for themselves, we asked them an open-ended question: "If you could produce an MTV video or a booklet for non-Muslim youth about being Muslim American, what would you want to tell them?" The participants were given space for three different responses. Across respondents, these young Muslim Americans want their peers to know:

1. *Who Muslims are.* Messages to educate others about Islam, religion, culture, being Muslim, defining *jihad*, and Islam's principles of peace and justice.
2. *"It is tough to be Muslim in America."* Messages about the negative impact of racism, prejudice, ignorance, and stereotypes.
3. *"We are normal!"* Messages to remind other youth that "we are normal; we are American; we are just like you!" and
4. *It's a balance and a struggle.* Messages about identity, balance, and the struggle of living between cultures.

Seventy-five percent of the participants wanted to educate others about Islam and Muslims in general.

"Islam is not just something that one has internally, but it is expressed in every aspect of life, character, mannerism, clothing, etc."
"Islam is a religion of peace that doesn't discriminate people or is intolerant to others. It is widely misinterpreted and misrepresented."
"Jihad: a thorough explanation/only allowed in instances when your religion is being attacked upon (open attack)."
"We too are American and care for the goodness of this country because our religion teaches us to be good citizens."
"Muslims do not support killing or revenge, Islam does not advocate events such as 9/11."

More than 54 percent of the participants offered explicit critiques of American-style racism and stereotyping. Echoing Maira's (2004) "dissenting citizenship," a critical and political perspective was offered by 22 percent who wanted others to understand the weight of discrimination, surveillance, stereotypes, the status of women in Islam, and the degree to which they had to contend with the ignorance of others about Islam:

"Muslims are not all terrorists!"
"Muslims don't pose a threat to society."
"We don't all hate the U.S.; if we did, why would we be here?"

"Just because we believe different things doesn't mean we are bad, evil people."

"To be open minded and non-judgmental, look at us as individuals and don't associate us with any "Muslim" terrorist groups the media has introduced you to."

More than 40 percent offered discourses of normalization and similarity. They wanted their peers to know that they are not very different from the rest of the population:

"*We are normal!* Just like all adolescents, we go through the same teenage difficulties."

"We're not different. We feel very similar family pressures."

"Islam doesn't hinder us from doing normal teen activities."

"Our God is the same God as Christianity and Judaism, and the three religions are very similar."

"We, just like others, are religious or moderate or do not believe in God at all."

"All Muslims are different, just like everybody around you."

Twenty-five percent simply wanted to let their peers know that they had to negotiate across different social and cultural terrains to balance the many, Muslim, American, and other ethnic/cultural influences in their lives. Some described the balance as a struggle, fraught with tensions, and others saw it as a smooth glide. But all wanted their peers to recognize the identity labors at the hyphen:

"There are struggles but we will be able to overcome."

"A balance between upholding Islamic practice while still adjusting to American culture and surrounding."

"The difficulties of assimilating to American non-Muslim ways without compromising our religious beliefs and practices."

"It is not that difficult to be a Muslim in America; you need to balance both sides of your life."

"Being torn between life as an American and life as a Muslim."

"Struggle to blend in with non-Muslim teenagers."

"It's difficult and challenging to be a Muslim adolescent in the U.S., for
    it often feels like a struggle of identity."
"How my parents' values interfere with values you grow up with in
    America."

It is apparent that these young Muslim men and women are deeply
aware of misconceptions about Islam in general and Muslim Americans
in particular. Their priority seems to be educating others about Islam as a
religion; they worry that most people in America do not understand the
basic tenets of this religion and also are anxious to challenge stereotypes
of Muslims. They urge their peers not to associate them with "terrorists"
who exploit Islam for their own political goals.

Just as important to these young people is that their peers perceive
them as "normal" in that they too experience typical developmental challenges and come in many different varieties. This point is significant because as in any other discourse about a unique social group, these young
people are highlighting the areas in which they have particular challenges
and are reminding us that they are individuals, not merely representatives
of a social group. They may be experiencing tough times right now by being Muslim in the United States, but this does not mean that they do not
also face the more typical "youth" issues of identity development (see
color map 23).

Conclusions

These young people are telling their peers, and us, that negotiating their
identities across contexts is both a challenge and a joy. On the one hand,
they find it difficult to balance the demands of Islam or home culture with
the demands of modern American youth culture (a challenge not unique
to Muslim youth). On the other hand, many also told us that this negotiation process is a creative adventure, which for some has been relatively
smooth. We discuss this further in chapter 5.

Meet Sahar

A Hyphen with Holes in It . . . Allowing Her to Sometimes Fall Through

Sahar is fourteen, in the seventh grade in Clifton, New Jersey, a predominantly white working-class town with a history of hostility to immigrants. Even though the schools have had an English-only policy, many immigrant families—predominantly of Dominican, Palestinian, and Colombian origin—tolerate the tense conditions because the school system's reputation is relatively better than that of the surrounding urban districts.

The fourth child in a family of six children, Sahar was born in the United States to parents from Rammallah. Her father finished elementary school, and her mother either graduated from high school or received a G.E.D. Her parents own a single-family home in a residential neighborhood, and Sahar lives with her siblings (all born in the United States), her parents, and sometimes a cousin or an aunt. She identifies as Arab American and Palestinian, receives grades between 60 and 94, studies for one or two hours a week, wears ḥijāb, prays often, and never goes to mosque. Sahar is more of a working-class child than most of our other interviewees, and she struggles academically. Held back in the second, sixth, and seventh grades, she is quite old for her grade and is now reading a book entitled *A Child Called It*, about a boy whose "mom abuses him for fun and doesn't let him do anything."

Sahar is very self-conscious about her weight and spends a great deal of time chatting online with her cousins and some friends.

She tells us she is stressed at home by family members and at school by "kids who make fun of how I look." Her self-portrait includes poses of herself shopping, playing baseball, with the book *A Child Called It* over her head, and then a box with question marks.

Although Sahar circled many items as "Moderately stressful," those that she marked as "Very stressful" are revealing:

I have more barriers to overcome than most of my non-Muslim friends.
I often feel ignored by people who are supposed to assist me.
People look down upon me if I practice customs of my culture.

She describes herself as "nice, friendly . . . I'm kind of athletic." On the survey she indicated that she is "afraid of certain animals, situations, or places" and described herself as "secretive, keep[ing] things to myself." She was one of the few respondents who said "Very true" to the item "I feel that no one loves me."

Sahar remembers being on safety patrol

in fifth grade . . . it was like after 9/11 and stuff. I'm standing on my post and then this kid walks past me and he called me a terrorist. And like I didn't like that so I told him I wasn't a terrorist or anything like that . . . he just kept walking . . . he knew that wasn't true . . . he couldn't say anything else about that. Because they can't just . . . see a Muslim person walking on the street . . . and accuse them of being a terrorist or a bad person, or anything like that.

Sahar tells us she has "Arabic friends, Spanish friends, Polish friends. I've got friends from Serbia and I've got friends from a lot of countries—from America, and they don't care what I am or anything. They just want to be your friend."

When asked, "Who are the people that you consider your friends?" She answered, "People that I trust. People that don't care what religion I'm from or where my parents are from or how I act or," thereby demonstrating her understanding of the kind of support she needs and deserves from her peers, her teachers, and her family.

Sahar wears a head scarf and seeks friends who "don't care" about her religion. She is bruised, often and easily, by those who focus on her "difference." She's frustrated when her family allows "my brothers . . . to go out with their friends and go to the movies . . . but us as girls, we are not allowed to go out like that." She related a time when she was most distressed:

Sahar: The other day, we were in math class and we're on the board. And this kid is standing next to me and he's like, "Oh, my God. It smells in here." And everything like that. And that offended me, so I went and I told the teacher and the teacher didn't listen to me. She was like, "Oh, OK," and she told him to stop but he didn't stop it. So then I got very like stressful and stuff. So I went to the office and I told them and they still didn't do anything about it. So I went to guidance, and she did something about it. She's like, "Do you want us to bring him in and talk to him?" I'm like, "No, thank you." And she was like, "Well if it doesn't stop, we'll take it to the vice principal."

> *Mayida (the interviewer)*: So what did you feel like you wanted them to do at that
>   point?
> *Sahar*: To do to the kid, to him?
> *Mayida*: Uh, huh.
> *Sahar*: I was going to throw him out of the window . . . because he's in every class
>   with me, so I at least wanted her to switch my schedule but she didn't.

While it was unclear whether the boy was referring to Sahar, she was highly
affected by his comment.

Frustrated by too many tasks for which she is responsible at home and sometimes "not understanding" what the teacher is saying in school, Sahar often feels
upset, and yet she is proud of being a peer mediator who can "help students
solve their problems."

Scared that high school will be "hard" and "mad" because "sometimes people
do give you like dirty looks because of the way you are . . . the place you're from
and stuff like that," she believes you have to "put that problem aside and just
focus on school."

With a strength that does not always come through, Sahar speaks with con-
viction about wearing ḥijāb:

> *Sahar*: Me, I always wanted to wear it since I was a little girl, because I'd see how
>   everyone's wearing it and stuff so I always wanted to wear it. So and then when
>   I started second grade—my second year of second grade—I started wearing
>   it. And I just got comfortable wearing it. And people ask, "Don't you take it
>   off?" . . . Some people even ask me if I take a shower with it or go to sleep with
>   it. And I'm like, "No! I take it off when I go home."
> *Mayida*: So how do those questions make you feel?
> *Sahar*: They make me feel like a normal person because they want to know a lot
>   about your country and where you're from and your religion.

When asked what advice she would give to a young Muslim American boy or
girl concerning life in the United States, Sahar rises to the occasion, swallows her
own vulnerabilities, and states:

> I would tell them not to be afraid of their religion or where they're from, be-
> cause people can't . . . because people don't know them as well to go and talk

about them. And that they should believe in themselves and not in what other people say to them or do to them.

Maybe this was the advice she was giving herself.

Sahar says about her faith: "I always liked being Muslim. And there won't be a time where anyone will put me down . . . because it's not their prerogative to make you . . . change your mind about it or anything. It's you."

Sahar does not feel supported in school. She failed social studies by one point and was ignored by her science teacher who would not answer her questions. Then when she spoke to the guidance counselor about it, her concerns were minimized and she was told "Oh, it's OK. Just try your best in his class and try to pass the year."

Sahar lives at the hyphen of ethnicity, biography, religion, gender, and class. Under stress at home and at school, she finds comfort in the "police in my school" who will protect her; in wearing the *ḥijāb*, in the second time through seventh grade, and in her safety patrol role. Vulnerable and often lonely, Sahar reminds us of young people's need for substantial support to buffer the blows on the hyphen.

3

■ ■ ■ ■ ■ ■ ■ ■ ■

Moral Exclusion in a "Nation of Immigrants"

An American Paradox or Tradition?

The structures, practices, and consequences of moral exclusion are at once political, social, psychological, and developmental. Susan Opotow writes that the practice of exclusion begins with a group-level "marking-off," which leads to "harm that can befall those who are excluded from the protections of community membership, including abrogation of rights, denial of economic opportunities and physical exclusion through institutionalization." Once so marked, those who fall outside the "scope of justice" come to be seen as less "beneficial" to society, less "similar" to a newly constituted "us," and less deserving of fair treatment (1995, 149, 62, 347). Political theorist Michael Waltzer argues that the creation of an ethnic identity and subsequent denial of community membership to that group signifies the first step in a "long train of abuses" (1983, 62). In addition, Opotow finds that severe social conflict accelerates the shrinkage of the scope of justice. Once a conflict erupts, "a social psychological process occurs over time that tears apart the relationship, gradually widening the psychological distance between people enough to sever their connection and the perception that they belong in the same moral community" (1995, 359).

The United States has a long and celebrated history of successfully integrating various immigrant groups. But the country has an equally long history of exclusions, denying full membership to various groups, a paradox, or tradition, that is currently at play. Muslim Americans are the most recent recipients of a long American tradition of publicly supported and institutionally sanctioned moral exclusion, enacted through legalized and institutionalized discrimination and followed by a massive unleashing of social prejudice, media stereotypes, and public hysteria.

In this chapter we examine two interrelated dynamics of moral exclusion built into U.S. history. First we discuss how particular ethnic groups have been historically and systematically produced as perceived threats to the nation and politically "racialized" with serious, often deadly, human rights violations.

Second, as these groups are targeted, we argue, they are homogenized; that is, they are constructed ideologically as if they were monolithic identifiable groups, through a forced *ethnogenesis*, or creating one people out of many. Currently, those labeled as Muslim Americans emerge from uncommon (sometimes contentious) backgrounds spanning from North Africa through the Middle East to South Asia. It is essential to understand this historical pattern of ethnogenesis if we are to recognize the current treatment of Muslims in America.

A Nation Built on a Foundation of Exclusions

The tone was set early with the Naturalization Act of 1790. To ensure the "purity" (read: whiteness) of the nation, exclusion became the norm. In the most sweeping act of legislative *ethnogenesis*, persons of Asian, African, and Native American descent were created as *the Other.*

> That any Alien being a free white person, who shall have resided within the limits and under the jurisdiction of the United States for the term of two years, may be admitted to become a citizen thereof on application to any common law Court of record in any one of the States wherein he shall have resided for the term of one year at least, and making proof to

the satisfaction of such Court that he is a person of good character. (Naturalization Act of 1790)

This act barred from naturalization all but *free white persons* (i.e., men) and excluded indentured servants and most women from becoming citizens. To be sure that those chosen to be "others" could not slip through the cracks, the act also limited citizenship to an arbitrary category of *persons of good moral character.* The Naturalization Act was not completely repealed until the Walter-McCarren Act of 1952.

But even before the Naturalization Act, Native Americans were the first to receive such treatment in the United States. In this case, their exclusion led to genocide and/or expulsion and the making of America as we know it. Beginning long before the U.S. Constitution was written, with the first organized cleansing of the then powerful Pequot tribe in 1637 by the combined New England colonial forces, Native Americans were almost annihilated by official and unofficial actions, legislation, and court decisions. In campaigns of colonization, oppression, and empire building, God was typically invoked as being on the "right" side. The assault on Native Americans was no exception. When 60 to 80 percent of New England's Native American population succumbed to European diseases, the Puritan historian and governor William Bradford confided in his journal, "For it pleased God to visit these Indians with a great sickness and such mortality that of a thousand, above nine and a half hundred of them dies, and many of them did rot above ground for want of burial" (Bradford 1967, 270–71).

In reality, the only rule in dealing with Native Americans was that were no rules, as affirmed in 1903 by the U.S. Supreme Court in the *Lone Wolf* decision. In this case, the Kiowa Nation argued that an 1868 treaty, contradicted by the Dawes Act, required tribal approval for land sales. But the Supreme Court ruled that the federal government had the power to abrogate *any* treaty with Native Americans. Whether the treaties were voided, superseded, or simply ignored, Native Americans were consigned, both de jure and de facto, to accept the unjust and brutal consequences.

Similarly, African Americans have borne the brunt of court-backed public and legislative horrors. Legislated to be counted as three-fifths of a person for census purposes in the Constitution, held as property by law with reaffirmation by the courts in the Fugitive Slave Act of 1850 and the *Dred Scott* decision of 1857, and consigned to second-class facilities through Jim Crow laws and again affirmed by the courts under *Plessy v. Ferguson*, African Americans have been subject to the most devastating forms of ethnogenesis, violence, criminalization, and pathology. Indeed, at that time, a person was considered a member of a particular race if only a single drop of the undesirable blood flowed in his or her veins.

We all have seen the horrifying photos of lynching. Most horrifying is that in these pictures the crowds invariably do not feel compelled to cover their faces, their smiles, because there was little fear of consequences. When a group is targeted, no matter how abhorrent the abuse, the powerful typically act with the knowledge and confidence that they will not be held accountable. Crowds of good, patriotic citizens circle around and smile as the bad one hangs from a tree.

Americans of Mexican descent too have experienced distinct forms of ethnogenesis and targeting by the U.S. government. The figurative hyphen in Mexican American was added with the signing of the Treaty of Guadalupe Hidalgo at the end of the Mexican-American War in 1848, suddenly making between 60,000 and 100,000 people no longer Mexican. Land taken, conquest secured, culture threatened, national identity hyphenated. For these people, citizenship was nearly impossible under a creative stretching of the Naturalization Act of 1790. Furthermore, article X mysteriously disappeared from the last version of the treaty. Article X was designed to protect Mexicans' landholdings in those territories ceded to the United States. Without this article, by the 1890s more than 80 percent of the landholdings of the so-called Mexican Americans had been lost, a loss that was confirmed by the highest courts. And with the loss of property and the possibility of citizenship came the refusal of voting rights.

Americans of Mexican descent also faced a number of laws directed at limiting their rights. California passed the notorious antivagrancy act, known as the 1855 Greaser Act, to *protect honest people from the excesses of vagabonds.* The vagabonds were *"generally, all people of Spanish or Indian blood."* The law enabled local authorities to arrest, deport, and seize the property of such people. In addition, the 1850 foreign miners' tax taxed only Spanish- and Chinese-speaking miners but did not tax Anglo miners. In several southwestern states until the 1940s, the birth certificates of children of Mexican descent born in United States read either *Mexican* or *Born in Mexico.* The "Other" was constructed again.

For a time, particularly after their property and voting rights had been stripped from them, workers of Mexican descent, both those born in United States and more recent immigrants, were sources of cheap labor, not just in the Southwest but throughout the nation. Then, with the onset of the Depression of the 1930s, a new form of targeting appeared. In order to provide jobs for "real" Americans, the federal government created the Repatriation Program, which led to the return of 400,000 people to Mexico. For many, this was often a first-time trip, since perhaps as many as 60 percent of such returnees had been born in the United States. Again, a group was recreated, now as foreigners, to be hated for taking jobs away from Americans, and once again, the courts supported this decision.

Twentieth-Century Moral Exclusion: Japanese Americans

After the bombing of Pearl Harbor in 1941, President Franklin D. Roosevelt signed Executive Order 9066, which justified actions for "national defense." More than 112,000 persons of Japanese descent, 70,000 of whom were U.S. citizens, were removed from their homes and relocated to concentration camps. More than 90 percent of the Japanese American population was confined for as long as four years, with neither a trial nor an individual review. Native Aleuts, living in Alaska, also were sent to live in canneries during this time. Ironically, at the same time 23,000 Japanese Americans were fighting in the U.S. military, defending "their" nation.

Most newspaper stories justified what was considered the regrettable "military necessity" of Japanese removal (Brennen & Duffy 2003). In March 1942, when loyalty committees were set up to evaluate the patriotism of German and Italian aliens, the *New York Times* reported that Congress's Tolan Committee stated that "a distinction was drawn between Japanese, on the one hand, and Germans and Italians, on the other. The committee said that the two latter groups have become thoroughly Americanized" (*New York Times* 1942, 6). But no loyalty committees were established for Japanese Americans, bringing to mind the distinction made with regard to "visible" minorities. While it may have been difficult to differentiate Italian or German descendants by sight, it was not difficult to identify Japanese descendants.

Social psychologist Donna Nagata writes that the internment provoked in the nisei (literally, "second generation") "a dissociation between reality and their perceptions that they were Americans just like everyone else" (1993, 30). Ironically, many of those who were interned felt a profound sense of shame. Nagata quotes a nisei woman as saying,

> Right after December 7 wherever I went I felt so self-conscious and embarrassed. I went to the library once and this handsome woman . . . looked at me and stuck her tongue out. . . . On the bus in Los Angeles, I heard two women in front of—they knew I could hear—they were saying: "One thing is certain, we should get all the Japs, line them up along the Pacific Ocean and shoot them." (1993, 31)

Another explained:

> The truth was that the government had betrayed us. Acknowledging such a reality was so difficult that our natural feelings of rage, fear and helplessness were turned inward and buried . . . [leading to] a deep depression, a sense of shame, a sense of "there must be something wrong with me." We were ashamed and humiliated. (Mass 1986, 160)

A full forty years later, the Commission on Wartime Relocation and Internment of Civilians (CWRIC) convened and concluded that "there was no justification in military necessity for the exclusion." The commission also noted,

> the President was unwilling to act to end the exclusion until the first Cabinet meeting following the President election of November, 1944 . . . the delay was motivated by political considerations . . . there is no rational explanation for maintaining the exclusion of loyal ethnic Japanese from the West Coast for 18 months after May 1943—except political pressure and fear.

In 1990, the U.S. government apologized, offering $20,000 to each of the survivors of the internment camps (Brennen & Duffy 2003). The CWRIC's final report details the nisei's trauma of their "sense of abandonment by their own country."

When the Supreme Court decided to intern Japanese Americans simply on the basis of ethnicity, Justice Robert Jackson's dissent forecast the heinous potential of continued state-sponsored exclusions on the basis of ethnic group rather than crime:

> But once a judicial opinion rationalizes such an order to show that it conforms to the Constitution, or rather rationalizes the Constitution to show that the Constitution sanctions such an order, the Court for all time has validated the principle of racial discrimination in criminal procedure and of transplanting American citizens. The principle then lies about like a loaded weapon ready for the hand of any authority that can bring forward a plausible claim of an urgent need. Every repetition imbeds that principle more deeply in our law and thinking and expands it to new purposes. (*Korematsu v. United States* 1944, dissenting opinion of Justice Robert Jackson)

Justice Jackson's dissent proved to be prophetic, given the current constitutional violations directed at Muslim Americans under the Patriot Act. Even though Muslims and Arabs have settled in the United States for more than one hundred years, Sarah Gualtieri reminds us that

> the distortion of Islam is an old habit in American orientalism, but it became more virulent in the post WWII period. Not coincidentally this corresponded to a change in the religious make-up of the Arab immigrant community during the 1950s and 1960s. . . . Many immigrants of this new wave were inspired by the politics of Arab nationalism with its secular, anti-imperialist stance, while others gravitated toward resurgent Islam and its call for a new politicized piety. By the 1970s, the majority of immigrants from the Arab world to the United States were Muslim and they developed an impressive institutional base for the religious and cultural needs of their communities. (Gualtieri 2004, 64)

In addition, Beveridge (2005) challenged New York City's commitment to profile young Muslim American males, arguing that this was not simply unethical and illegal but also *demographically impossible*. He pointed out that "profiling by origin is the sort of policy that seems appealing during periods of stress and hysteria, but in hindsight is almost always seen as a mistake—such as the internment of Japanese Americans during World

War II. In this case, however, it wouldn't even be possible" (2005) because of the unique nature of this new identity category.

Nonetheless, on June 15, 2006, a federal judge in Brooklyn ruled that under immigration law, the government could create ethnic groupings of noncitizens who were, by virtue of demographics, deemed suspect and may therefore "detain non-citizens on the basis of religious, race or national original, and to hold them indefinitely without explanation." The judge wrote, "The executive is free to single out 'nationals of a particular country' and focus enforcement efforts on them. . . . This is, of course, an extraordinarily rough and overbroad sort of distinction of which, if applied to citizens, our courts would be highly suspicious" (Bernstein 2006a, A1). David Cole, a legal scholar and cocounsel, announced that the ruling makes New York "an equal protection-free zone," permitting the government to detain immigrants at will. "What this decision says is the next time there is a terror attack, the government is free to round up every Muslim immigrant in the United States, based solely on their ethnic and religious identity and hold them on immigration pretexts for as long as it desires" (Bernstein 2006a, A1).

Since then, according to Swiney (2006), between twelve hundred and three thousand Muslim noncitizens have been detained, with an estimated 40 percent from Pakistan. More than five thousand investigatory interviews of male noncitzens from "Middle Eastern" or "Islamic" countries have been conducted, and minor visa violations have been thoroughly investigated. New York State has conducted mass deportations of Pakistani nationals (Maira 2004). In June 2002, the National Security Entry-Exit Registration System (NSEERS) was implemented, mandating that all males over the age of sixteen from twenty-four Muslim-majority countries, as well as North Korea, be photographed and fingerprinted at federal immigration facilities (for a review, see Swiney 2006).

Racial profiling has thus become a state-sanctioned form of constructing and targeting ethnic groups. Before 9/11, national polls indicated strong opposition to racial profiling, with 80 percent of Americans believing that racial profiling was wrong (Maira 2004). After 9/11, however, 60 percent favored racial profiling, "at least as long as it was directed at Arabs and Muslims" (Howe 2001, 3).

Even in 2007, the majority of the U.S. public believes that Muslim

Americans glorify suicide bombings and condone violence (*Newsweek* poll 2007). Perhaps more alarming is the finding from the Gallup–*USA Today* poll that more than 39 percent of Americans today favor requiring Muslim Americans, including U.S. citizens, to carry a special ID to prevent future terrorist attacks (Elias 2006).

The Psychology of Moral Exclusion: Implications for Youth

We are obligated developmentally to ask whether young people are affected by these historic contexts of government-sponsored exclusions and official and unofficial surveillance.

We turn again to history to see the effects of state-sponsored exclusion of youth development. In 1886, the agent for the Utes Indians decided that education would be the means of "civilizing" Indian children:

> It is food for thought to note the number of handsome, bright-eyed children here, typical little savages, arrayed in blankets, leggings and gee-strings, their faces hideously painted, growing up in all the barbarism of their parents. A few years more, and they will be men and women, perhaps beyond redemption, for, under the most favorable circumstances, but little can be hoped from them after growth and matured, wedded and steeped in the vices of their fathers. It is rather the little children that must be taken in hand and cared for and nurtured, for from them must be realized the dream, if ever realized of the philanthropist and of all good people, of that day to come when the Indian, a refined, cultured, educated being will assume the title of an American citizen, with all the rights, privileges and aspirations of that favored individual. (Adams 1995, 19)

In his book *Education for Extinction: American Indians and the Boarding School Experience 1875–1928,* David Wallace Adams details how the Bureau of Indian Affairs used boarding schools to instill in Native Americans the so-called values of civilization and erase any vestiges of their native culture, as well as encourage

> individualism, industry, private property; the acceptance of Christian doctrine and morality . . . ; the abandonment of loyalty to the tribal community for a higher identification with the state as an "independent

citizen"; the willingness to become both a producer and consumer of material goods; and finally, an acceptance of the idea that man's conquest of nature constituted one of his noblest accomplishments. (1995, 15)

Education was one of many tools of state-sponsored cultural extinction. Recall that Native Americans had to be "cleansed" of their belief in collective ownership to make way for the white appropriation of Native lands. The aim of Indian education from the 1880s through 1920s was thus explicitly assimilation, if not extinction (Marr 2006). Reformers challenged the view that Indians were uncivilized and advocated instead a campaign to train them to be patriotic and productive members of society.

General Richard Pratt, a nineteenth-century assimilationist, argued vociferously for off-reservation boarding schools. Drawing on his Civil War experience with "Negro troops," he advocated that the best way to "civilize" the Indian was to "immerse him in civilization and keep him there until well soaked" (Utley 1964, xxi, in Lomawaima 1994, 4). In 1879 Pratt founded the Carlisle Indian School in Pennsylvania, which sought to "kill the Indian and save the man." Using a series of chilling "before" and "after" photos of the youths, Pratt and other so-called reformers demonstrated the effectiveness of beating the Indian out of Native children. With their hair cut short, beaten if they used their native language, and discouraged from engaging in traditional religious practices, the children were forced into Christian doctrine and required to speak English. Trained mainly in vocational and family skills, gender stereotyped, and strictly divided, this form of "education" for Indian children—removal from family and community—was law in 1893, and parents who refused to send their children to school were threatened with annuities withheld and/or jail.

The historic accounts offered by Adams, like those by Frederick E. Hoxie (2001) and K. Tsianina Lomawaima (1994), describe the macro- and micropractices and cultural genocide built into these educational projects, as well as the complexity of these schooling experiences in the minds and communities of Native youth.

The Japanese (American) Evacuation and Resettlement Study gathered oral interviews, memoirs, unpublished letters, a diary, camp newspapers, and school newspapers from the Japanese American internment camps. Letters written by Japanese American children and adolescents interned at Poston Camp were collected by librarian Clara Breed in San Diego. For example, Louise Ogawa, who was seventeen in 1943 wrote, "This camp is so far away from civilization that it makes me feel as if I was an [sic] convict who is not allowed to see anyone." The shock of displacement can be felt in the letters, particularly those by adolescents (Josephson 2003, 48).

Some of the children sound as if they identified fully with the United States, blaming "those Japs, what are they doing that for?" (age nine). Another wrote, "It doesn't have anything to do with us because I'm an American, you know. I was completely American" (age ten).

The "youths were bewildered by the fact that they had been treated as enemy aliens even though they were American citizens" (Tong 2004, 21). At the same time, these young people developed a heightened racial consciousness, and race became "one organizing principle of citizenship." For the nisei youth,

> the swift, forced imprisonment in a racially homogeneous environment isolated from American mainstream society followed by repeated attempts to question their birthright (and even United States congressional attempts to divest them of their citizenship) led to self-questioning and the germination of ideas of race and difference as a conscious reality . . . unlike their Issei [first-generation] parents who had endured much bitterness in the long interwar years, their racial exclusion came swiftly and the color line was drawn so sharply in spite of their United States citizenship. (Tong 2004, 24)

Ultimately these young people fought hard to claim their American identities. "They had to assert their faith in the fairness of the American government and in doing so they submerged any critical appraisal of state authority" (Tong 2004, 28). People were allowed to leave the camp for school or a job as long as they signed a loyalty oath, were clearly not a risk to national security, and could produce proof of sponsorship.

Social psychologist Donna Nagata (1993) describes in detail the cross-generational legacy of this injustice carried into the third generation of Japanese Americans. She writes about herself:

> At the age of 6, I discovered a jar of brightly colored shells under my grandmother's kitchen sink. When I inquired where they had come from she did not answer. Instead, she told me in broken English, "Ask your

mother." My mother's response to the same question was, "Oh, I made them in camp." "Was it fun?" I asked enthusiastically. "Not really," she replied. Her answer puzzled me. The shells were beautiful and camp, as far as I knew, was a fun place where children roasted marshmallows and sang songs around the fire. Yet my mother's reaction did not seem happy. I was perplexed by this brief exchange but I also sensed I should not ask more questions. As time went by, "camp" remained a vague, cryptic reference to some time in the past, the past of my parents, their friends, my grandparents and my relatives. We never directly discussed it. It was not until high school that I began to understand the significance of the word, that camp referred to a World War II American concentration camp, not a summer camp. Much later I learned that the silence surrounding discussions about this traumatic period of my parents' lives was a phenomenon characteristic not only of my family, but also of most other Japanese families after the war. (1993, vii)

We hear in these testimonies of Native and Japanese American youth the political manipulation of fear mobilized through racism and economics, abandonment and betrayal by the state, the theft of land, a threatened annihilation of culture, a cross-generational cloud of outrage, silence, and, for some, shame. We hear the long reach of injustice stretching across generations and fundamentally unacknowledged by the nation. Today, we are in the midst of a parallel legacy, infiltrating new bodies, minds, souls, and communities of youth, this time Muslim American, trying to make sense of a nation that has, again, betrayed its young. The schools and the media are implicated in fanning the flames of Islamophobia. As Leti Volpp argued:

Simply because the state does not officially sponsor an activity does not mean that the state does not bear a relationship to that activity. In simultaneously advocating policies of colorblindness for citizenry while engaging in racial profiling for non-citizens, and publicly embracing all religions while particularly privileging Christianity, the administration has, in the name of democratic inclusion, disingenuously excluded. Thus, that an epidemic of hate violence has occurred within the context of "private" relations does not mean that such violence is without "public" origins or consequences. (2002, 1583)

Representing "the Other": The Role of the Popular Media

As children of immigrants who identify with Islam, young Muslim Americans find themselves in an internal "community [that] is deemed suspect" (Nguyen 2005, 140) by the state and the newspapers and on the screen. They are at risk of being adversely affected by a number of "social mirrors," including "the media, the classroom, and on the street" (Suárez-Orozco & Suárez-Orozco 2001, 99) that depict Muslims as barbaric desert dwellers, violent thieves, terrorists, misogynists, and four-year-old "jihadist" boys pictured with guns (El-Amine 2005; Shaheen 2003, Wingfield & Karaman 1995). Fueled by and justifying the state's acts of exclusion, the popular media circulate images that feed the public panic.

Critical media scholars have documented a long history of the media's racist representations of Islam, Arabs, and Muslims in the United States. For instance, Stockton (1994, 138) traces the U.S. media's representations of Arabs, which have historically echoed older stereotypes of Blacks and Jews, drawing on themes of "sexual depravity, physiological and psychological inferiority, conspiracy and secret powers," grafted onto Arabs during moments of political tension, including the oil embargo of the early 1970s. Gualtieri reported that in 1989 a carton entitled "Reading the Arab Mind" reflected many of the elements of a ninety-year-old cartoon entitled "The Jewish Mind." Wilkins and Downing analyzed the 1998 film *The Siege* as a "mediated representation of terrorism, serv[ing] as a vehicle for Orientalist discourse" (2002, 419), in which Islam and the Middle East are represented as "unitary, absolutist, fatalistic, patriarchal, unreasoning, obsessional, anti-modern and punitive," with Muslims portrayed as "culturally and psychologically primitive, prisoners of their emotions, trapped in a patriarchal vise and locked into 'jihad' (interpreted . . . as sanctifying bloodthirsty violence against all Westerners)" (2002, 420).

We see the explicit linking of Islam to violence in Karim's (2002) analysis of *Time's*, *Newsweek's*, and *Maclean's* (Canadian) coverage of two events from 1993: the suspected involvement by Sheikh Omar Abdel-Rahman in the 1993 World Trade Center bombing and the violent confrontation between the Branch Davidians and U.S. federal agents in Waco, Texas. In all forms of media, Karim found that "Islamic/Muslim" was consistently used to describe the terror of the first attack, but no reference was made to the Branch Davidians' Christianity, whose leader claimed to be Christ or a disciple of Christ. By functionally decoupling Christianity and violence, the media helped fuse Muslim and terrorism in the American mind. Drawing from Gordon Allport (1954), Karim argued that these ethnic identifiers "act like shrieking sirens, deafening us to all finer discriminations that we might otherwise perceive" (Allport 1954, 175; also see Karim 2002, 109).

A deep orientalist bias has long permeated the media. Comparing newspaper coverage of the attack on Pearl Harbor with the 2001 attack on the World Trade Towers, Brennen and Duffy (2003) traced the journalists' strategies by which Japanese Americans, and then Muslim Americans, were systematically linked to violence and framed as the "Other" in need of containment. As if in historic echo, the media called for a national "pragmatism" that rationalized in the public imagination a curtailment of civil liberties for Japanese Americans and, later, Muslim Americans. As calls for national unity became louder, newspapers helped justify the isolation and separation of "them." Distinctions between citizens and "aliens" blurred, and alternative media perspectives were difficult to find. In both cases, government sources were the primary spokespeople, though they said little, owing to national security concerns. Ultimately, the writers argue, "The coverage of Japanese-Americans as well as Muslim and Arab-Americans [was] framed to evoke a pervading sense of fear about the Other" (Brennen & Duffy 2003, 13).

After 9/11, the well-oiled discursive wheels of "Islamic peril" were set in motion. As Karim wrote, "Whereas mainstream journalists do not always subscribe overtly to official views on terrorism, the field of meanings in which they choose to operate inevitably leads them to produce only certain interpretations of political violence" (2002, 23). Extending this analysis to the social implications of these constricted views on "Islamic peril," Karim continued, "The unremitting panoptic gaze of the Northern powers that Muslim conservatives use as an argument against the establishment of greater freedoms" only serves to strengthen the hold of fundamentalist beliefs because "when the enemy satellites are keeping watch, it is not the moment to wallow in one's individuality" (Karim 2002, 107).

Annabelle Sreberny draws our attention to how the international media also invoked an emotional, inclusive, and rational "we" across national borders in support of "America," positing Muslims as the dangerous and irrational "them." Most journalists, even progressive journalists from out-side the United States, "somehow merged with Americans in a cultural ge-ography of attachment" at the moment of the 9/11 attack (2002, 223). In a close textual analysis of the "we" in British left journalism, Sreberny asks, "Who do 'we' think 'we' are"? "Was the 'we' a retreat into some kind of collective security?" (2002, 227, 228).

We see the divisions represented and reinforced in popular youth mag-azines as well. In November 2004, *Seventeen* magazine published a short feature on Muslim and Catholic youth in what was called "a town divided" (Piligian 2004). The Hamtramck, Michigan, City Council permitted a lo-cal mosque to broadcast the call to prayer, five times a day, on an outdoor loudspeaker. In the magazine's interview of two young women, Shahlar, age eighteen and Muslim, explained that the call to prayer lasts for twenty minutes and gathers Muslims into a community of prayer. "In May, when I heard the call for the first time since we moved here [from Bangladesh in 1994], I finally felt complete. I like having different cultures here. Church bells ring all the time. . . . The U.S. has freedom of religion—so why aren't we free to have ours?"

On the other side of the thick black line literally dividing the feature story, we meet Sarah, age twenty-one and Catholic, who introduced her-self as follows:

> I'm Polish and Roman Catholic and I've lived in Hamtramck my whole life, just like my mom. This has been her home for 65 years—now she cries over what's happening to our city. I noticed the Arabs moving in when I was 11; it felt like Aladdin had come to life. Now I have Arab friends I love. But it's just gone too far. This town used to be Polish, now they're taking over.

The visual and discursive in this article underscore the line separating "us" and "them." While the young Muslim woman speaks through a dis-course of human rights and freedom of religion, the Catholic American woman claims original ownership of the town and resents the invasion.

Unfortunately, oblivious to the distinctions and variations within the Muslim community and with no attention to language, the media produce, legitimate, and circulate stereotypes like this one about Muslim Americans as binaries. We could easily dismiss these statements as extreme ideas put forward by a minority, but unfortunately these views are common on TV and talk radio and in print.

Although the precise relation of media coverage to public opinion is difficult to discern, it is well recognized that anti-Muslim sentiment, Islamophobia, preceded 9/11, was inflamed in 2001, and has remained high and become even worse since then. Many prominent media personalities, including religious leaders like Revs. Franklin Graham, Jerry Falwell, and Jerry Vines, the past president of the Southern Baptist Convention, were frequent guests on primetime shows denigrating Islam and its prophet as "inherently evil and violent." Rev. Graham, the head of the international missionary agency Samaritan's Purse and son of the evangelist Billy Graham, stated that Islam is "a very evil and wicked religion." Rev. Vines described the prophet as "a demon-possessed pedophile." Rev. Falwell joined this discourse in a *60 Minutes* interview by arguing that "Muhammad was a terrorist." Partly as a result of this powerful "othering" process reproduced on a daily basis, a majority of Americans in 2006 believe that "Muslims are disproportionately prone to violence" (Deane & Fears 2006, A01).

Sociologist Andrew Beveridge reports (2001) that in September 2001, 34 percent of teens said that they viewed Arab-Americans as potential terrorists. In a March 2006 *Washington Post*/ABC survey, one-third of polled Americans believed that "Islam helps to stoke violence," up from 14 percent in September 2001 (Deane & Fears 2006, A01). In the same survey, 43 percent had heard negative remarks about Arabs, and 25 percent admitted feeling prejudice toward Muslims. More recent polling data show that the dynamics are probably becoming more negative. In a *USA Today*/Gallup poll conducted on July 28–30, 2006, about four out of ten respondents favored requiring Muslims, including U.S. citizens, to carry a special ID in order to protect the United States from a terrorist attack (Elias 2006).

James Zogby, president of the Arab American Institute, explains the currents connecting political discourse and popular opinion: "The intensity has not abated and remains a vein that's very near the surface, ready to be tapped at any moment. . . . Members of Congress have been exploiting this . . . issue. Radio commentators have been talking about it nonstop" (cited in Deane & Fears 2006, A01). Bayoumi, the editor of *The Edward Said Reader*, recently summarized the current context and how it shapes the emerging Muslim "race":

> The persistent racism of the past half-decade [is] a new prejudice concocted out of old-time religious chauvinism, classic ethnic bigotry and a hefty dose of political repression. Arabs, South Asians and Muslims around the country have had to deal with a series of laws, executive orders and policing strategies—dubbed "designer" laws by some American Muslims—that target them almost exclusively. Many have become accustomed to drawing links with the wartime fate of Japanese-Americans.
>
> But "designer" laws produce more than historical comparisons. Japanese internment occurred at a time in American history when Asian exclusion laws were still on the books. Jim Crow was alive and racism was formally a part of the American system. Today's "war on terror," by contrast, plays out in our post–civil rights era. In a society that mouths the virtues of multiculturalism, the present war has legislatively produced the first virtual "race" for the twenty-first century, the Muslim race. (www.the nation.com, September 25, 2006)

The Effects of Media Coverage on Youth

> You don't want to be alienated, but it's like being pushed in a corner when you stand and you just listen all day to Muslim bashing on every single channel—these people are violent, these people are this, these people are that you know.   —Javaid, nineteen years old

Suárez-Orozco writes about the "pattern of intense exclusion and segregation between large number of immigrants and the larger society" (2004, 143), making it difficult for youth to participate in the opportunity structure or the psychological sense of a national "we." When she talks about "identity formation under siege," she is borrowing from social mirroring theory, disassembling how negative social imagery and practices penetrate the souls of young people in the United States. If these messages are "predominantly negative and hostile" and if "these reflections are received in a number of mirrors, including the media, the classroom and the street, the outcome [can be] devastating" (2004, 148). As Suárez-Orozco predicted, we heard a great deal from the participants in our studies of how they are depicted in the media. When we asked the adolescents in our younger group about media coverage, only about 40 percent agreed with the statement that their culture "is respected in the media," and a smaller proportion, less than 30 percent, agreed with the statement that their religion is respected. Similar sentiments about the media were evident in the focus group's discussion:

> I think the media supports this historical idea that Islam is a religion spread by violence and I think it's a deeply spiritual religion and they try to make it seem very superficial and the media just tries to reinforce that idea that even if it doesn't manifest transparently I think that's what it is always mentioning. And I think the media, not just with Islam, but is very negative with, here in America I have read studies about this, very negative for all religions. I think, but especially Islam, that's the thing that bothers me that most and I actually went to a private school, and you would actually hear a lot of professors, at least one professor, that Latin professor, he would say stuff in class like, "these people spread their religion by the sword." . . . It blocks people from experiencing each other more and being open-minded and hearing the other side and not just assuming like these people are you know, violent people. By far, I think we are very non-violent, we are very passive.

Another Muslim American teenager agrees:

> Most of the stuff that you see on the news, on TV, in the papers, about Muslims it's not me and it's not any of them [pointing out others in the focus group] and it's probably not any of the 99 percent of Muslims I've met. They are going to sensationalize stories and they are not going to talk about the average person living in our age, the average person living on Atlantic Avenue in Brooklyn, they are going to talk about that plot that was uncovered at Grand Central Station or something like that. I mean the news is a special case and America's image of Muslims unfortunately has been fabricated.

A Pakistani young man, age twenty, pointed out the hypocrisy in the way Muslims are treated by the U.S. media and politicians: "How can you call one sixth of the world fascist or some kind of cult that's been around for fourteen hundred years?" Another young man angrily stated:

> I really get frustrated. People like the media and our politicians are like so intellectually dishonest when they start talking about these issues. It's like they assume that we as a nation are like morally somewhere in the sky and that everyone else is somewhere down on the ground, and so like we can look down and tell them, "hey you guys don't know how to live." That really troubles me.

Partly as a result of misrepresentation of Muslims and Islam in the popular media, many young Muslim Americans seek out news and information in alternative sources. A nineteen-year-old young man told us that "instead of going to CNN.com, or instead of going to whatever broadcast media there is published in the U.S.," he checks out international sources such as BBC.com or the *Guardian*'s homepage. A much younger, fourteen-year-old girl surprised us with her elaborate system of getting the news: "I listen to CNN, Fox News, Al-Jazeera, and French news every night." Both contended that because of their efforts, they probably know more about the issues than "the quote unquote average American." These young people understand well that they are being framed as the cause of a moral panic over "terror."

Moral Panics: The Case of Muslim Youth

Historian Corey Robin argued that political fears have been systematically manipulated throughout U.S. history to mobilize a national identity and to justify both international and domestic aggression:

> Convinced that we lack moral or political principles to bind us together, we savor the experience of being afraid, as many writers did after 9/11, for only fear, we believe can turn us from isolated men and women into a unified people. Looking to political fear as the ground of our public life, we refuse to see the grievances and controversies that underlie it. (2004, 3)

Drawing on Hofstadter's notion of "the paranoid style of American politics" (1964, 77), Robin noted that "though this fear is also created, wielded or manipulated by political leaders, its specific purpose or function is internal intimidation, to use sanctions or the threat of sanctions to ensure that one group retains or augments its power at the expense of another" (2004, 19).

In such campaigns of fear, it is not unusual for the government to create and deploy varied technologies of surveillance, enabled by both machines and people (for contemporary as well as historic analyses of youth as a target of national moral panics, see Ayers et al. 2001) and to pin a badge of moral suspicion on groups under surveillance, both outside and inside the United States. Keeping us all afraid, ever dependent on authorities who seem to know best, Americans are shockingly willing to sacrifice their own and others' civil liberties to remain "free." Moral panics often funnel collective anxieties onto the bodies of youth of color who attract a disproportionate share of the watching, the "catching," the arresting and serving time. Today, these sights may fall on Muslim American youth.

Moral panics have the effect of creating costly vulnerabilities in the targeted communities which, at the same time, bolster the white/good/rational/civilized side of the binary. In moral panics, victims often are recast as threats. Two stories about missing Muslim daughters reveal how Muslim American youth have been repositioned as a threat to "America."

On April 7, 2005, two sixteen-year old girls were arrested in New York City after the FBI said they planned to become suicide bombers. One of them, Tashnuba, had stopped attending her small New York City public high school in September 2004 because of problems at school about her Islamic dress code. Just a few years after her family had entered the country without papers, Tashnuba began wearing a full-length veil and teaching religion at a local mosque. She wanted to attend an all-girls Islamic school, but her family could not afford the tuition. So she was being homeschooled and was working toward a GED.

Her father grew quite concerned about his daughter. A watch salesman from Bangladesh, he labeled himself as

far more devoted to American education than to prayer. . . . Then last fall, the daughter, whom her father describes as loving Bollywood soap operas and shopping with girlfriends, startled him and her mother by seeking their approval to marry a young American Muslim man they had never met and whom she barely knew. (Bernstein & Lichtblau 2005, B1)

Her father refused. "A few months later, when the teenager stayed out overnight for the first time, her father, fearing elopement, went to the police for help. . . . It is a decision he regrets deeply."

On March 24, two agents who claimed to represent Immigration and Customs came to Tashnuba's home and told her mother that

the reason they were taking Tashnuba was because of an asylum case and because she did not show up at her appointment date. . . . They confiscated Tashnuba's computer, her personal journals, and her mother's cell phone. They took Tashnuba, to Federal Plaza . . . for 11 hours, and told if she did not comply, her brothers and sisters would be sent to foster homes and her parents would be deported to Bangladesh. (Bernstein & Lichtblau 2005, B1)

At Federal Plaza, Tashnuba met Adama, another Muslim American teen, from Guinea. Adama also was sixteen at the time of her detention by federal authorities. In 1990, shortly after her birth, Adama and her parents arrived in the United States, also without papers. Her father was arrested for immigration violations. According to friends and teachers at Heritage High School in East Harlem, Adama wore "jeans under her garb, [displayed] a lively classroom curiosity about topics like Judaism and art, and . . . after school [she] cared for four young siblings [all U.S. citizens]" (Bernstein & Lichtblau 2005, B1). Her teacher, Kimberly Lane, told reporters, "This is a girl who's been in this country since she was 2 years old. She's just a regular teenager—like . . . her biggest worry was whether she'd done her homework or studied for a science test" (Bernstein 2005, B3). Raised as an "orthodox Muslim," her teacher explained that Adama was "completely integrated into this school. She's a wonderful girl" (Bernstein 2005, B3). This teacher recalled a moment when she overheard a crowd of students cheering in the hallway of her school. When she looked out her classroom doorway, she saw that

the teenager [Adama] had stopped wearing her veil and she beamed as
her fellow students, seeing her face for the first time, cheered. . . . After
the class read *Night*, the Holocaust memoir by Elie Wiesel, the girl wrote
a paper about genocide in the Sudan. . . . She was so excited about a field
trip to see Christo's Gates in Central Park, that she skipped an appointment at immigration—a teenage impulse the teacher now worries might
have set off problems with federal authorities. (Bernstein 2005, B3)

The FBI and the Immigration and Customs Enforcement failed to
charge either Tashnuba Hayder or Adama Bah with a crime, but the two
still were subjected to weeks of substandard detention and interrogation, and Tashnuba and her U.S.-born siblings have now been deported
to Dhaka, Bangladesh. Although Adama was released, her father was returned to Guinea, separated from his five children.

Later Adama returned to the news:

After three hours of testimony behind closed doors yesterday, an immigration judge adjourned a hearing in the case of a young woman seeking
asylum from Guinea's practice of female genital mutilation. The delay, until March 1, disappointed supporters of Adama Bah, 18, who had hoped
for a decision on her petition. Ms. Bah had been detained and questioned
by federal agents who asserted that she was a potential suicide bomber—
an assertion that was dropped when she was released in May 2005. But
she still faces deportation to Guinea, which she left at age 2, because her
childhood visa is invalid. (Bernstein 2006b, B3)

Two young women go missing, one religious and the other secular.
Their eyes meet, and their fates become entwined. One has already been
deported, and the other awaits a decision. These are simple stories of
adolescent girls testing their freedoms modestly and paying a high price,
the devastating consequences of moral panics launched on the backs of
youth.

As Nguyen wrote,

There's very little room left, within a national climate of fear and growing intolerance, for any infraction. . . . In a political imagination that has

shifted so far to the right, people without status and with a certain profile must earn and deserve their place in society, must prove why they should not be suspected, jailed, and shipped away. (Nguyen 2005, xv)

Like Nguyen, we worry that there is "very little room left," and so we close this chapter on moral exclusion with the hope of making a bit of room. In the next few chapters, we want our readers to meet the wise, vibrant, challenging, funny, scared, thoughtful, confused, chatty, and quiet Muslim American youth who generously shared their lives with us. We ask our readers to remember that these young people are thoroughly American, just like the Native, Mexican, African, and Japanese American youth who were internally exiled years before them. Relentlessly committed to this country and disturbed by the national movement to exclude them, these youth seek to shape the political landscape of tomorrow.

Meet Yeliz

A Young Woman of Conviction, Distinct across Contexts

Yeliz's self-portrait is of a beautiful young woman, head covered with ḥijāb, with the letters MUSLIM floating overhead. An A student in most of her courses, Yeliz studies three to five hours a week, considers school to be "very important," and is now reading *Of Mice and Men*. She describes herself as "Caucasian/white/Euro-American." Her mother and father are from Turkey, and both are high school graduates.

Yeliz is well aware that her behaviors, her perspectives, and her practices vary according to the situation. "I draw that because I used to live in Paterson , we used to walk around on the way to the mosque . . . but I'm partly Muslim." Selcuk (the interviewer) asked, "What is she looking at?" Yeliz responded, "Everybody." Selcuk pressed a bit, "Do people look at her?" "Ahh, well, some people. It depends. Well, not in Paterson, but if you are here [suburban New Jersey] people will stare at you." Then Selcuk asked whether the staring made Yeliz uncomfortable. "No, if someone says something to me, I just argue back and . . . they wouldn't dare . . . I get into fights too much."

Remarkably reflective about her tendency to get into "fights," Yeliz also was mindful of her prayer behavior. In the midst of the interview, she announced to Selcuk, "I'm going to start today, I used to do it [pray] once in a while, but now I'm going to start five times a day."

An extremely assertive young woman, Yeliz is delighted to educate others about Islam and to argue if necessary.

> See now in social studies class, we are now learning about Muslims, and I am the only Muslim in my class and the teacher tells me if we say something wrong, correct me, can you bring in things to show everybody, so I told them, yeah. I'm gonna bring in stuff. . . . It feels good 'cause no one knows about it. I teach them.

Yeliz had been planning a career as a lawyer, and then "I switched to FBI" and now maybe "detective." She likes to go outside, . . . talk a lot. I talk a lot. . . . we hang out with friends, go on the computer sometimes, talk to my friends . . . sports, I like to play with my cousins and I was gonna join the basketball team this year, but I couldn't so they opened karate here so I'm going to start karate again. . . . I write stories and stuff. I like writing.

She is not stressed except "when others make jokes about or put down Muslim; when people consider Muslim Americans to be more dangerous than other groups; and when loosening the ties with Islam is difficult." Although she rated almost all the physical and psychological problems as "Not at all true," Yeliz rated "I argue a lot" as VERY TRUE.

It came as no surprise, then that when Yeliz hears "TV and news and everything . . . about Muslims,"

I feel like beating them up . . . because you can't judge anybody. That's just one person's mistake . . . there is actually two kids that sit behind me in social studies class, and I kept hearing "the Muslims, the Muslims"; that's what they kept on saying and I guess they were making fun of the teacher when she was teaching, and I asked them about it but not when they were like "Muslims" to stop it, if not I was gonna turn around and yell at them. What are they gonna do? It was two boys, I even know them, they shouldn't be saying anything. I got really mad. My sister was, like, "Forget about it." I don't forget things.

Acutely attuned to contextual slights or assaults, Yeliz could "pass" as Caucasian and non-Muslim, but instead she responds assertively and passionately to any bias she encounters. Her friends are Muslim, Bosnian, and "American" . . . but "my mom says 'watch who your friends are' . . . be careful." Yeliz notes that her older sister is

even more strict than my mom. She is serious . . . more strict . . . she's annoying, she'll say, let's see, don't talk to this person, I don't like who he is who she is, you know, she knows them and so she tells me not to hang out with them. . . . Sometimes I get really mad . . . [but] I have to be [OK with it]; yeah, she'll kick me out.

"If I [Yeliz] want to go somewhere, it's like take Gio with you, take a boy with you." Gio is her little brother.

When asked about her personal identification as a Muslim American, Yeliz was clear. She's Turkish, and she loves all the lessons she learns from her mother.

I learn everything from my mom 'cause she, like, she will teach me different things about religion about the culture she teach me, like she would tell me stories if she has time, you know? When I was little, we used to be in the car and she would play music for me. She used to teach me everything, so like I learned from her 'cause I guess she knows more first generation.

Although Yeliz's appearance may be ambiguous—that is, people would not know she was Muslim or Turkish unless she told them—she is committed to telling them.

Selcuk: Given all that you know about American teens and Muslim teens, what is truly unique about you?
Yeliz: Hmmm, that I express my feelings and everything, that I'm open. I don't say anything like, you know, if I think something is bad, I tell them. If I think something is good, I tell them. I explain myself with everything, like I don't keep everything inside.

Asked to offer advice to a young Muslim American girl five years younger, Yeliz told us:

I'd tell her that she should stand up for herself if someone messes with her, that she should always be, like, not be scared of anybody if she needs to wear it, she needs to wear it like her scarf and she is gonna wear it, like I'd tell her not be scared of anybody, to show and to be proud.

Yeliz dances on the hyphen, daring anyone to challenge her right to live in multiple worlds.

Map 3. Muhammad, Male, Arab, Age 14

4

■　■　■　■　■　■　■　■　■

The Weight of the Hyphen
Discrimination and Coping

In *Black Skin, White Masks*, Franz Fanon wrote about the painful shock of seeing oneself through objectifying eyes:

Look, a Negro!
  I came into the world imbued with the will to find a meaning in things, my spirit filled with the desire to attain to the source of the world, and then I found that I was an object in the midst of other objects. Sealed into that crushing objecthood, I turned beseechingly to others. Their attention was a liberation, running over my body suddenly abraded into nonbeing, endowing me once more with an agility that I had thought lost, and by taking me out of the world, restoring me to it. But just as I reached the other side, I stumbled and the movements, the attitudes, the glances of the other fixed me there, in the sense in which a chemical solution is fixed by a dye. I was indignant; I demanded an explanation. Nothing happened. I burst apart. Now the fragments have been put together again by another self. (1967, 109)

Many immigrant children and adolescents, Suárez-Orozco argues, respond to the "othering" of their group with similar self-doubt, shame, low aspirations, and disengagement: "We should not underestimate the toll that these experiences and shattered dreams take upon the souls of developing children. The positive attitudes of recent immigrant children are a remarkable resource; as a society we would be best served by harnessing rather than crushing those energies" (2000, 221). Here we consider the toll.

Numerous studies reveal that individuals from marginalized groups are exposed to stress as a result of their social status (Meyer 2003). Stress associated with immigrant status also has been widely documented in the literature as "acculturative stress" (Berry 1997; Nesdale, Rooney, & Smith 1997; Suárez-Orozco 2000). Thus, "stress" originates not only from the prejudice and discrimination stemming from one's minority status but also from the developmental challenges of reconciling multiple cultural systems of reference (LaFramboise, Coleman, & Gerton 1993).

One of the most disturbing findings from our studies of Muslim youth over the past five years was the degree to which they have absorbed discriminatory acts into their lives. Muslim young men and women told us through surveys, focus groups, and maps, about the joys but also the burdens of being Muslim, young, and American at this point in history. In addition to worrying about how to cope with and protect themselves in a state of heightened surveillance and suspicion, they also worry about the social scrutiny and discrimination to which their families are subjected.

In our two survey studies of younger and older Muslim Americans, we asked them to cite the frequency of discriminatory acts they had experienced during the previous twelve months. Using a modified version of Krieger and Sidney's (1996) checklist, they documented the frequency of discrimination experienced at school, while shopping, on the street, on the playground, and in a public setting—just because they were Muslim. The participants reported their responses in a scale ranging from 0 (never) to 5 (almost daily).

About 84 percent of the younger cohort, aged twelve to eighteen, reported one or more acts of discrimination during the previous twelve months. More than 10 percent, equal numbers of girls and boys, reported experiences of *daily* discrimination. About 60 percent of the participants reported that they experienced discrimination at school, the setting where they were mistreated the most, and the remainder reported being mistreated while they were shopping, that is, in public spaces.

The results were slightly worse for the older group, aged eighteen to twenty-five. Using the same scale, we found that over the past year, 88 percent of the participants reported having been subjected to at least one act of discrimination *because they were Muslim*. Furthermore, 13 percent of the participants indicated that they experienced discrimination on a daily basis in at least one of the settings. Again, as chapter 3 showed, school was where Muslims had to deal with discrimination most often. The older group also seemed to have experienced less discrimination while shopping, compared with other settings, for which 54 percent reported being mistreated because they were Muslim.

At a suburban northeastern college campus, Sirin (2005a) conducted another comparative study of 145 undergraduate students, 71 of whom were from Muslim and 74 of whom were from Euro-American Christian backgrounds, to understand the degree to which students experienced "culture-related stress" on campus. Sirin measured culture-related stress using four scenarios illustrating cultural discomfort on campus on a variety of issues such as sexuality, human rights, and religious beliefs. The participants rated their stress level and also the various ways in which they could address each issue, such as talking to the professor, requesting another assignment, or refusing to complete the assignment. We created two valid instruments, one assessing the stress level and the other assessing the participants' ability to address the issue. The results, presented in figure 1, show that Muslim students experience more cultural stress on campus

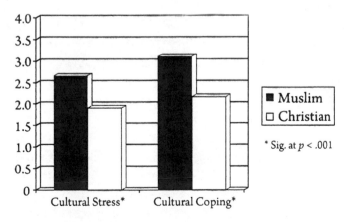

Figure 1. Cultural Stress on Campus

but that they also seem to address the issue by seeking help from their professors.

Unfortunately, many young people from all backgrounds experience a certain degree of stress and discrimination in their everyday lives in the United States solely because of their background. In a nationwide study, 44 percent of African Americans, 24 percent of Latino/as, 56 percent of Asian Americans, and only 7 percent of Euro-Americans reported being the target of discriminatory treatment during the previous year (Hogue, Hargraves, & Collins 2000). Fisher, Wallace, and Fenton (2000) also found a higher prevalence among minority youth, with 57 percent reporting having been called a racially insulting name, 31 percent reporting having been threatened by peers because of their race or ethnicity, and 42 percent believing that they had been given a lower grade in school because of their race or ethnicity. What these bleak numbers confirm is that Muslims are in the substantial ranks of those who feel mistreated in the United States simply because of their background.

Not only do these alarming statistics reveal the frequency of discrimination against this generation of Muslim youth, but in our conversations with young men and women and through focus groups, interviews, and maps (see map 14), we heard about layers of exclusion and scrutiny. Those from the younger and older groups representing the diversity of Muslims in both ethnicity (e.g., Arab, Pakistani, Iranian) and denominations (e.g., Sunni, Shi'a) offered stories of surveillance from varied sources: national and local media, the Immigration and Naturalization Service, the FBI, police, schools. As youth, they also were watched by the Muslim American community itself: parents, older siblings, "Muslim uncles and aunties," as well as from God or Allah. They described being watched, talked about, or suspected in public spaces, on the subway, at school, at home, and in their neighborhoods.

In response to what we label a *scaffolding of scrutiny*, we heard a range of responses. Like Japanese American young people sixty years ago, some of the Muslim Americans spoke of great loyalty toward the United States. Those who feel "thoroughly American" have been reminded on the streets, however, that they are "aliens." Zahra feels "misunderstood" and judged. "We do live in a society that does, you know, not understand us. They do judge us. And it's very difficult to, you know, try to break away from that."

She later related how she was verbally assaulted on the street after September 11, 2001:

I was standing outside my mosque, and I think it was like a month after [9/11]. I was wearing a scarf, and this guy starts cursing at me. "You're Osama bin Ladin's daughter." . . . It was awful, awful stuff, and that is one of the biggest things high on my mind when it comes to discrimination and just feeling so not welcome. That doesn't happen to me on a regular basis, because I don't wear *hijāb*. But I'm sure people who do, people who are obviously Arab or obviously Muslim, they get it a lot more than, you know. So on their behalf, I think it still exists a lot.

Likewise, Asma fears that her name alone may signify an invitation to discrimination:

So, at times, yes there is a lot of discrimination here. When people meet me personally, they have a totally different aspect of me [than] when they just know me through, let's say, a job application. I have my name filled out, my religion and everything. They look at it like they're racist about that. They wouldn't probably accept me just by looking at a job application, but if they were to meet me personally, they'd have a better view of who I am. And my last name is Hussein. That's another problem. They look upon me like, "Oh, my God. She might be related to Saddam Hussein," . . . there is a lot of discrimination. There is.

Many of the young people in our study relied on "being American" as the basis for their criticism of American policies and practices. This combination of claiming citizenship and the right to dissent mirrors the work of Sunaina Maira. In her study of South Asian Muslim youth in Boston, Maira found that young people used various discourses to narrate their sense of citizenship. *Flexible citizenship*, a term borrowed from Aihwa Ong, is a social practice by which youth engage simultaneously in the political and social practices of several nations. Other youths embrace a *multicultural or polycultural citizenship* by which they mark their social networks as diverse, bridging not only nation of origin and United States but also stretching across racial and ethnic groups of peers. A subsample of the young people in our research engaged in what Maira calls *dissenting citizenship*, posing a

> critique [of the] imperial feeling of U.S. nationalism after 9/11 through their linking of warfare within the state to international war. It is this link between the domestic and imperial that makes their perspective an important mode of dissent because the imperial project of the new "Cold War," as in earlier times, works by obscuring the links between domestic and foreign policies. (Maira 2004, 15)

Maira continues,

> These young immigrants are simply—but not merely—subjects of both the "war on terror" and the "war on immigrants." Their exclusion from processes of "being-made" as citizens, legally and culturally, and their emergent political "self-making," highlight the ways in which civic consent to state policy is secured by imperial power. The targeting of a population demonized as "other," and the absorption of previously targeted communities into a unifying nationalism and climate of fear, shift attention away from the ways in which the war at home and the war abroad actually work in tandem, at the expense of ordinary people everywhere. (Maira 2004, 16)

In an example of Maira's *dissenting citizenship*, twenty-four-year-old Manal, who has a degree in political science and is pursuing a master's degree in education, decorated her identity map with symbols of surveillance and exclusion: "political—war—economic, no-fly list, wire tapping, hate, terrorism" (see map 15).

Leila, a twenty-two-year-old college student, felt personally judged and violated by the scrutiny and by the hypocrisy of a government that says it stands for freedom. A college senior on her way to law school, Leila told us:

> What America means to me is freedom. If you take away that freedom, it's not America anymore. This country has these laws and the ways of living and what it represents. It no longer is representing what it was, it's different now. . . . But have I been pleased with those laws? No. I don't like

the Patriot Act. I'm totally against it. This is America. America represents the American dream—freedom, having a house, having everything, but just be free, you know. Not having anyone track your moves or see what you're doing, who you're sending an e-mail to. Why? This is my life. No one has the right to intrude in my life.

Positioning herself as deeply patriotic and critical, Leila, like several of the other young people we interviewed, worries about her civil and human rights as a Muslim in the United States. And she has good reason to fear. As noted elsewhere, many national polls show that almost half the U.S. citizens polled nationally said they believed that the U.S. government should in some way limit Muslim Americans' civil liberties (Friedlander 2004). Many of the young women already know this because they live it. Rabab believes that "even if you're a U.S. citizen, they'll take everything you have." Fatima does not trust the system designed to protect her civil liberties. "We have all these amendments and everything that are protecting us, but there's always a loophole. There's always . . . some way that something can happen that shouldn't have happened but did happen." Aisha worries about the Patriot Act and phone taps, saying,

> I think that's wrong, and I think, you know, they're just slowly taking away like all *our freedom*. And I think like years from now we're going to look back and we're really not going to be able to say anything. It's going to be like a dictatorship country basically.

Suha asks, "Why is [this country] treating me like an outsider? I'm not. I don't feel as an outsider, and I shouldn't be treated like one, and neither should any other Muslim who resides here. They shouldn't be treated like outsiders." Fatima adds: "I think all *we* ask for is respect and acceptance, because *we, as Americans here*, haven't done anything directly to hurt any other Americans, so why are we being treated like this?"

Iman talks about the experience of traveling with a Muslim-sounding name:

> There's always that element of like am I being racially profiled. . . . I was traveling with my sister and she has a different last name because she's married. . . . Americans . . . think her last name is more Muslim than my

last name . . . they're probably like equal. . . . We were traveling and had to take like a few planes to get to wherever we needed to get to, and every time, there was always a security check on all her bags. Every single time . . . they claim it was random, but I mean, we always feel like there is a side to it that's not random. You know, as they say "random selection," we always feel like we're picked for that random thing [laughs], and it's just like how random is it really when I'm always the one being searched?

Ivette explains the multisensory nature of surveillance: being watched is not simply a visual act but applies to all the senses. A blind woman, Ivette is well aware "of who's watching, who isn't."

I asked this one guy, I said, "Excuse me, can you tell me what street this is?" And he turned around and he spit at me. I mean I argued my case and then walked away, and I found help somewhere else. I just eventually walked until I realized where I was. Or me and my friends, we went out to eat, and this happens to me a lot. We went out to eat two weeks ago and I got horrible service. It's not the first and only time. And everyone got their food except me to begin with, everyone was asked what they wanted to eat, but the guy walked away from me without even asking me, like I wasn't even sitting there. . . . It's a lot of things for me. It's, I am Muslim; I wear the scarf; I have a dog. And it's a lot of issues, but mainly it was because I have the scarf and he just didn't feel like dealing with me. It's not the first time it's happened to me. It's happened to me quite often. It used to really, really rile me up, but now, "Just give me my food. I'm just hungry!"

Patrice talked about her emotional reactions to the renewal of the Patriot Act:

I think I really get stressed out about it sometimes when they do things like renew the Patriot Act and, all these detainees and . . . how they exploited people because they found out they were illegal. I've heard that so many young men have been interviewed and thousands of them have been deported. A lot of people's lives have been affected. I think it's really tough, and it gave me a negative perspective of American politics, you know.

Inas is extremely disturbed by the violations of her civil liberties. As if she were speaking to the government, she asks the group, "What are you going to do? Arrest me for being American? I was born and raised in this country, you know." Ivette follows with her questions about the government's policies: "I just think it's amazing. This government with the policies. . . . How you can do this and say this is a democracy? But if you're being policed by everything, then you really can't, you can't do anything. And they have the nerve to criticize other governments!"

The Price of Discrimination

One's reputation, whether false or true, cannot be hammered, hammered, hammered, into one's head without doing something to one's character.

—Allport 1954

Adolescence is the moment in which international, national, social and personal "crises" erupt most publicly and spontaneously, and yet they often are misread by adults and youth as simply personal, hormonal, disciplinary, or developmental "problems" (Abu El-Haj 2005; Appadurai 2004; Fine et. al. 2004; Sen 2004; Sirin et al. 2004; Sirin & Rogers-Sirin 2005). Paul Willis argues that youth embody and perform for the culture the very economic, technical, and, we would add, cultural, conflicts that constitute global politics.

> Youth are always among the first to experience the problems and possibilities of the successive waves of technical and economic modernization [cultural crises] that sweep through capitalist societies. Young people respond in disorganized and chaotic ways, but to the best of their abilities and with relevance to the actual possibilities of their lives as they see, live and embody them. These responses are actually embedded in the flows of cultural modernization but to adult eyes they may seem to be mysterious, troubling and even shocking and antisocial. (Willis 2002, 461)

We consider here the cost of discrimination for young Muslim Americans. The vast literature on adolescent experiences of discrimination shows adverse effects on both psychological well-being and physical health. The perceived frequency of discrimination and the cumulative

ecological risk (community disadvantage and stress) predict a more difficult psychological adjustment for African American than European American youth (Prelow et al. 2004). Simons and colleagues (2002) found racial discrimination to be closely associated with depressive symptoms in
African American youth, and Rumbaut (1994) confirmed this relationship
for immigrant youth (see also Simons et al. 2002). Rosenbloom and Way
(2004), like Fisher, Wallace, and Fenton (2000), documented the substantial rates of "discrimination distress" across racial and ethnic groups.
In both studies, African American and Latino youth reported higher rates
of institutional discrimination, and East and South Asian American youth
reported higher rates of peer discrimination.

Our analyses of the surveys of young adult Muslim Americans also
reveal the significant physical and psychological health consequences of
moral exclusion. Youth who feel morally excluded, experiencing discrimination-related stress in the mainstream U.S. society because of their status
as Muslim American, are far more likely to report anxiety, depression, and
somatic complaints than do those who do not report high levels of exclusion stress. Specifically, we found significant moderate-to-high correlations between discrimination-related stress and psychological withdrawal,
somatic complaints, and anxiety/depression. In addition to discrimination-related stress, we also found significant correlations between the perceived frequency of discrimination and psychological withdrawal as well
as between discrimination and symptoms of anxiety/depression. In combination, these quantitative findings confirmed what we heard from the
youth in the focus groups and interviews, that the toll of moral exclusion,
in both discrimination-related stress and perceived discriminatory acts,
extends far beyond identity negotiation and affects the psychological well-
being and health of young people at a critical time in their developmental
process.

We also found positive evidence of resistance to discrimination in our
younger group study. Those who tried to challenge the discrimination reported significantly fewer incidences of religious and ethnic discrimination than those who did not,[1] and those who resisted discrimination also
appeared to be significantly less worried than their counterparts who accepted discrimination as a fact of life.[2] In other words, adolescents who accepted discriminatory treatment as a fact of life reported more discrimination and more anxiety. There are many ways to interpret these differences.

Perhaps those who internalize and do not challenge their experiences feel and appear helpless ("it is a fact of life"), rendering them more vulnerable to continued discrimination and anxiety. Alternatively, young people who experience more discrimination may be more likely to believe that it is a fact of life, and those who experience less discrimination might have more confidence to challenge injustice when they do encounter it.

We also found in our surveys that young men and women experience cultural and political stressors quite differently. We used a modified version of the SAFE measure, an instrument originally designed to measure "acculturation stress." We included items such as "Because I am Muslim, I feel that others often exclude me from participating in their activities," "People look down upon me if I practice customs of my culture," and "I am upset that most people consider the Muslim American community to be more dangerous than other groups." The participants in the older group study were asked to rate thirteen of these items, from 0 (have not experienced/not at all stressful) to 3 (very stressful).[3] Compared with Muslim men, Muslim women seem to experience, or report, more discrimination-related stress.

While there was no significant gender difference between females and males in the perceived frequency of discrimination, a closer look at the survey data shows that those women who cover their hair report more discrimination.[4] These findings confirm our expectations that Muslim girls who are veiled and therefore more visible would have a more difficult path than relatively invisible Muslim boys would (for a very interesting discussion of visible minorities versus minorities who can "pass," see Helms 1994). To varying degrees, Muslim girls must endure the stress of living in a world that demonizes them for their religious affiliation, equates Islam with terrorism, and locks them into a "simple binary of resistance/subordination" (Mahmood 2005, 9), at once invisible and hypervisible (Boyd-Franklin, Franklin, & Touissant 2003).

This variation by gender echoes a more general finding about immigrants' different expectations for daughters and sons. Much of what people think is unique to this generation of Muslim Americans is typical for immigrant families. Dion and Dion (2001) found that pressures for "traditional socialization" are particularly strong for second-generation daughters across immigrant groups when the new country seems to threaten important cultural values. Dasgupta (1998) discovered that struggles over "cultural continuity" are launched in and over the bodies of second-generation daughters and in their intergenerational conflicts, even though young women and their mothers seemed to endorse similarly strong "egalitarian" attitudes. Suárez-Orozco and Qin documented this phenomenon across time and nation:

> One of the most consistent findings across studies in immigrant families is the different socialization strategies that parents have for their daughters and their sons . . . this finding cuts across nearly every ethnic background as well as across different historic periods: stricter parental control of immigrant girls has been documented in second-generation Chinese women in San Francisco in the 1920s . . . , Italian women in Harlem in the 1930s, . . . Mexican girls in the Southwest during the interwar years . . . , daughters of Caribbean . . . , Asian Indian . . . , Hispanic, . . . Yemeni . . . , Chinese . . . , and Hindu, Muslim and Mexican . . . immigrant girls in the last two decades. . . . Similar findings are also shown among South Asian immigrant groups in Canada . . . and among Muslim immigrants in France. (2006, 171)

But in a nonclinical sample, Suárez-Orozco and Qin also found less family conflict in immigrant families than in white American families. Next we examine some of these family dynamics.

Dynamics at Home

Living in a culture of scrutiny penetrates even the most protected and seemingly private spaces of family life. "PARANOIA, PARANOIA, PARANOIA!!!" wrote a young man in response to an open-ended question about daily stressors, stating that his "father becomes very scared for me and at times attempts to control this." Another young man asked an unexpected question to others in a focus group: "Are your parents, like, paranoid?" Everybody in the group, from diverse ethnic backgrounds, jumped into a lively conversation. In the focus groups we conducted and in the open-ended questions we asked, young people spoke of great pressure from their parents not to be too visible as Muslim in the United States. At the same time, they thought they had to "take care of" their parents, defusing their "paranoid" thoughts. At some point, someone would admit that the children, too, sometimes harbored these very thoughts. Nadim, a nine-teen-year-old son of immigrants from Pakistan, told the following story about his relationship with his mother:

> I live near the mosque so I would go there for prayer—and my parents wouldn't want me to go 'cause I remember one time I was in a class, and *Time* or something was there watching and they took a picture. I wasn't in the picture, but just like you can imagine this is the picture, and the little corner my head was in it, 'cause I was right in front of the camera lens. There was the top of my head in the picture. Only I knew it was me. My mom looked at the picture, and she saw the top of my head and was like, "This is you! This is what I am telling you! You can't be going to the mosque and doing all this stuff, you don't know what is going to hap-pen!" You know, it was a good article too. . . . I was barely in the picture. . . . She knew it was me. She was going crazy. She was like, "You don't know who is watching you."

As funny as this sounds, we heard about many similar situations in which even jokes created awkward moments of fear and suspicion at the dinner table. One young man offered this:

> I'm oblivious to all this stuff 'cause if they wanted to do something to me, let them do it to me. Empires fall. I'm not really scared of them. But my parents are very paranoid. I was talking to a friend of mine, and we were talking about the war in Lebanon and just by saying Hezbollah or Allah [was enough to upset her]. . . . The surveillance . . . am I against it? Most definitely. It's not right, but am I going to waste my time and become par-anoid when I can't do anything about it? I know people who are. Like one day I was talking to my friend and he was joking and said, "Let's convert to Judaism, . . . and then convert back to Islam," and his parents heard the word *Jew*, and they were like "FBI! FBI!" He was joking; he said it jok-ingly. I think that's very paranoid.

Another young man, Faisal, pointed out his dilemma as an activist and a "good son." As a civic-oriented young man, he believes in participating in the mainstream activities beyond the Muslim community and is commit-ted to be part of the dialogue on his campus. At the same time, he must continuously assure his parents that it is fine for his name to be printed in the student paper.

> My parents are extremely paranoid, especially my mom, not so much my dad, but it's not really about when I go to the mosque or something like that. They are like, "Go to the mosque, please go to the mosque." It's more because I am majoring in political science so I am constantly debating with someone and constantly having to prove my point reluctantly. So my mom hates it. Every day when I leave my house, she tells me, "Be careful of what you say and may God be with you" 'cause she is really worried, you know? She really thinks that something is going to happen. And I don't really pay much mind to it because we grew up here; we're like, "yeah, it's all good."

Of course, over time, all this so-called paranoia takes a toll on the relationships between children and their parents. A young man talked about these difficulties:

> I dropped my mom off at Bloomingdale's. I have nothing better to do so I go to the Ninety-sixth Street mosque to just chill out there, you know, read or something, you know, do homework. It's almost like a club area; it's not like I'm excessively religious. I wish. And my father gets mad about that. He's like, "You are going to the mosque too much," and I'm like, "What was I supposed to do?" [Our parents] are very paranoid, and I think that they should take into consideration that they are messing with too many people's lives and what are they catching in the end? They need to work with us.

What the young people call paranoia is, not surprisingly, related to their parents' dreams for and fears about a better life for their children. The young people understand why their parents are concerned: "They usually say that they came here for us, and they don't want us to ruin the opportunity they gave us. They didn't grow up here. I think when we grow up here, we're more like, easy about it, we're like, it's OK, nothing is going to happen." Oram explained, "In my [Albanian] community, a lot of people be like 'Listen, keep quiet, the country is falling,' 'cause they experienced the fall of Yugoslavia."

Like all immigrants, Muslims also bring their history with them. With that comes their history of religious and ethnic struggle in their home countries, not only in the Middle East, but also in other parts of the world. In other words, their parents' "paranoia" reflects their experience of both the United States and their countries of origin.

At the same time, however, bubbling up in the focus group was the fear that maybe their parents were right, or maybe they—the youth—had been anesthetized by the American sense that "it couldn't happen here." Questioning themselves just a bit, the young people, especially the sons, wondered aloud whether they were simply not seeing the gravity of the threat so apparent to their elders:

> We are a bit naive. It's 'cause we grew up here, we automatically assume, and I do, too, just because someone is American, that they are very nice people and they won't . . . but anything can happen here. It can happen just as bad as the worst conflicts in the world. You know, those were normal people too before it happened. Everyone was getting along, friendly and then all of a sudden something happens. So I feel that's where it comes from, it's like "Don't worry about it, this is America, it won't happen." It can happen anywhere, I think. I don't want to be paranoid, you know it's a waste of brain cells.

As youth see their safe and comforting, supportive and engaging world shrinking in the webs of surveillance, they become confused about how to read the dangers.

What was once "public" has been privatized (Low 2003); what could be taken for granted must be approached cautiously. Casual behaviors like hanging out, going to parks, walking down streets, laughing aloud with friends, talking on a cell phone, and sending money home are now publicly scrutinized. The Internet is monitored more and more; schools have adopted extreme "zero tolerance" policies; and stores, parks, malls, and streets are watched for youth, particularly youth of color, including Muslim Americans. African American and Latino youth have long read these messages in accordance with the advice of the elders. Now Muslim American youth are joining the ranks of "dissenting citizens" (Maira 2004). The difference is that the Muslim American youth must enter this new territory without the experience of earlier generations.

Surveillance at Home

From focus groups and interviews, we learned that while the Muslim American community was being watched from the outside, both globally and in the United States, young men and especially young women also must contend with more intimate scrutiny within their families and religious communities (see Khan 2002). These political, social, and psychological dynamics extend well beyond the Muslim American community. Indeed, political scientist Cathy Cohen, discussing the African American community in the United States and its treatment of HIV/AIDS, argued that historically persecuted and marginalized communities typically generate internal policing mechanisms in dialectical relation to their history of oppression: "These internally created, community based definitions of identity . . . center not merely on easily identifiable physical characteristics, but also use moralistic and character evaluations to appraise membership" (1999, 74). Nira Yuval-Davis considered the gendering of such policing: "The mythical unity of . . . 'imagined communities' which divides the world between 'us' and 'them' is maintained and ideologically reproduced by a whole system of . . . symbolic 'border guards' . . . women's roles [function] as symbolic border guards and as embodiments of the collectivity, while at the same time being its cultural reproducers" (1997, 23).

At the nexus of these multiple forces of surveillance and exclusion, it is not surprising to find Iman admitting that she feels "atypical," "outcasted," and "disconnected," "not welcomed," "judged," and "too outspoken" even when she is with other Muslim Americans.

> Oftentimes, I feel like I think too much about truth in religion and where it came from and who said what, and I ask too many questions. I feel like I'm more cultural than religious. . . . And I feel because I ask twenty questions, I'm not welcome there, just like being judged for that. . . . But it's also sad in the sense that you're saying that about your own people, you don't want to be a part of them because you feel like they expect you to be a certain way. And because you're not that certain way, they won't accept you.

Like Iman, Zahra feels judged, but in a different sphere, by her family. "I think there is a part of me that doesn't come out with my family. And I think . . . I don't even know if I could say my family knows who I am. I definitely can't voice my opinion on certain issues, because, they will think I've lost my way."

Iman completed Zahra's thought: "You're being too American." Similarly, a young man who considers himself a devout, practicing Muslim nevertheless finds it difficult at times to please the judging eyes of the Muslim community.

> It's like I don't have my pants above my ankles. I don't have a beard down to here. I don't put mascara in my eyes. Those are nice things, I don't discredit them. If you're at that level of religiosity in which, you know, you can change every outer form of your identity to fit this model of the prophet, it's great. I'm not at that level, so don't judge me. And that's something within Muslims that we have to address too. That we can assume a variety of identities. That's what being Muslim is.

Cennet, a fifteen-year-old nondevout Muslim girl who does not wear *hijāb* but "practices all the religious traditions," told her focus group, "I feel like *the bad Muslim girl*. The aunties—friends and relatives of her mother—see me as the corrupt one because I talk to boys. They think I'm loose or going to get pregnant or something." As she spoke, her friend Selina, much more devout but also without *hijāb*, explained: "I feel like I want to be pure Muslim inside, but I don't have to wear *hijāb* to show that." Another young woman, Ima, who was the only nonveiled female in the coed group, simply justified her flowing hair: "I'm just not mature enough. I have to be honest, I love movies and makeup and the mall. I swear I'm going to wear *hijāb*, but I'm not mature enough. And [giggling] I really like my hair." The decision of these three young women not to wear *hijāb* needed to be justified in their small group discussions.

Some young women and men referred to their relatives who were "not good Muslims." In fact, in the all-women group, both of the young women who did not wear *hijāb* seemed a bit worried about being judged by other Muslim American women and offered stories of veiled cousins who have been labeled "bad Muslims" (Khan 2002). They also participated in inconsistent judgments, labeling who was "good" and not "good." At different times, young men and women condemned nonconformity to both Islamic and U.S. expectations. When describing a cousin, one young woman stated, "We're all mad at him. He joined the army! The U.S. Army to fight in Iraq!!!" Another chimed in, "My family is really mad at my cousin 'cause he says, 'I hate America. America sucks.'" So on the two extremes of patriotism, military loyalty and protest, intrafamily and intracommunity judgments flourish. These young people are nevertheless anxiously enforcing the work of external judges from within.

Not only do the youth feel obligated to "hide" some of their identities at home because they travel between worlds, but they also worry about the price their parents might have to pay for the choices they, particularly the daughters, make. Samira's decision about college, for instance, was strongly influenced by the scrutiny her mother anticipated should her daughter choose to live independently while attending college in New York City:

> I want to move away for college . . . even though I'm probably going to stay in the city. My mom flips out and she says, "If you're living in the city, you're like a couple of miles away from me and you move out, what would people say?" So, it's . . . it's tough. But it's doable, I think.

Asma worries that her actions might create an uncomfortable situation for her father, who is well known in his community. In addition to her feeling both responsible to and protected by her family, Asma describes how she feels watched by Allah.

> The way I act at home is the same way I act at college. . . . The only reason I'm a little cautious when I step out on campus . . . is because . . . my dad sits with those people. He communicates with them. . . . You have to keep in mind little things for your parents. At the same time, you could have your fun. You could enjoy your life. As long as you know that you're doing the right thing, you're enjoying your life. Even if my parents are not here, Allah's here. So, you know, if they're not watching me, he is, so I'd better do this right or I better not do that. . . . It just works out that way.

There is an acute "mindfulness" (Langer 1997) evident in the stories narrated by these young people, a persistent social vigilance. Conscious of being watched by their religious communities, their families, and their friends, they sometimes censor or monitor themselves. Whether or not it is "true" that they or their families are being listened to on the telephone or tracked on the Internet—as several have been warned by their parents —the sense that they are being controlled or watched, is enough to "induce . . . a state of conscious and permanent visibility that assures the automatic functioning of power" and the achievement of the "major effect of the Panopticon" (Foucault 1995, 201). According to Foucault, the Panopticon serves

> to arrange things so that the surveillance is permanent in its effects, even if it is discontinuous in its action; that the perfection of power should tend to render its actual exercise unnecessary; that this architectural apparatus should be a machine for creating and sustaining a power relation independent of the person who exercises it. (1995, 201)

It is this intense effect of scrutiny from everywhere that leads many of the young people to make changes, even small ones, in their daily lives. The gazes and the stares seep into their beings, and they feel as though they are being interrogated and intensely scrutinized. They live with interior doubts, ghosts, and censors, are always deliberate in their actions, and are rarely able to ignore external or internal cues.

Parenting Parents

According to Donna Nagata (1993), Japanese American elders typically say little about their internment and relocation. They do not rehearse at home the trauma that tore through Japanese communities in the United States. Nagata maintains that both issei and nisei parents refuse to discuss this with their children. From the Muslim American youth in the United States at the beginning of the twenty-first century, we also hear a similar, if somewhat reversed, dynamic. Adolescent Muslim children today are hesitant to burden their parents with the stories of the everyday discrimination they endure. Bhatia and Ram (2001) argue that racialized immigrant communities keep alive the memories of discrimination and hardship through individual and collective remembering (see also Apfelbaum 2000), and yet we hear, over and over, that young Muslim men and women do not want to make it even harder for their parents. So they endure alone.

It is not that young men and women do not tell their parents about their struggles over their religious identity but that they also feel they have to protect, and at times educate, their parents about the ways of things in this country. Zahra, for example, worries that her parents will "be investigated for no good reason, just for sending money to poor families over there. . . . I think it's important to find balance between being like naive and then being paranoid. And I think that's just being cautious." In the face of this tiered surveillance, these young people are determined to speak with, but not complain to, their family.

Protecting parents from knowledge of persistent discrimination and reminding them of their rights in the United States appear to be two of the tasks of immigrant youth parenting their parents. Salma, who was fourteen years old at the time of the interview, talked about how she argued with her father on numerous occasions about not hiding his religion. Originally from Macedonia, her father works in the food industry at a major hotel. Accustomed to hiding his Muslim identity, he remains silent at the hotel about his ethnic and religious commitments. Once, asked by the hotel chef to taste a new chicken dish made with wine, he politely refused and later told his family that he told the chef he was "allergic to chicken." Salma laughed, "Dad, this is America. You can say you are Muslim, and you don't drink wine." And then turning to the focus group, she continued, "My parents hide everything, but we're free here."

In another case, one of the young men told us that his sister had to convince his mother that it was all right to call the police when they were in trouble, when they were the victims of a hate crime.

> They were just taking a walk by the shore, my sisters, my mother and my aunt. A group of men started yelling out, "You smelly Arabs, go fuck yourself and get the fuck out of our country." My sister picked up the phone, called the cops, these guys are harassing us, ta-da ta-da ta-da. The cops came by and they just drove away. That really got to my sister. My mom was just like, "Shut up, shut up, you know we'll just get out of here." You know, like, "don't worry it's no big deal." I think that's where all the confidence comes in with being born here, you know, my sister was like, "I'm gonna fight this." The parents would just be, like, "be quiet and go home" until nothing happens.

The silence at home concerning discrimination and surveillance contrasts with what Diane Hughes and her colleagues found in their work with African American families (Hughes & Chen 1997) and in their review of the literature on parents' ethnic/racial socialization practices (Hughes et al. 2006). At this point in history, it is hard to know whether Muslim parents will follow the Japanese American path of silence at home about discrimination outside or will devise cultural narratives of discrimination that can help their children negotiate the structural and relational violence they will endure.

Youth Coping with Discrimination

The young people in our studies were wonderfully innovative in the face of discrimination. Religion was the most popular coping strategy. Our two survey studies that assessed coping (using the COPE scale developed by Carver, Scheier, & Weintraub 1989) found that whereas youth effectively use a multitude of coping strategies to deal with stress and discrimination, ranging from planning, emotional, social, and religious coping, they tend to rely most heavily on religious coping. This finding was evident as well in Sirin's (2005b) comparative study of 145 college students, in which he found that Muslim youth ($N = 71$) more often used planning and religious coping strategies than did their white Christian peers ($N = 74$), as shown in figure 2.

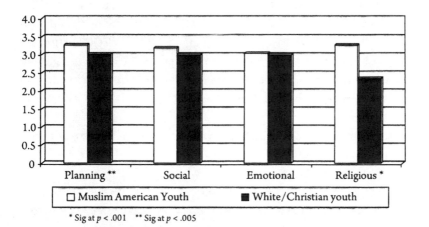

* Sig at $p < .001$ ** Sig at $p < .005$

Figure 2. Coping Strategies by Religious Groups

Muslim Americans' heavy reliance on religion and spirituality also was quite evident in their identity maps (see map 3 and maps 20 and 29) and in the focus groups, in which many of the participants referred to their religion when explaining how they dealt with discrimination and stress in their everyday life: "At the end of the day, you seek spiritual guidance from your creator." Many of these young people seemed to rely on their religion not only as a spiritual coping mechanism but also as a powerful metaphor that allowed them to situate their individual experience in context:

> In Islam, God is going to test us all. It's part of the game, you know, and I actually I feel like the more there is, the better. Like for the Lebanon thing, I am not happy the war happened but at the same time I took my dad's van, we went around filled it up, the van, with as much stuff as I could to donate. . . . Maybe it's good that they are discriminating against us. It's part of history. When the Romans discriminated against the Christians, what happened to the Romans? They all became Christians. So it's the way I see it.

Another young man put it this way:

> I think we as Muslims, we put our faith in Allah and that helps us get through every day. If you always keep in mind what's important and you continue to practice your faith. . . . I'll tell you. In high school, most of my friends were not Muslims, but after I went to Palestine, and slowly there was a transition in my life where I became very active in our Muslim association. Most of my friends are Muslim now and the discrimination has probably gotten worse since then and yet I'm much happier as a person. So the benefits, you can weigh them out. Discriminate me all you want. It's OK. I mean, as much as I hate it but . . .

One younger boy, age thirteen, expressed a kind of fatalism about dealing with discrimination:

> Yeah, basically, my opinion on the whole thing is that wherever you are and wherever you go, you're always going to face racism. So, basically, the only thing you have with you is your faith and you have to have a strong faith in God. You have to have humility and humbleness among other

people. God will help you and you'll start gaining respect from other people for it.

This heavy reliance on faith in God, combined with the substantial amount of discrimination endured, may also explain why this generation of Muslims is so heavily engaged in religious practices (see map 4). About 93 percent of the participants report that they fast during Ramadan, one of the five pillars of Islam. Furthermore, more than 63 percent report that they pray on a daily basis, another pillar of Islam, and nearly half the participants wear religious dress.

We do not have any historical data on Muslim youth to compare these

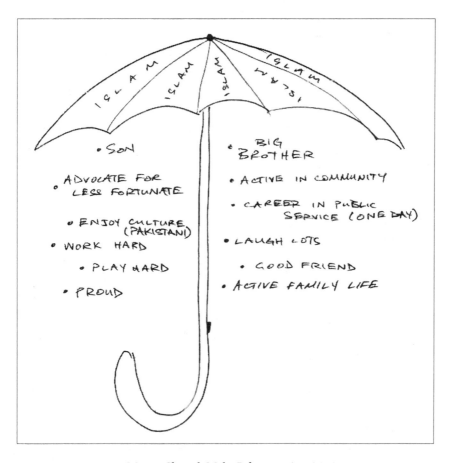

Map 4. Shawal, Male, Pakistani, Age 25

statistics with those of previous generations of Muslims in the United States. But we were surprised that many of the participants told us that they had chosen a more religious path than their parents did. Their choice sometimes created tensions at home. When we asked the older group about stresses they had at home, several mentioned this point. One young Indian American woman noted that her parents "sometimes get concerned that I am becoming too Muslim and that my religiosity may in turn get me into trouble." Another made a similar point: "My priority tends to be Islam, [my parents' priorities] are the more material things." A Palestinian teenager in our interviews observed that her parents "don't like me going to the mosque too much because they are afraid I might get brainwashed or become too religious." In chapter 3, Aisha made a similar point about how difficult it had been for her to figure out her religion without much help from her parents.

In fact, many of the veiled women in our studies told us that they started to wear *hijāb*, or decided not to take off their veil after 9/11, even when their parents objected (see color map 25). One young girl, age fifteen, who decided to cover her hair despite her mother's resistance, explained to us how that helped her in her everyday life: "I finally figured out what to tell people about the *hijāb*. I wear it like a bicyclist wears a bike helmet. It protects me from danger, and it gives me the freedom to wander where I dare not without it. Then they leave me alone!!"

Turning to Friends and Taking Action

Besides religion and God, we also asked the young people specifically to whom else they turned when they were treated badly because of their Muslim background. Most of the participants in the younger group admitted in unison: "I don't really tell my parents. They have enough to contend with." Another boy added just as much: "Tell nobody . . . because I don't want to upset my parents, they have too much to deal with, and if I tell my teachers, I can get in big trouble. So I work it out myself." The older group, however, although they continued *not* to tell their parents, seemed to find great comfort in having Muslim friends with whom to talk things over (see color map 16).

When we asked whether they turned to their non-Muslim friends, only one boy in the younger cohort and one young man in the older one believed that their "non-Muslim buddies" would understand and defend them: "I love him just as much as I love the rest of my friends." For the rest of the people in our groups, this was not an option: "They wouldn't understand, so I don't bother." As one young man stated it, having to explain his situation to a non-Muslim friend was not easy: "If I was to tell, for example, that you are not supposed to date, I would only talk to Muslims. And I wouldn't talk to non-Muslims because you'd be like, "Hey, I don't date," can you give me advice? What's a non-Muslim going to tell you, to the Muslims about that?" They also pointed out how differences across cultures created some very practical questions in everyday life:

> You are not going to hang out with somebody who drinks if you don't drink. Someone who parties if you don't party. You need to find people to get that base and who can give you support when you are away from home. And most likely, by choice the ones you can identify yourself with most, that's Islam for us.

They also find it easier to practice Islam if they are surrounded by other Muslims: "It's much more practical being that I see Islam as a way of life, it's like when we are all around each other, we actually enforce each other a lot more, you know." "The wrong foods, the wrong drinks. If I was alone, I guarantee you the pressures from the non-Muslims who do those kinds of things." In other words, for these youth, peer support is not just about having others around but about having others around who understand their way of life and whom they are not worried about hurting by sharing their troubles.

They also noted the difficulties of trying to educate their non-Muslim friends about their experiences as Muslims in the United States. With a sense of resignation, most admitted that they wouldn't "confide in them" because "[we] have a lot of issues I'm not sure how they would react to." They're afraid that their peers would not be willing to listen to them about "certain political things" and "discrimination things." Instead, they "rely on people who you can relate to. Who have gone through the same things as you. It's characteristic of how new immigrant communities develop."

These justifications for keeping their struggles to themselves or their "own" group and not finding much support from nongroup members echoes what Beverly Tatum (1997) had to say about why black students in desegregated schools "sit together in the cafeteria." Searching for spaces of comfort and recognition, young people across racial and ethnic groups prefer to tell their stories to a caring group who not only can relate to them but also do not question the authenticity of their experiences.

Civic Engagement and Political Action

After religion and friends, the third most common coping strategy was civic engagement. Most, if not all, the young people with whom we spoke agreed that there has been a shift in the Muslim community toward civic participation. Because of "things like the Patriot Act," they now have no choice but to "really engage in the society we live in and make that movement toward politics." They call for more interfaith dialogue and more mainstream civic engagement to make a difference at local and federal levels. One young man described the changes since 9/11 as dramatic in regard to the degree of political involvement among this generation of Muslims: "Now you see the sentiment of trying to change society from within. You see Muslims getting more involved in civil rights movements." They all pointed out the recent increase in voter registration among Muslims, as well as the election of the first Muslim U.S. representative, Keith Ellison (D-MN), as signs of these new times. Many saw these developments as the beginning of a new era in which they could take control of their destiny as American citizens. One young man, full of optimism, explained how "especially in this nation, when one strives to do something, anything is possible."

While recognizing the importance of civic engagement, young people also were aware of the challenges ahead of them. They knew that despite the convergence of forces among Muslims across racial, ethnic, and denominational groups after 9/11, there was still a great deal of "confusion and uncertainty" about building a unified movement. In regard to mainstream U.S. political alignments, they also recognized the challenges for Muslims who were, for example, "pro-life but anti-war," as one young man put it. Young people also see the Muslim community at large as not being active enough: "We are educated, we have a lot of money . . . but there is no political say."

For many immigrants, including Muslims, civic engagement requires social traffic with mainstream U.S. society. Young people of all age cohorts recognize that "while there is some integration, it's not to the extent that should be happening because there's just this sense of pessimism." They see Muslims' active participation in the American civic life as a challenge for the Muslim community: "We have to engage ourselves within the society that we live in." For Muslim Americans, civic engagement is a way not only to deal with the current crisis but also to claim their rightful position as fully engaged members of the mainstream U.S. society. Besides the frustration, pessimism, and anger, the young men and women also see Muslim Americans as critical bridge builders both between their community and the mainstream society and between the Muslim world and the West: "The entire Muslim world looks to us for advice, looks to us as a sense of inspiration, looks to us as a sense of direction."

Simon and Klandermans's model (2001) explains why these young men and women see political engagement as one of the ways of dealing with discrimination and surveillance. According to their model, people develop a politicized collective identity through an awareness of shared grievances, adversarial attributions, and involvement in the society at large. It therefore is not surprising that many of the young man and women in our focus groups identified themselves as Muslims enduring trials and struggles as Muslims in the United States and, most important, chose to address their grievances to the mainstream U.S. society.

Trying to Find Psychological Balance

Besides relying on religion, Muslim friends, and active civic engagement, these Muslim American respondents used various psychological coping strategies to deal with discrimination and surveillance. Some denied, deflected, or diluted their experiences of discrimination. Some questioned their own reality, balancing between caution and paranoia, and some feel guilty about internalizing the stereotypes and suspicions of others. Noor speculated that these odd reactions were related to being monitored: "Many times when we receive mail from Iran, it's always been opened. . . . And even a few times on the phone when conversation gets a little too risky, the line goes out." Samira joined the conversation:

> I didn't really get paranoid because of the surveillance, but sometimes I
> do get paranoid when I'm on the train and I see someone . . . who might

not even look that Muslim, but has a bag or something. I hate that, you know, that you have to feel that way towards some people who might be . . . of the same religion or the same culture, you know.

Despite their sense of moral exclusion, some of the young people psychologically situate themselves as Americans who are under attack, defending the actions of the U.S. government. Erum explained:

They stare. I personally don't find any problem in that. Because if I were to be in that position, if I put myself in their shoes . . . being a police officer and after being hit by some terrorists, I would do the same thing. I would be very, very overprotective. I would say, this is my job to protect the society and I would try my best.

A few insisted that they had not personally experienced any discrimination or altered their lives as a result of the increased surveillance. As Manal stated, "I know a lot of people changed their names, and they stopped wearing hijāb and stuff like that after 9/11. Personally, I haven't changed anything about myself. I'm the same. I still wear my Allah [pendant]. I don't hide anything. I don't feel the need to."

Others project their anxieties onto kin, worrying about their mothers, sisters, brothers, and uncles who are easily identifiable as Muslim Americans because of their facial features or style of dress and for those who try to be less visible by changing their ethnic- or Muslim-sounding names. While positioning herself at a distance from a position of "victim," Manal expressed great concern for her mother:

I think of my mom wherever she goes. She always dresses in her cultural clothes. . . . I've never really faced discrimination, but she's faced a lot of discrimination because of that. . . . If we'd go to a doctor's office, or we would go shopping and ask a question . . . they would react differently to her than they would react to me . . . [they'd] probably belittle her more than they would to me.

Many simply minimize their feelings about being mistreated as Muslims, prepared not to give in to the pressures and the demands of the current atmosphere of fear and surveillance. One young man, darker skinned than the other Muslims in the group, spoke of the sting of hypervisibility on his college campus:

> I think when I walk on campus sometimes, I think people look at me with a caution sign, kind of like, "Oh be careful with this kid!" I think there are a couple of other students that also have this caution sign on them on my campus, but honestly it doesn't mean anything to me. They can think of me whatever they want 'cause the people that I care about and that care about me are all I have to worry about. I don't really pay any mind to anybody else. They are not going to shape my life and I won't let them.

Another young man in the group agreed with this strategy and suggested that people were worse off:

> [When I am discriminated against,] I always say there are people who go through much worse than that. All these things we go through in this country and I always say there's people who don't have food to eat. Speaking of discrimination, you have the companions who went through worse. They were happy to do that.

Some questioned why this was happening to them, as the "other" Americans: "I've become so used to being discriminated against and having to go through extra obstacles just to express my freedom of speech, which I thought was an American value. But I guess it's an American value only for non-Muslims."

Others learned from the racialized history of the United States by looking at other groups who had to endure relentless exclusion within the country, for example, "African Americans who faced racism" and "stigmas that Jews face," with the hope that the circumstances for Muslims in the United States would improve over time:

> The derogatory terms for them [Blacks and Jews] were used left and right, but obviously, we, society, have stepped away from that, and it's going to continue to step away from that. Eventually I guess you have to just stride, stride through it, and hopefully you'll hope that one day when people say Muslims, they don't associate it with terrorists or vice versa,

when they say terrorists they don't associate it with Muslim. Or you hope that one day, out of the U.S. Airways flight or whatever, you know the seventy-nine people that got off board, and you're the one brown guy, you hope that one day will come that they don't pull just you to the side and ask you a million questions. But yeah, I think that's kind of the frame of how civil liberty has formed in this country.

Gendered Responses to Discrimination and Surveillance

In our surveys we found no significant variation by gender in the extent to which Muslim American young people use particular coping mechanisms. But in our focus groups and through the maps we observed that men and women seem to receive, interpret, and respond distinctly to discrimination and the surveillance surrounding them. According to the identity maps drawn by high school students, we can see how Muslim American youth craft "hyphenated cultural selves" amid contested global and local relations and representations. How young people negotiate at the hyphen varies widely and often by gender, but they all work the hyphen. Consider map 3, created by Muhammad and shown at the beginning of this chapter. At age fourteen, Muhammad humanizes what we heard from so many of the young men we interviewed, that the difficulties of being Muslim and being American have broken him in half, filling him with "tears for racism," a frown, a severed soul. Living with the haunting ghosts of "terrorist" looming around him, he, like so many other young men, feels swallowed by a representation he cannot resist, lest he embody the hegemonic trope of a young Muslim man filled with rage. To resist, he tries to contain the anger, to protect himself and his family.

Selina, age fifteen, created a different yet equally powerful visual narrative of fluid selves—American and Islamic—at the hyphen, voicing what so many of the young women told us (see color map 27). Refusing to separate the currents of Islam and America moving through her body yet still recognizing the distinct pools of water from which they flowed, Selina insisted on the psychological project of synthesis, a fluid sense of identity, in which she could rightfully claim both currents at the same time, decorated with smiles and a beautiful blending of shades.

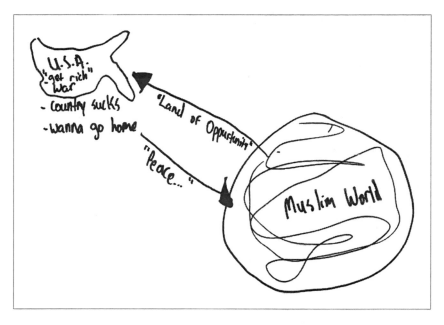

Map 5. Omar, Male, Arab, Age 16

Both boys and girls conveyed a geographic sense of living in a vibrant but troubled diaspora. The psychological labor of "working the hyphen" varied among them by gender and community. In our conversations with Muslim youth in the United States, we discovered flexible connections, longings, and commitments to both their "home" country and the United States (Suárez-Orozco & Oin-Hilliard 2004). Although both young men and women spoke of a sense of self connected to multiple worlds that were breaking apart, the young men's stories were marked by a sense of despair and defeat and a strong romance with "peace in the Muslim world" (see map 5). A young boy, Malik, age twelve, joined the focus group late, listened for a bit, and then, when asked about what it's like to be Muslim in New Jersey, he mumbled, "It's just hard." We pressed him to say more, but he was unwilling to elaborate. "Just hard."

In marked contrast, many of the young girls in our focus groups spoke with a sense of authority and mission to educate others. Many mentioned times in school when everyone "turns to me, like about the war. Like I am supposed to educate them." We asked if she minded being singled out as an authority, and Hadice, age fourteen, elaborated:

> I guess it's better that I educate them than they stay ignorant. I want to tell them there is more to know than just today, them alone, the mall, boys, music. I want to tell them to learn about what's going on in the world. But they don't watch the news or read the paper. I listen to CNN, Fox News, Al-Jazeera, and French news every night. So maybe it's best that I do answer their questions. There is a big world out there, and I personally believe I am just one small dot in this world. There is something much bigger than any of us. I wish the American students understood that.

In contrast, the following is how Hasheem responded to the same question, which was a typical response of the Muslim young men we interviewed: "I just get angry at them. I just don't want to. They're ignorant and I don't want to deal with them. I don't necessarily let it go, but I just, you know, to hell with them" (see color map 20). Another was infuriated with requests like "Prove to me that you are not working with our enemies," an actual question asked on CNN of Keith Ellison, the first Muslim U.S. congressman. In many cases, young men keep their anger and frustration to themselves: "It's like when you converse with people who are non-Muslim and they say [derogatory] things about Muslims. You just laugh with them and say you just say shut the fuck up, you know, like in your mind, you know. Like it's just stupid, it's a waste of breath."

It appears that for the young men with whom we spoke, the options to respond to stereotypes and discriminatory acts were either deep anger and frustration or silence and resignation, none of which opens up a dialogue, a laborious act carried out mostly by Muslim young women.

While all Muslim youth are equally frustrated by the absurdity of the questions asked them ("Are you a terrorist?" "Why do you dress like that?"), the girls and young women were more eager for others to "just ask me a question . . . don't assume I'm gonna throw bombs . . . or I'm an uneducated woman!" They want the opportunity to share themselves, to teach, and to change minds. Not at all naive about the stereotypes held about Muslim women as uneducated, oppressed, or dupes of religion, one young girl in our focus group explained that she looks for ways to educate those who stereotype and "don't know any better." To challenge the assumption of "oppressed woman," these young women exhibit strength, authority, and confidence.

Conclusions

The results of our surveys, focus-group interviews, and identity maps highlighted a wisdom derived from discrimination and surveillance, a wisdom gathered at much too young an age. These young U.S. citizens antici- pate the onslaught of misrepresentations, delight in the (rare) goodness of strangers ("Our neighbors were so great, they went everywhere with us! And women from the next town knitted scarves with the U.S. flag and ac- companied us everywhere. The support was great!"). They remain buoyed by the Qur'an, structured spiritual and religious beliefs, and strong com- mitments to culture, religion, and ritual. On the one hand, these youth must pay the price, discrimination and anxiety, of a global conflict, but on the other hand, many of the participants also seemed to reject such treatment as unacceptable. They tried to do something about it, mostly on their own. They do not use family as a support for their experiences of discrimination, as they were anxious not to burden their elders further. Indeed, it is the job of the second (or one and a half) generation to calm the home space.

Meet Ayyad

"A Regular Cute Guy"

At age sixteen, Brooklyn born and bred, Ayyad insists that he is just a "regular cute guy." A tenth grader attending public school, he describes himself as an athlete who spends three to five hours a week on schoolwork, is committed to going to college, and prays only during Ramadan. Both his parents were born in Palestine, and he visits there "almost every summer." By all accounts, Ayyad is a "typical American teen," and his interview revealed no tension at all in his hyphenated identities.

> *Dalal*: What about your identities as a Muslim and an American, where do they fit in?
>
> *Ayyad*: What do you mean?
>
> *Dalal*: So being Muslim: is that a part of you or a part of how you see yourself?
>
> *Ayyad*: Um, like on the holidays, we go out to the mosque, and like Ramadan my whole family fasts.
>
> *Dalal (still trying)*: And what about being an American: is that part of your identity as well?
>
> *Ayyad*: Yeah . . . like we do a lot of American holidays like Thanksgiving . . . Christmas . . .

Ayyad moves across his worlds with relative ease. Indeed, he was comfortable in the interview but slightly resistant to our interview questions that bordered on presuming some tension at the hyphen: To the question of whether there was a time when he felt proud to be Muslim, he responded, "No, not that I remember." And to the question of whether there was a time when he felt it was difficult to be a Muslim American, he referred to 9/11, recalling that "some people talked . . . 'you're Muslim so you're a terrorist' but some just said, 'Oh, doesn't matter 'cause he's Muslim means he's a terrorist, no he's not, that's not true.'" "I'm just a regular Palestinian kid. I do everything the same as every other. . . . I'm proud to be a Muslim."

His friends are "all mixed." They play basketball, "go places, joke around, chill . . . play pool." He also is on the Debka team and performs Arabic dance.

Ayyad's dad owns a supermarket, "so I go help him out." Although he is committed to going to college, he feels some pressure, as a man, to work rather than to stay in school. But his mother encourages him to "stay in school," telling him that "school is the better way out."

On his survey, Ayyad indicated that he is most comfortable with people from the United States and from Palestine; his best friends are "both," as are his holidays, foods, and "the way I do things and the way I think about things." Quite at home across racial and ethnic lines, Ayyad personally feels little tension in his school, friends, and community.

Although he rated eleven of sixteen items to be "not at all stressful," his stress levels rose in regard to hearing jokes about or put-downs of Muslims or stereotypes of Muslim Americans as more dangerous than other groups. Most stressful to Ayyad are media portrayals of Muslims.

Aware of social injustices, Ayyad tells the story of a cousin who was in a fight with another youth, but only his cousin was arrested. "Why did [only] my cousin get arrested for no reason and the kid didn't do anything?" When pressed on why this happened, Ayyad said simply, "Discrimination." His mother tells him, "Don't get into no fight, see what happened to your cousin, it could happen to you."

When asked about tensions in school, Ayyad explained, with delight, that a teacher initiated a classroom conversation about injustice in the Middle East.

> *Ayyad*: My teacher brought it up once, that she is pro-Palestinian so she started talking about it, and she said how it's not fair like on TV it won't show the stuff that's really happening, and stuff like that. And she got to go to Palestine and saw what happened and she found out the truth.
> *Dalal*: And how did it feel to be sitting there in class?"
> *Ayyad*: It didn't bother me.
> *Dalal*: Did you feel proud maybe? Like someone's on your side?
> *Ayyad*: Yeah.

Later in the interview, Ayyad described another incident, in school, when he was able to share his knowledge and expertise with other students:

> *Ayyad*: When they built the wall, the big wall, and then they like, my friend said, "Oh, I heard that they built a wall," and then I told him, "Oh yeah, they built a wall and like we can't get through where we want to go and there are a lot of checkpoints," and all that stuff.

Dalal: And what did they say?

Ayyad: "Oh, that's not fair." And they started saying like what should happen, . . . they should change that rule . . . if they want to take over, they should just all act as one, be equal with each other.

Dalal: How did it make you feel to be able to . . .

Ayyad: It felt good 'cause they finally knew what was going on.

With little edge, generosity of spirit, a soul in Palestine, and very much born and raised in the soil (and cement) of Brooklyn, Ayyad knows and thinks about "everyday life in Palestine . . . it's not easy. Maybe we got it easy but in Palestine they don't."

When pressed to elaborate on his views of Americans, Ayyad answered even-handedly, "There's some good people and some bad people everywhere you go."

In his "mostly black" high school, he says, "I feel accepted," so too in his Italian neighborhood. Ayyad also expects the same generosity of spirit from others.

When asked what he wants people to know about him, he was pointed: "That I'm not a terrorist, I'm just a teenage boy doing what a teenage boy does. . . . I play basketball."

"Pro?"

"I'm gonna be the first Palestinian [in the Pros]."

5

■　■　■　■　■　■　■　■　■

Negotiating the Muslim American Hyphen

Integrated, Parallel, and Conflictual Paths

Adolescence (Erikson 1980) and young adulthood (Arnett 2000) refer to a developmental period in which young people form, and then re-form, their cultural identities. This may be a particularly complex psychological task for those youths living in contentious political contexts. In this chapter we consider how young people generate identities, relationships, and a sense of purpose when one social identity is contested by formal institutions, social relationships, and/or the media.

Immigrant minority youth form their identity by becoming a member of a collective group based on racial, ethnic, or religious background and by negotiating among different cultural frameworks (Berry 1990; LaFramboise, Coleman, & Gerton 1993; Suárez-Orozco 2004). Berry (1990, 1997) formulated the most widely researched framework for immigrant adjustment, which suggests an acculturation model with two independent domains: (1) the degree to which one is willing to identify with and is allowed to participate in one's home (e.g., Muslim) culture and (2) the degree to which one is willing to identify with and is allowed to participate in one's host (e.g., broader U.S.) culture. Several studies investigated the relationship of ethnic (country of origin) and national (host country) identities (Berry et al. 2006; Birman, Trickett, & Buchanan 2005; Phinney et al. 2001). According to Berry's model, a positive correlation between measures of home and host identifications indicates an integrated identity, or biculturalism. In contrast, ethnic and national identities are experienced as irreconcilable if they are negatively correlated (i.e., revealing either a strong home country orientation or a strong host country orientation). Alternatively, the two identities may vary independently, which would suggest that they are not incompatible but also are not related. The two identities live in separate baskets of identity (for an updated review of this model, see Berry et al. 2006).

A study of immigrant Muslim youth in the United States provides many opportunities to understand how young people find their paths as Muslims and Americans. Beyond bicultural identifications, these youth craft their identity from multiple sources of social identification (see color maps 15 through 18). The following is how Azhar, an eighteen-year-old man, described his identity, which is similar to most of the other stories we heard in our studies:

> Basically I feel that there are three main facets of what I feel are priorities in my life. What shape my decisions. One being my Pakistani heritage. My father and mother are from Pakistan, and growing up I was really ingrained in Pakistani culture, meaning that I was always exposed to the music, the culture, the tradition, the poetry of Iqbal, the whole family style of being Pakistani. I mean, I think every aspect of being Pakistani, I felt like I was exposed to. I went to Pakistan every year almost, during my vacations to visit family there. . . . And all of this stuff is tied into my identity. Then there comes the American aspect of my identity. I love pop culture, I love watching Steven Colbert and Jon Stewart on the *Daily Show*, I love rock music. I love being part of America in general. It gives you so much freedom to express your ideas in whatever ways you want. And then comes Islam, which ties into everything. And it sort of gives me a direction in which I look to. From the start, as far as I can remember, I was always ingrained in an Islamic household. My parents always emphasized that you should be a good Muslim. We should have strong moral values, you should be very inclined to being following the *sunnah* of the Prophet.

And along with that came a lot of education. I was really involved in going to a lot of educational seminars, I was part of some Muslim youth organizations.

Here is how one young woman expressed her identity (see map 6):

I am proud of who I am as an Iranian, as a Muslim, as an American, and I think I've just come to accept that, and the strength really lies in having confidence in the person that you are and for me it goes back to my faith in God. I must have some purpose for this, and it must mean that I have to do something. I have faith in that. That's personally where I get my strength.

The work of social psychologist Kay Deaux has been foundational for our research. She defines social identity as

a general concept . . . [which] implies both the existence of socially defined categories—what Verkuyten (2005) calls social fact—and the subjective experience of defining oneself in terms of the available categories. . . . In using the term self-categorization . . . we require that the category label be one that the person is willing to consider self-descriptive. (2006, 95, 101).

Borrowing from Deaux, we argue for the notion of *hyphenated selves* in order to understand how youths create and enact their identities when political or social conditions place them in tension. We use this idea to help us think about how youth negotiate, embody, and narrate their multiple selves, at the hyphen, in a fractured world, nation, community, home, or school.

We are most interested in understanding how young people experience the psychological and political jolt of "excluded citizenship" (Pinson 2008): how they think about, embody, and represent the pivot on which their identities join or split. We also seek to understand how historic and contemporary political conditions enable, complicate, or eviscerate the very delicate hyphens at which young people struggle to construct meaningful narratives of themselves. And we want to understand under what conditions these hyphenated selves move toward critical

Map 6. Chitta, Female, Bangladesh, Age 22

consciousness and activism. By theorizing about hyphenated selves, we are exploring what happens socially and psychologically when young people craft narratives of themselves from identities that hyphenate and then perforate, when they are separated from the larger body politic, and when they become internal exiles in their own nation.

The "Clash" Hypothesis: Being Muslim *and* American

Particularly since 9/11 and at those other times when the conflict in the Middle East is on the news, a debate ensues about whether Islamic values are compatible with Western values (Huntington 1993). Recently, Huntington (2004) took his assertions about the "clash of civilizations" to a new level in his book *Who Are We: The Challenges to America's National Identity*, in which he labels Muslim immigrants in the West the "indigestible" minority (Huntington 2004, 188). Journalists and scholars alike have argued the same point, sometimes to great fanfare on TV, that Muslims who live in Western countries, including the United States, have difficulty reconciling these two cultures. The ideology of a "civilization clash," disseminated widely by the media, is indeed part of the moral exclusion process. It is reasoned that if a certain group (e.g., the Muslim minority in the United States) fails to reconcile the differences between these two clashing "civilizations," they deserve to be morally excluded from the mainstream society. Our preliminary work challenged the "clash" hypothesis and suggested instead that most Muslim youth were migrating relatively smoothly between worlds and inventing new hybrid spaces.

To test the clash hypothesis directly, we gathered data from surveys, maps, and focus groups. In the surveys we asked the older cohort, aged eighteen to twenty-five, about the degree to which they identified with Muslim and mainstream U.S. identities and their preferences for social and cultural activities involving their home and U.S. cultures. Our measurement model for identification was novel because instead of forcing the participants to position themselves on a continuum between Muslim and American identities—which inherently assumes that they are at opposite ends of a scale—we tested each mode of identification (i.e., Muslim and American) independently. This approach allowed us to assess directly the potential links between these two identifications.

In addition to identification, we were able to examine through our social/cultural practices questionnaire the degree to which youth choose to engage with or separate from the mainstream U.S. society. We also used the maps for a more textured understanding of loyalties and desires. The maps provide data in a nonverbal format on how young people present themselves. Finally, we supported our findings with focus-group data.

Muslim and Mainstream U.S. Identification

To challenge the "clash" assumption, we examined the correlation between the two collective identity scores: identification with Muslim community and identification with the mainstream U.S. society. For this portion of the analysis, we used Muslim and American versions of the Collective Self Esteem scale (Crocker et al. 1994; Luhtanen & Crocker 1992). The versions we used were designed to assess the perception of one's identification with a certain group on three domains: private regard, identity importance, and membership. The Muslim version of the scale focuses on identification with "Muslim communities," and the mainstream U.S. version focuses on identification with "mainstream U.S. society." We found that the modified versions of the measure (see appendix A) are both reliable and valid for the Muslim American samples that we studied (for more detail, see Sirin et al. in press; Sirin & Fine 2007). In our measurement strategy we deliberately avoided the forced-choice dilemma in which participants are asked to pick one of two identities (Shih & Sanchez 2005), as this makes it difficult to examine the clash hypothesis by eliminating the possibility of a working hyphen. Independently assessing the identification with Muslim communities and the mainstream U.S. society enabled us to test whether they were related in the first place.

Interestingly, we found no *negative* correlation between how Muslim American youth view their Muslim and mainstream U.S. identifications. These young people seemed to value (or not value) both affiliations in all three domains in unrelated ways. More important, when we looked at the correlations among the scale's three domains across the Muslim and American affiliations, we found a *positive* and significant relation between how they viewed their membership to American mainstream society and the Muslim community at large.[1] The more that the participants saw themselves as engaged members of the Muslim community, the more likely they were also to see themselves as engaged members of the mainstream U.S. society. Together, these findings suggest that Muslim and American identities are not mutually exclusive. On the contrary, they are highly compatible, as beautifully summarized on map 26, drawn by a twenty-one-year-old Iranian American woman. For the most part, these young people have modeled a commitment to a hyphenated identity with great respect for multiplicity, difference, and dissent (see color map 24).

Thus when the two groups are in conflict, it may not necessarily mean that individuals who negotiate across the two cultures/groups experience that conflict internally.

In addition to examining whether identifications with two "cultures" were related, we also wondered whether Muslim American youth identify more strongly with one of the two groups. In our survey study of the older group, we found that young Muslim men and women identified more strongly with their Muslim community than with the mainstream U.S. society.[2] These findings may appear to contrast with the earlier assertion we made with regard to the "clash" hypothesis, as it shows that young Muslims report deeper bonds with the Muslim community than with mainstream U.S. society. But it is important to note that both ratings were above the neutral point of 4 on a scale of "1 = strongly disagree" to "7 = strongly agree." In other words, these youth characterize themselves as Muslim regarding the importance and valence of that identity, but their American identities are important to them as well (the average scores on the Muslim and American identification scales are in note 2). A similar finding was also reported by the Pew Research Center (2007) in a recent survey of a nationally representative sample of 1,050 Muslim Americans. This survey found that although 47 percent of all Muslim Americans identified as "Muslim first" and 28 percent as "American first," this figure was reversed among those Muslims whose religious commitment was low. More interesting, this identification pattern was similar to that of U.S. Christians, who were almost equally split between a "Christian first" (42%) and an "American first" (48%) identity overall, but devout Christians tended to be more polarized (59% and 30%, respectively). In our study, the correlations between Muslim and American identities suggest that Muslim identity was not favored at the expense of American identity. Together, these findings regarding identification with Muslim and American identities are intriguing in times of substantial surveillance, scrutiny, and media stereotyping. Despite the pressures of discrimination and public surveillance, Muslim Americans seem to find a way to highlight their belonging to both cultures, illustrating once again that identity negotiation is not a zero-sum arrangement.

Finally, if the identifications with Muslim communities and mainstream U.S. society were compatible, we wanted to know what factors contributed to each identification. Our survey study focused on several factors that might help us understand the Muslim American identity. Specifically, relying on earlier research on other immigrant minority youths, we identified discrimination-related stress and acculturative practices, such as one's choice of music and food, as well as religiosity and gender, as possible factors. Overall, we found that the best predictor of a *Muslim identity* was religiosity. In fact, perceived frequency of discrimination, acculturative practices, and gender did not seem to directly shape the degree to which one identified with a Muslim community.

As expected, those who practiced Islam were more likely to identify with their Muslim identity. Discrimination-related stress, however, contributed negatively to Muslim young people's identification with the mainstream U.S. society. The more discrimination they experienced, the weaker their bond was with the mainstream U.S. society. At the same time, the more closely they were engaged with mainstream social and cultural activities, the more likely they were to identify positively with the mainstream U.S. society.

Social and Cultural Preferences

We also wanted to know more about the actual social and cultural activities of young Muslims. What do they do? Dream about? Eat? Listen to? Unger and colleagues' 2002 Acculturation, Habits, and Interests Multicultural Scale for Adolescents (AHIMSA) was designed to measure immigrant and "bicultural" adolescents' engagement in a variety of social and cultural activities. Respondents check whether they engage in these activities with people from "the U.S." (Assimilation), "the country my family is from" (Separation), "both" (Integration), or "neither" (Marginalization). Table 4 shows that the majority of adolescents are engaged in social and cultural activities characteristic of both mainstream U.S. and Muslim communities. In fact, for seven out of eight items, the most common preference was for integration, that is, "both," emphasizing the strong commitment to engage in social and cultural activities across the home and mainstream U.S. cultures. The only area that showed a strong preference for home-country orientation was celebrating religious/cultural holidays, but even for this, the participants were divided almost in half, with about an equal percentage preferring to celebrate either only the U.S. holidays

Table 4

Percentage of Preference for Cultural and Social Activities $(N = 209)$

Items	Mainstream U.S. *Assimilation*	The Country My Family Is From *Isolation*	Both *Integration*	Neither *Marginalization*
I am most comfortable being with people from	12	14	71	3
My best friends are from	27	16	51	7
The people I fit in with best are from	18	23	53	5
My favorite music is from	38	12	42	8
My favorite TV shows are from	67	6	21	5
The holidays I celebrate are from	4	46	43	6
The food I eat at home is from	2	24	62	1
The way I do things and the way I think about things are from	14	14	69	3

or both the U.S. and ethnic/religious holidays. The overwhelming preference for "integration" illustrated once again that claims about Muslim Americans' reluctance to join the social and cultural life in the United States cannot be empirically validated, at least for young Muslim men and women. Integration, moreover, does not mean erasure or assimilation but engagement in "mainstream" activities as a Muslim American (see color map 18).

Our identity maps also revealed a deep desire for "peaceful coexistence" at the hyphen of Muslim and American identities. In two separate studies (with younger and older groups), only a small minority of the participants drew maps representing conflicts between the two identities. The great majority of the samples depicted psychological processes of integration or parallel identities. Specifically, 61 percent of the participants constructed maps reflecting an integrated Muslim American identity; 29 percent of the participants constructed maps showing parallel lives/separation between Muslim and American identities; and 11 percent of the participants constructed maps indicating an unfinished, conflictual identity negotiation. That is, most young Muslims appear to be experiencing their Muslim and American selves either as a coherent whole (integrated),

Map 7. Amber, Female, Egyptian, Age 14

as illustrated by one of our participants in map 7, or in separate domains of life (parallel).

In our interviews with young people, we did not hear much about the so-called clash or incompatibility of Muslim and American ways of life. Many of them saw the current conflict as induced by political leaders rather than inherent in religious or cultural practices. "First I used to view it like, OK, this is an Islamic/West conflict but now I realize that this is a power struggle, something that, you know, historically there's imperial power; they have done this and used this, this is nothing new." That is, the young people locate the tension in political, not cultural, conflicts.

The combination of findings across surveys, maps, and focus groups provides strong evidence that these youths embody a deep sense of themselves as both Muslim and American. These findings also show the substantial variability in how young people negotiate their hyphenated Muslim American identities. Together, these findings refute the "clash of civilizations" perspective (Huntington 1993, 2004) and suggest development of "hyphenated selves." These youths take up residence in the middle of the hyphen, where they play with multiple allegiances to, and experience multiple stresses from, both their Muslim communities and the mainstream U.S. society. As Arnett (2002), Suárez-Orozco (2004), and Yuval-Davis (1999) observed in the context of a global world, today's youth of all groups are bound to develop transnational identities. To that we add that those young people from the East and the global South are even more likely to generate *hyphenated identities*, that is, rich, complex, and highly salient identities cutting across borders and going beyond the fixed, geographic, nation-bound binaries.

The "Rejection-Identification" Hypothesis

Branscombe (Branscombe, Schmitt, & Harvey 1999; Jetten, Spears, & Postmes 2004) suggests that groups that are under siege, those whose identities are contested by others, value their ingroup identification more than their outgroup identification.. According to this rejection-identification model, perceptions of discrimination and related stress strengthen one's identification with one's own group and weaken one's identification with the outgroup. In other words, one identifies more with one's own collective identity particularly when one is rejected by the dominant group. We tested this hypothesis with our data from Muslim youth to explore the role of surveillance and stereotypes in the identity negotiation process. Because we used a multidimensional measurement framework rather than one that dichotomizes identifications across contexts as a binary variable, we were able to determine how discrimination and stress affected Muslim and mainstream U.S. identifications.

Our results showed partial support for the rejection-identification hypothesis. On all three domains of Muslim identification that we measured, we found that the frequency and stress resulting from discrimination and stereotypes strongly and significantly strengthened the importance of, membership in, and private regard for *Muslim collective identity*.

Furthermore, although not as strong and uniform, we also observed significant *negative* correlations between discrimination/stress measures and two of the three domains of mainstream U.S. identification, namely, the importance of and private regard for this identification. The data here are correlational and static rather than longitudinal, so they do not provide full support for the causal direction implied in the rejection-identification hypothesis. Nevertheless, it is possible to argue that those who are discriminated against are more likely to identify as Muslim and less likely to identify as "American."

The young people in the focus groups vigorously debated this issue. Some agreed that they intentionally and publicly claimed their Muslim identities in response to the politicized context in which they found themselves, as would be expected by the rejection-identification model. Others claimed that the United States did not support them, so why should they identify with it? "This country doesn't stand for who I am, it never respected me. And when it comes to my identity, and my religious views, that's another reason why it's difficult for me to accept the fact that I'm American, even though in many aspects I am." Others, however, argued that they stood firm as Americans despite the surveillance:

> I differentiate between America as a society and America as a government. I feel that these ideas which are being propelled by this conservative move in the government are not the ideas that represent the overall public in the United States itself. . . . rather than saying I am not American, I say I don't support this government.

Suha, a college student involved in the Muslim Student Association, challenged this position: "If we don't tell someone that we exist, no one is going to know." As we show in detail in chapter 4, following Simon and Klandermans's (2001) politicized collective identity model, there is a distinction between those who continue to engage politically and those who withdraw.

As theorists of the media and psychologists contend, the very stereotyping and surveillance activities in which the United States has engaged have raised the rates of perceived discrimination and discouraged young people from identifying with being "American." That is, empirically, their experiences of discrimination seem to encourage them to distance themselves from their American identities and lead them to see identifying with "mainstream U.S. identity" as less important. Such practices actually *exacerbate* their alienation from U.S. society and diminish their sense of social belonging.

Following up these findings with focus-group interviews, we were surprised to find that partly because of the shifts in the identification processes of young Muslims who came of age after 9/11, many explained that their parents were more closely identified with the mainstream U.S. culture than their children were. The following is a dialogue among three of the participants in one of our focus groups:

Abdul-baqi: My dad has lived here for more than thirty, or more than half his life he has been in America. Even though he didn't grow up here, he likes westerns and cowboys and stuff and that's like, I guess, American history or whatever. He very much likes Christmas carols and stuff. I don't know, maybe he likes American culture because it gave him an opportunity. Maybe it was a little bit different back then than now.

Mihran: That's interesting 'cause I felt the same way. Now my dad has a friend who is Christian. This guy was really good friends with my dad 'cause they do business together. They spend a lot of time—this guy has been at my house I think more than me. This is a really nice guy and his wife, they are always over and like they are really nice people. So me and my sister, we always make fun of my dad about that because you would never see him hanging out with Muslims. And he also has this Jewish friend, too, from Israel, and I'm like the radical in my house, quote unquote.

Besim: There's always been this struggle even in my household to be a bit more European. More Westernized. And I've actually struggled against that 'cause I don't prefer adapting to anyone's whims unless it's completely logical. The only thing I adapt to strongly is perhaps my religion.

The current social and political climates seem to have a pronounced negative impact on the way that some Muslim young people approach mainstream social and cultural activities. Unlike their parents, at least some of the young men find it difficult to imagine singing Christmas carols or hanging out primarily with non-Muslims.

Another aspect of the rejection-identification hypothesis is that identification with a minority group has a positive impact on well-being outcomes (Branscombe, Schmitt, & Harvey 1999). We found, as others have (Ethier & Deaux 1994; Fuligni, Witkow, & Garcia 2005; Romero & Roberts 2003; Rumbaut 1994; Waters 1999), that a strong commitment to cultural identification (being Muslim American) has a protective effect on a youth's development. We found that for young adults, a Muslim identification in general was significantly correlated with positive developmental assets, such as positive values and positive identity,[3] indicating that those with a strong Muslim identity present with more positive identities and a higher sense of self-worth, as would be expected by the rejection-identification paradigm (Romero & Roberts 2003). Furthermore, it is important to note that the importance and strength of the identification with the mainstream U.S. society do not have a positive correlation with physical or mental health. On the contrary, identification with mainstream American society seems to increase the reported levels of somatic symptoms and depression/anxiety.[4] In short, while both identities are powerful and important to the everyday lives of young people and the meaning-making process, a deeper identification with the Muslim community seems to have more positive health consequences, and a deeper identification with the mainstream U.S. society seems to have more negative health consequences.

These findings confirm what others (like Anzaldúa 1987; Ethier & Deaux 1994) have found for various immigrant populations: identification with multiple cultural backgrounds is not always an "either/or" proposition; the distinctions are not linear, fixed, or clear-cut; and identification with the home culture may be an important buffer, protecting youth from dominant cultural stress. As Mary Waters stated about immigrant identities:

> Racial and ethnic identities are not zero-sum entities; it is possible to hold several at any one time, and they are very clearly situational. In one situation a person can feel very American, at another time Irish, and yet another time white—one could hold all identities simultaneously. But the recognition of the multiplicity and situationality of social identities does not mean that people are free to choose any identity they want or to attach any meaning they want to their identity. History and current power relations create and shape the opportunities people face in their day-to-day lives, giving some people "ethnic options" and

others "racial labels." There are also shared or contested meanings attached to different groups that affect individuals' way of thinking about themselves. (1999, 47)

Together these findings suggest that Muslim and American identities are loosely (and positively) related to one another and that they are shaped by two very distinct processes, religiosity for Muslim identification and discrimination-related stress and acculturation practices for mainstream U.S. identification.

Negotiating the Muslim American Hyphen

Beyond measuring the degree to which youth identify with their multiple cultures, we also wanted to understand qualitatively how they negotiated, both psychologically and socially, these sometimes unrelated, sometimes parallel, and sometimes conflictual lives. Through the maps and focus groups, we tried to determine how young people create meaning at the hyphen. Overall, we found that young people devise very complex dynamics at the hyphen, mainly with their "American" and "Muslim" identities but sometimes also with their ethnic identities, political engagements, school, music, or fashion. That is, they engage across contexts in what Verkuyten and de Wolf called a "flexible expression" of identities as social practices, across a wide web of contexts, often having to "explain and justify their identity, not only in interactions with dominant group members but also in relation to their own group" (2002, 371). We relied on maps, surveys, and interviews to unearth these identity-negotiation processes with a focus on "change, hybridity and self-determination" (Verkuyten & de Wolf 2002, 375) As Sunil Bhatia has pointed out, immigrants engage in "ongoing negotiations between voices of assignation and assertion," reflecting a dialogical model of acculturation in the context of cultural difference, identity politics, and increasing globalization and transnational communication (Bhatia 2007, 186).

In our survey of the younger group, we grouped maps using the general framework found in the "bicultural identity" literature showing that although some perceive their dual cultural identities as "integrated," others perceive them as "oppositional," more challenging to integrate (Benet-Martinez et al. 2002; Phinney & Devich-Navarro 1997). For the older cohort, with data from 118 young adults, we were able to test these differences further using a more refined framework with three metacategories: integrated, parallel, and conflictual. Specifically, the maps were coded as (1) "integrated" if the Muslim and American identities were fully blended in a nonconflicting way, (2) "parallel identities" if both identities were depicted as separate worlds, or (3) "conflictual" if the maps represented tension, conflicting elements, hostility, or irreconcilability of the identities. With this coding framework, we were able to better differentiate parallel and conflictual paths, emphasizing the important difference between living in multiple different worlds and struggling with tensions between worlds.

We also examined the maps, like map 8, by gender. We found a pattern of interest: young Muslim women were more likely to display "integrated" identities than men were, similar to the trend we observed in the younger group.[5] About 70 percent of the young women, compared with

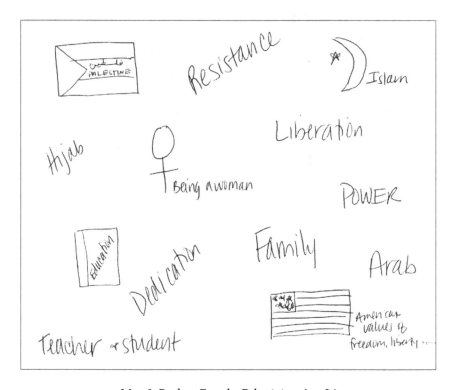

Map 8. Bushra, Female, Palestinian, Age 24

half the young men, constructed "integrated" maps. The young men, however, were more likely to construct maps representing parallel identities than young women were, 45 percent versus only 17 percent, respectively. More interesting, when we looked at the small minority of the participants who constructed conflictual maps, we found that about 80 percent of them were female. Together these findings show that in both groups, the girls and young women, compared with their male peers, were more likely to produce maps representing a dynamic tension between their identifications with Muslim and American selves. For the boys and young men, however, the modal path seemed to be a process of living in parallel worlds, sometimes with struggle, an important point we will revisit in chapter 6.

The young people chose each of these three commonly observed paths in order to make sense of their Muslim and American identities in a highly contentious moment in history and place. Next we explore these paths as integration, parallel lives, and conflict.

Integrated Paths

Several of the participants, mostly women, told us that their layered identities gave them wide "access to the rest of the world." Iman described an almost chemical transformation that came from the layering of her many selves: "You're like a new culture. It's like those new restaurants that mix . . . you're like a *fusion* . . . a new fusion. And it's just interesting to be you, you know, because you're fusing two cultures in one" (see Bhabha 1994, and color maps 22, 24, 25, and 27).

Through focus groups and identity maps, we discovered the many different ways that young men and women combine creatively several different aspects of their personhood. When describing her map (a colorful flower), Rabab explained how she embodied her flexible identities:

It's uneven . . . I made all wiggly and whatever, because no one is defined by lines. Because things keep shifting, at least some things keep shifting around. . . . I was coloring in yellow on the sides, because that whole thing is the effect of Islam on me . . . it ended being the biggest piece out of all of these, so I guess that's just a coincidence, but a great coincidence.

Map 9. Patrice, Female, African American, Age 22

Amir, a twenty-year-old Albanian, spoke of the many identities he had "acquired" over his young life:

> There are many things in an identity, and I think as an American, a big part of my identity is American. My mentality has been shaped by the way things are run here, but I also see myself as a Muslim. I have to adapt to the religion, and that's more like a way of life. You know it could also affect my mentality. I see myself as not just being American but having other identities as well. I lived in Switzerland for two years [so] I feel I actually acquired a lot there . . . Swiss taste. Also, I was in the Italian part of Switzerland, so, you know, you get their style a little bit. And I come from Albania, so the culture there also has an influence on the way you think. When people limit [identity] to one or two things, I think I struggle with it because, let's say somebody is from . . . I don't know where . . . Mongolia, and he immigrates to this country and somebody tells him "you're American." He might actually get sensitive and say "no I'm not," or vice versa. I think, in fact, if we acknowledge that we are all these things, it makes it much more simple, you know? 'Cause it's the truth, you know? Some people refer to their ethnicity as their identity, you know, and I don't think that's the case, you know? Who knows. Well, my ethnicity is, I can claim I'm Albanian, but I can be anything, you know. I can be Roman, Turk, Arab, so many different things you don't know what you

are. If you look at it from a scientific perspective, identity is just what you acquire.

Amir's life story travels across multiple geographies and cultures. Such a journey is not uncommon among Muslims, as the United States is often not the first country to which Muslims immigrate after they leave their country of origin. Many Palestinians, for example, came to the United States from South America, Europe, or Africa. Many refugees from the Iranian revolution, the Bosnian war, and the first Gulf war arrived from Europe. It is quite possible, therefore, that these diverse experiences of living and having relatives in many different countries provide a global context for developing transnational identities, particularly for second-generation Muslims (see color map 17).

Once these immigrants arrive in the United States, however, they find only a few substantial Muslim communities, such as Dearborn, Michigan; Bay Ridge, New York; or Paterson, New Jersey. Even those who move into these enclaves when they first arrive in this country often move out to other parts of the country once they begin raising their children. As a result, a large number of second-generation Muslim immigrants are living in places without a sizable Muslim community. Tariq, a nineteen-year-old Pakistani man attending college in New York City, told us how he negotiated his identity in one such town.

> I grew up in the U.S. my whole life but I never really adapted to my family's culture. I mean I did to a certain extent, but I never really spoke the language too much in my area. There weren't a lot of Muslims, so I had all American friends and did a lot of American things. You don't necessarily agree with the government or the policies. Maybe some of the cultural things that go on, but to me, America is like a melting pot of all these cultures. I'm one piece of that. I don't think when you say you are [an] American Jew, there's one thing you can identify with. I guess there is the government, the things you see on TV, and the front that we have, but to me there's so much more than that. There's so many more parts to our culture, the American culture. . . . In my house there are some things like my parents don't let me watch at night, you know, like filthy movies or whatever, listening to bad music, but it's part of American culture here. And you know, I had those values of like Pakistan or Islam, but I also

have the American customs and culture too 'cause I grew up here, I can't, I don't totally alienate myself from it 'cause if I didn't like it, I wouldn't live here anymore. But I do like it, as much as we say we don't agree with it. Yes, there are some things that totally don't agree with Islam either, but I'm living here and I choose to live here, 'cause I do like some of the stuff, whether it is un-Islamic or not. . . . I don't see why I can't call myself American and Muslim.

Several of the young people feel it is "definitely an advantage" to be aware of and part of more than one ethnic or cultural group. Twenty-four-year-old Inas exclaimed, "It's beautiful to be so multicultural. . . . I'm Syrian, Circassian, *and* I'm American." Leila, a twenty-two-year-old college student, observed that "it would be boring . . . to be just Pakistani." When Marina, a fifteen-year-old Egyptian girl, presented her identity map, her beautiful face was framed by a pale blue flowered *ḥijāb*, she spoke excitedly about the thrilling challenge of the hyphen: "Islam gives me meaning and the U.S. holds the promise of freedom to wear *ḥijāb*, practice religion like my brothers, to be educated and to educate others." In the hyphen, she can embrace what she loves about her religion and culture, but she can also separate from what she finds oppressive. Azarene agreed, showing an identity map that painted freedom and education as central to women's well-being across Islam and America.

While all the youths identified their Muslim selves in their identity maps, they varied greatly in the levels of their religiosity, ranging from cultural to spiritual to pious to questioning. Iman used "balance lines" to explain her position along several continua:

On one end it says "Muslim"; [on] the other end it says "non-Muslim." . . . My star that, like, shows who I am is closer to non-Muslim. . . . Whenever somebody asks me what my religion is, I always say Muslim, although I don't practice as a Muslim. I always feel that it's intertwined with my culture. Then, the next line, one end says "religious," the other end says "spiritual." And there is some religious aspect of me, but it's pulling more toward the spiritual, so it's . . . closer to spiritual than it is to religious. And then the third line on one end says "belief in God"; the other says "atheist." The star is right on the beginning of that line, on the top of belief in God.

Sula explains her religious identification is carried in faith and tradition but not dress: "Although I don't cover, I am very in touch with Islam." Some of the women differentiate their religious practices from those of their parents. Erum, who considers herself "traditional," explained that while she is "not a very religious person," her mother and her siblings are. In addition to specifying their levels of religiosity, several differentiated between their connection to their Muslim faith and their connection to the Islamic community. Manal, a graduate student who said that Islam was a "huge part" of her identity, also noted that she was *not* connected to the Muslim community.

Living in Parallel Worlds

A smaller group of our interviewees told us that they live in, and commute between, two parallel, separate worlds. These youth experienced their Muslim and American selves in different compartments of life, with seemingly little tension (see maps 10, 11, and 12). Our surveys revealed that those who live parallel lives were significantly more involved in social and cultural activities of their home culture than were those experiencing conflict or integration. With identities rooted firmly in two worlds, these young people engage substantially in the social (i.e., hanging out with people from their home culture) and cultural activities of their home countries (i.e., eating food, listening to music, and watching TV originating from one's home culture).

While commuting between worlds may sound effortless, a number of the young people described the burdens of living in parallel worlds as "suppressing." They selectively enact specific parts of their identity at home and in school with peers. Farid, an eighteen-year-old Afghan freshman, spoke through his identity map about how he negotiated his identity across contexts.

I didn't grow up around any Afghan people at all. I grew up in a completely white neighborhood, so the music that I listen to, the culture that I was brought up in, was completely white American. And at the same time I am clearly always going to be different [from] American people, because it is hard to ignore the difference, physical appearances and stuff like that. I do have a few Afghan friends, and I have cousins and when I hang out

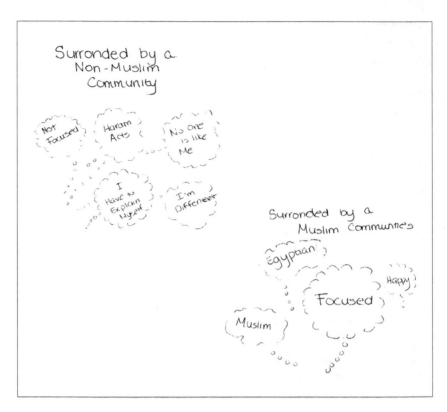

Map 10. Fatimah, Female, Egyptian-Italian, Age 20

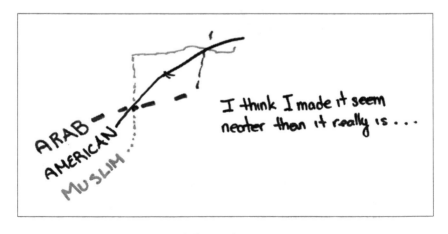

Map 11. Widad, Female, Egyptian, Age 20

with them, I am like the white kid. But when I hang out with white kids, they treat me well, but I don't know I always feel I am different, and I don't think they notice that I am different . . . for instance, I don't necessarily like football, but I would go to football games and be bored there because I felt like that was what I was supposed to be doing. You know what I mean? There is just a lot of stupid stuff that I did that I didn't really want to do just because I thought that it would help me fit in.

Manal described the burdens of constantly negotiating between two very different cultures: "After a while, you do get really tired of carrying two selves around." Zahra also struggles with having her identity contested in both the worlds to which she belonged: "You're kind of nowhere in that aspect. With like Americans, you're just Muslim; you're different.

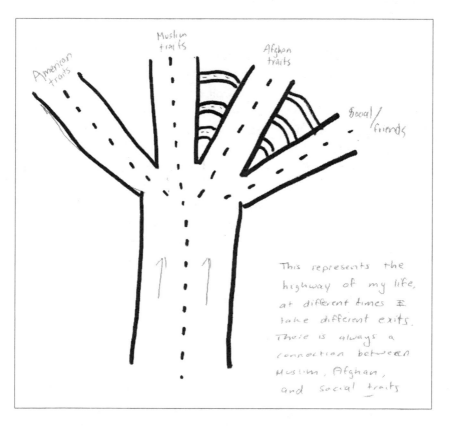

Map 12. David, Male, Afghan, Age 22

But with Muslims, you're not Muslim enough. You're not good enough of a Muslim. You're still different. You're just not accepted anywhere."

Noor expressed feeling more comfortable with her "Iranian friends than with [her] American friends." Some move easily, "finding balance," while others feel the burden of living in two different worlds:

> No, it is a huge problem. Whenever I want to go do something—my parents have this weird idea of what American kids are like, they get it from TV. We are all just doing drugs and having sex when we are out together [laughing], so they hate letting me go out. They wouldn't even let me sleep over at my best friend's house until I was like in eleventh, twelfth grade. When I wanted to go to prom, they gave me such a hard time about that. After graduation parties, such a hard time about that. It's been all right since I have been here because I never see them—when I was back home, I hated it.

While the youth elaborated on how Islam shapes their identities, they were explicit about what it means to be "American." Loyal to religion, ethnicity, community, family, and the United States, the young people spoke with both pride and concern about their nation, the United States. When discussing patriotism, they listed the "freedoms" and "liberties" available to them in the United States, and then they quietly listed the violations they had witnessed and experienced. Although they highlighted the differences between their home cultures and mainstream U.S. culture, they had not yet learned how to live in both worlds with ease. The process of identity negotiation for youth who take a journey on this path involves learning how to switch on and off between two parallel worldviews, that is, jumping between the sides of the hyphen. There are developmental questions here that we cannot fully answer at this point. For example, we do not know whether those youths who choose to live in two parallel worlds have tried (and failed) in their efforts to develop hybrid identities, or whether they simply never attempted to do this.

Conflict at the Hyphen

Reconciling and claiming both American and Islamic values in the United States at this moment in history is a struggle for some young Muslim men and women. Despite the popular imagination and scholarly claims about the incompatibility assumption, however, we found only a small number of young people who seemed to experience being Muslim in direct conflict with mainstream U.S. values and traditions (see map 13, color maps 14, 20, 21).

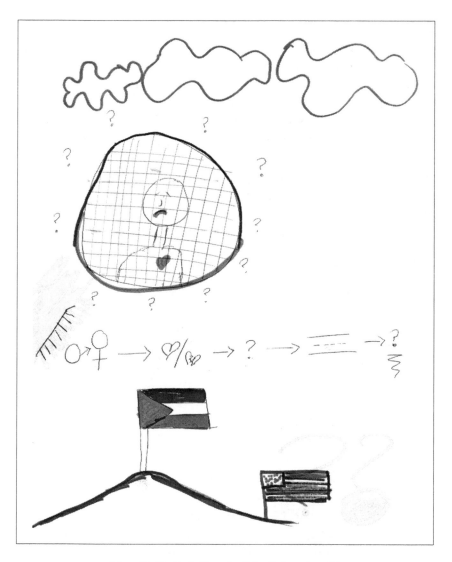

Map 13. Nadirah, Female, Palestinian, Age 22

Conflict at the hyphen is sparked not only between religious (e.g., Muslim) and national (e.g., American) identities but also between ethnic (e.g., Palestinian) and national identities or between war (here) and peace (over there). Azhar, an eighteen-year-old Pakistani man, eloquently explained how he was negotiating across his Pakistani, American, and Muslim identities, sometimes encountering a great degree of conflict and struggle along the way:

There has always been this struggle of sort of conflating or managing all these identities within me. The main conflict comes from Islam and America. I am American born. I have lived all my life in America. I love everything, that is, I love a lot of things about America. I love the civil rights movement. I love the fact that you have this sense of individuality. But at the same time, you look at what Islam has been in conflict in the West with. You look at Orientalism, you look at imperialism. These are the sorts of things that create a backlash within Muslim communities and countries in the twentieth century. Being the child of twentieth-century-born Pakistani parents, there is definitely some of that sentiment that is ingrained in me. If you look at Sayyid Mawdudi, he is one of the premier twentieth-century Islamic scholars, and he is a very anti-Western person. Those ideas get grouped in with family values sometimes, and then sometimes it brings upon this stereotype within you that everything that's with America is wrong. . . . So you always see this struggle within me saying that Islam is the ideal. You know there is always this struggle to define Islam as the ideal way of life within me. There is always this constant struggle between defining my values as a Muslim or an American.

Another Pakistani man, twenty-two-year-old Usman, summarized this tension over reconciling conflicting worlds:

As [a way] of reconciling my Pakistani heritage with my American background, I feel that it happens quite seamlessly. There isn't that big of a drawback in that the problem comes when I try to bring together my Islamic background and my American background, and there are certain problems and there are certain things that are not exactly pleasing, as you would say, to our Creator.

While many of the young men and women celebrate the advantages of their multicultural and religious identities, they also were keenly aware of the weight of living "between" and "within" multiple cultures or selves (Sarroub 2005; Wiley, Perkins, & Deaux 2006). Meda described how she carried her multiple selves across contexts:

> I am Muslim, I am Pakistani. American has a whole . . . like a really big part of me, and you know, you can't come to another country and be like . . . and try and separate yourself from that country, because you grow up there. . . . My parents are from Pakistan, and Pakistan is a huge part of their identity. Islam is a huge part of my identity, too. But I have three different things going around: I want to be the young, the American, college student. But at the same time, I have to be, you know, the good Muslim daughter at home, too. So, balancing is very difficult at times.

Fatima used a sports metaphor to depict the conflicts she faces volleying between identities:

> I used to play handball when I was in high school. These are the walls that it's hitting against constantly. It's always having some sort of clash or colliding with these things in my life. There is me, a family person . . . but there's also that I have to conform to my culture in some ways. Not completely, because if anyone knows me, I am very outspoken, so I won't ever be put down by anyone if they're wrong. There's the friend part of me . . . I get along with everyone.

Usman, a twenty-two-year-old senior at a prestigious private university, pointed out the difficulties of negotiating across contexts and the challenges he expects to encounter in the professional world after graduating from college:

> I am a Pakistani Muslim American, and I have had trouble in the past reconciling all three facets of my life. Those being a Pakistani, a Muslim, and being a U.S. citizen. And, umm, the problems that I face, especially now, I will be graduating in May. And the field that I am going into, investment banking, and the future, I am looking to go into law. I see moral and ethical values being questioned which I was obviously raised with more of

an Islamic foundation, which those backgrounds such as law and banking sort of deflate those values. And they deflate them to a degree to which I myself question if those are the correct future endeavors that I am looking to go into . . . I would say with [my] professional goals that they absolutely do not coincide with my religious background.

When we began our work with the Muslim American youth, we thought we would find a large segment going through what Usman described here. To our surprise, however, only a small portion seem to report the kind of identity conflict that is so prevalent in both the scholarly literature and public discussions of youth who negotiate their identities across racial, ethnic, religious, and national boundaries (see color map 21). We certainly need more time and more data to determine the long-term developmental implications of the current historical context, but the early evidence suggests that young people are innovative, creatively reconciling the many challenges of living on the precarious hyphen of Muslim American (see color map 22).

A Flashpoint: Critiquing Muslims

As expected from any group under pressure, Muslims in general and particularly Muslims in the post-9/11 United States find it quite difficult to articulate their internal criticism of their religious backgrounds or the Muslim world in general. The difference between a "sellout" and an honest critique is not always clear in the minds of many. In the context of expansive surveillance, loyalty oaths loom large, and those who betray their own run the risk of being ostracized or exploited by the dominant group.

Because of these challenges, we did not hear much criticism of Islam. However, to our surprise (and we did not ask such questions in our surveys!) we noticed that those who were willing to criticize Islam or the Muslim world, as well as U.S. government policies, tended to be the young people whose maps represented deep integration. That is, those who portrayed their lives as integrated were more likely to be critical of Muslims ("Muslims should better educate themselves") as a community or Islam as a culture ("Imams in the Middle East are not high-class people; today they're like the local shepherd. His views may be very black and white, and he might call for like dangerous kinds of things"). Indeed, firmly rooted in both worlds, with a creative "fusion" identity, these young people offered rich, complex, and critical views of U.S. governmental policy and Islam. They also were likely to analyze local politics with a critical eye: "One guy doing a hate crime against a Muslim guy on the street does not equal all Americans. One Muslim doing a hate crime against America does not equal all Muslims."

As arbiters of many allegiances, they also show a willingness to take responsibility, that is, to note the points of tensions without feeling like a "sellout." Tariq, for example, explained the current relations between Muslims and the West by placing the blame on both sides: "You know it is not always like there is one right side or that there is one completely wrong side. Obviously both sides must be doing some wrong deeds. There must be something wrong on both sides that has led to a result of this." Another young man agreed, "I don't want to be the one to blame the West and say oh you guys initiated it first. Obviously Muslims have to do work within the communities to dispel these anti-Western feelings." Those who connect with both the Muslim and American communities also seemed to be able to be critical of not only American society but also the Muslim community in the United States and at large. Though without enough survey data to conduct a direct comparative assertion, we nonetheless suggest that those who develop integrated identities are probably more motivated to make such criticisms because they care about both their identities and the relationships between them.

Conclusions

We identified three important points about how young Muslim men and women form their identities. First, we found strong empirical evidence that Muslim American youth indeed develop strong commitments to both their Muslim identities and their American identities. This finding fundamentally challenges the dominant "incompatibility" hypothesis, which proposes that Muslim and "American" cultures are mutually exclusive. Second, we determined that two very different processes lead to an identification with the Muslim community and the mainstream U.S. society. Third, we identified three forms of psychological work engaged by youth at the hyphen. Most young people have creatively *integrated* aspects of their Muslim and "American" selves. A smaller group—mostly male—describe *parallel* and relatively non-intersecting lives, between which they commute. Last, a quite small but important group embody and experience substantial *conflict at the hyphen.*

Meet Taliya

Seeking Safe Spaces for
Social Analysis and Action

At age seventeen, growing up in Florida, Taliya is a soft-spoken but ambitious young intellectual with exciting dreams for her future. Born in Pakistan, she came to the United States when she was two years old. In the ninth grade she moved from an Islamic school to a public school. Today she plays tennis and soccer, likes to make films, and "loves books . . . mostly historical . . . they're very interesting and they help my vocabulary." On her survey, the only "very true of me" item she checked was "I feel that I have to be perfect." A voracious reader, she studies history and is a dedicated social analyst. Concerned about the Muslim diaspora and global conflict, she speaks eloquently about the Ottoman Empire, conflict in the Basque region of Spain, and Protestant-Catholic violence in Ireland.

Today Taliya wears traditional dress, covers her hair, prays five times a day, and attends mosque twice a week. Five years ago, the events of 9/11 shook her twelve-year-old world:

> After 9/11 . . . because of the seriousness of the event, and the rest of civilians whose innocence was . . . it was all like really fast. You know, like one moment I was sitting at school and the next moment on TV, there's like the news about terrorists and people committing that crime. And then, you know, I experienced a sense of confusion that particularly because . . . like you know, I was twelve. So that was kind of like, "Whoa! What was going on?" . . . you know? But now, I've kind of understood it better, in a sense, because probably I have matured more.

Later in the interview, she elaborated on the relentless and dangerous forms of racial profiling that have followed the U.S. "war on terror":

> *Taliya*: OK, right now they are racial profiling Arab Muslims, right? And that was in the beginning and then they started doing like different Muslims, because they came to realize that they don't just come from an Arabic country but from Pakistan . . . and other . . . So they kind of like broadened their profiling

—Muslim profiling. And like, like, before they only used to pay attention to the men. I think it is because like it's like, in the Palestinian lands, like the men used to do suicide bombings first. . . . And then they moved onto [women], because . . . the women started doing it, you know.

Madeeha (*interviewer*): So they crossed that gender divide?

Taliya: Yeah, yeah, and like so I think like if you stop one way, you know, you're going to find out another way to do it. Oh you know, you may be paying attention to our men over here, but there might be a Mexican who is doing the same thing . . . you know, killing civilians, that's wrong. But then I mean you can't take it out on the people who are not responsible.

Taking the position that the United States should "back off" from global warfare and imperialism, she offered numerous examples of cultures and civilizations that "despite their conflicts, they dealt with them *on their own*, and so, you know, without interference." In contrast, she's most concerned that

President Bush decided to go into Afghanistan because of, you know, the Taliban and all that stuff. And then he decided, "Oh, why not go into Iran or, you know, Iraq," and so, in a way, you kind of see he's moving because in a way, he's moving . . . like he's paying attention more to the Muslim world instead of like other parts of the world. For example, Spain. Spain has problems, too. Like they have terrorists, too and then Ireland too. Like Spain has like . . . there are regions that are divided. And the northern region is fighting with the southern region. The northern region wants liberty. They want to create their own nation. And so they're using this means of terrorizing people and like taking their policemen away . . . Also in Ireland, the Protestants and the Catholics are still fighting . . . taking it out on the innocent people. Like . . . the Ottoman Empire, like it was one of the greatest empires and I mean they did have their conflicts. And like during the sixteenth and seventeenth centuries. But at the same time, they dealt with it . . . and still produced like one of the greatest mathematicians, scientists.

Taliya roots her identity in the Islamic diaspora. Her identity map represents a "'tree of knowledge' . . . the star, the crescent represents Islam, and it's like the foundation for all of the other things, like family and tradition and history. And it all comes together from like the foundation . . . and that is religion." She extended this analysis later in the interview when she explained that "language is very important, because it brings people together and it goes back to Islam, because there's people from all over the world who converted or have originally been in Islam."

Madeeha, the interviewer, asked her, "I mean . . . it's like you're saying their common language is Islam?"

Taliya responded with a sophistication beyond her years: "Yeah, like in a way, if you think about it metaphorically."

For Taliya, "Being Muslim is a way of life. And being an American allows me to really practice our way of life . . . because some other countries don't just necessarily acknowledge that." The blend of Islam as the foundation, and American soil as the space where she feels she can engage as a young Muslim woman, is a blend that satisfies her, despite her analysis of racial profiling. A knowledge of history and global politics gives her a sturdy basis on which to critique, and appreciate, the social and political possibilities for young Muslim American women.

Taliya sculpts her "conservative" Muslim identity and practices firmly within the "protected freedoms" of American soil. She thrives in her small "magnet program" in a public high school, filled with

> all kinds of minorities. . . . Fortunately, I do not face much discrimination. Perhaps [because] the people whom I am surrounded by are not ignorant and consist of different ethnic backgrounds. In other words, there is much diversity at my school, and I am in a program [magnet program] whose students are intelligent and thus do not base on race or religions.

Working the hyphen with delicacy and intense social analysis, Taliya organizes her world through small, safe spaces where she engages thoughtfully and deliberately with Muslim youth and non-Muslim youth, spaces where she is protected and can be analytic.

> We have a club . . . at my [public] high school, Islam Club and we do various activities in order to . . . allow other students to become more aware . . . there are some students . . . whose parents are very strict in terms of like, you know, religion, if you're Christian their parents are like real strict not letting them associate . . . but they still come anyway, because it appealed to them.

Returning to her magnet program, she noted, "Yeah, it makes a big difference . . . it created a wall between like me and the bad side. I'm not very into the outside world 'cause I'm protected like because . . . probably because I don't have a lot of classes with those types of people [e.g., people who smoke cigarettes]."

From behind the veil and within the confines of her magnet school and a home in which "I don't question my parents," Taliya is committed to educating her Floridian peers about ḥijāb, dating, and even "to clarify like the role of Jesus in our religion . . . we don't just eliminate him completely." Throughout the interview, she talked about how wearing ḥijāb reflected her signature, her stance in the world, a statement to others:

> It represents how religious you are . . . if you don't wear it, you know, they're probably just thinking you're just another kid. But then if you do wear it, then people are going to wonder and then probably start asking questions. And then want to learn more and eventually you know get an understanding.

Taliya's social relations are closely connected to the wearing of head cover. "The first impression is when they first see you, they never met you before and is probably that you're all serious and you don't take things lightly. And then, once they get to know you, they're like, 'Oh, OK, she's cool.'" But the "weird questions" and "blurt[ing out] random things" follow her, like "'Is your hair really long or curly?' in the middle of English class . . . so it kind of shows that they're thinking about things, even though they don't express them." With a smile, she admits, "I think, like perhaps in my opinion, I think they take me more seriously than I really am."

Turning to the future, Taliya intends to study medicine, "perhaps because it's the most challenging and I tend to stick to the most challenging options for some reason perhaps because it gives me satisfaction that I've done choices the hard way." A pioneer in the young Muslim world, she also is cultivating an interest in filmmaking as a hobby in the future. A young woman of the world, with great vision in her everyday life, Taliya is carving out safe spaces for comfort, peace, reflection, and identity building—to analyze the many hyphens on which her dreams rest and to stretch a broad canvas for a life of meaning.

6

∎ ∎ ∎ ∎ ∎ ∎ ∎ ∎ ∎

Contact Zones

Negotiating the Hyphen between
Self and Others

Rashid describes a much repeated scene:

Rashid: I've been stopped by the police once, and that was really quite un-
nerving because he asked me what religion I was. I was not happy with
[that].
Interviewer: Wow.
Rashid: I felt kind of angry. On my American side I felt kind of betrayed a
little bit in that.
Interviewer: Well, what did you say?
Rashid: I told them I was Muslim, and basically the police officer was concerned because someone called the police because I was praying near a
train station.

Sabreeha (Pakistani, age twenty-two) told us a different sort of contact
story:

I was taking a terrorism class and there was this girl who sat next to me.
She was really trying to be friendly with me, and she was Israeli and the

teacher was talking about terrorism and she looks at me and says, "They don't know terrorism like us," I'm like, "Excuse me?" like "What do you mean?" She says, "You know, I'm Israeli and you're Muslim, you know, you understand." I say, "I'm American, I don't know what you are talking about. I know just as much about terrorism as they do." I haven't experienced any more than the kids in the class, the American kids. [I explained] I'm not Palestinian. She's like "Yeah, but you're Muslim." I was like "What??" I was just really surprised. I mean September 11 was the first time I have actually firsthand experienced terrorism. How would I be more in tune with terrorism? I was really upset at the fact that just because I wear a *hijāb* and I would sit next to her in the classroom that I would have more insight into terrorism than anyone else in the class would.

Sabreeha continues by telling a story of being protected by an unsuspected ally:

Back home, we are the only Muslim family within our community, so right after 9/11 I was the only Muslim in my high school, the whole district. I was walking around, the security guard pulled me to the side and said, "If anything happens, let me know first, I will take care of it, even if the students are joking or anything, just let me know." As he was telling me this, these two kids were walking by—I think they were freshman—and they said, "Hey, let's go to 7-11 and blow up those Palestinians." The security guards grabbed them and said, "First of all, they are from Pakistan, get it straight!" and the guy was like this Caucasian white guy and was like, "Second of all, what did you say?" And they were just joking, they weren't serious at all, but the school took it very seriously . . . I mean my local community was very open, and they wanted to make sure that people understood the difference. Me and my sister, they knew us very well, we had a good image so they just wanted to make sure that people understood the difference so they opened the doors for us actually. I feel that because it was small, it was that way, but if it had not been, it would have been a lot different.

Rashed and Sabreeha told very different stories of contact with non-Muslims and their reactions. We have collected many of these stories, along with responses as varied as these. In this chapter we move from an analysis of the *intrasubjective* work of hyphenated selves to a look at the *intersubjective work* of social relations at the hyphen. In order to understand how young Muslims in the United States encounter "others" and how they respond, across context and relationship, we created focus groups in which self, other, and the "spaces between" could be observed. Challenging the traditional psychological partition of interior and exterior, self and social, we tried to connect our understanding of *hyphenated selves* as a psychological rendering of self-in-relation to an analysis of how Muslim American young adults experience and engage in *contact zones* in relation to others. If people feel conflicted about their identities, how do they negotiate the space between self and other in a social setting? If people are trying to integrate their many selves, how do they negotiate "others" when the interaction feels threatening or aversive?

Methodologically, we shift from looking at individual-level surveys and maps and toward considering collective discourses deployed in single-sex focus groups in which self, other, and the relations between them come to life (Benjamin 1998; Cushman 1995; Guidano 1987). Based on what the maps and individual interviews have suggested to us, in this chapter we analyze how the hyphen is lived in conversations with others. That is, in this chapter we look at under what conditions, and for whom, contact with "others" provokes a recoiling and silencing of self, and under what conditions, and for whom, contact is experienced and embraced as an opportunity to reach across borders, to educate and to engage.

We borrow the language of contact zones from Maria Elena Torre (2005), who draws on the writings of Mary Louise Pratt (1992) and Gloria Anzaldúa (1987). Pratt introduced the term *contact zone* to describe "social spaces where disparate cultures meet, clash, and grapple with each other, often in highly asymmetrical relations of power" (Pratt 1992, 4). Torre extended the notion to the psychology of intergroup relations, suggesting that within contact zones, psychologists could find a textured understanding of human interactions across power differences. Analytically, according to Torre, this is an opportunity to push our psychological theorizing beyond simplified binaries such as oppressor and oppressed, self and other, and colonizer and colonized in order to understand the dialectical relations between them. By interrogating social relations in contact zones, critical psychological inquiry can examine the praxis of the *space between,* of what Anzaldúa (1987) calls "the border-land," or the "work at the hyphen," as we call it in this book. A contact perspective "foreground[s] the interactive, improvisational dimensions of colonial encounters so easily ignored by diffusionist accounts of conquest and domination. . . . [It] emphasizes how subjects are constituted in and by their relations to each other . . . in terms of co-presence, interaction, [and] interlocking understandings and practices" (Pratt 1992, 5).

Our interests are in the existential challenge posed to self by the contact zone. We ask to what extent young Muslim Americans experience what Iris Marion Young called a "justice of [mis] recognition" in the zone, and how they respond. Immigrant youth import to social settings both their anxieties and their desires to belong; their collective memories of oppression, colonization, and cultural pride; their fantasies and projections; their fears and longings.

Specifically, in our interviews and focus groups with young Muslims, we chronicled numerous scenes of contact with white Americans, people of color, and other Muslims; with the media, books, the police, family, and strangers. The young Muslim Americans experienced some of these contacts as assaultive and suspicious; others, as loving and protective. In response, the young people told us they felt outrage, shock, fear, psychological withdrawal, and sometimes the inspiration to teach. One young woman, who often wears a scarf, told us that she decided to walk up to the person who had just misjudged her, insisting on "educating him . . . if I don't, who will?"

Ali recounted a political rally at his university. Muslim Americans were protesting against a local event showing the infamous "Muhammad cartoons" that incited an international controversy in 2006 because Islam prohibits showing any figures resembling Allah (God) or Muhammad (the Prophet). To mark their disturbance, students organized a sit-in:

> I just remember before the protest we were allowed to sit in when they actually allowed the thing to happen, so we had to sit in the building where it was going to happen, and the president of the University came and higher officials came, Jewish kids came, and then we prayed in the park out here. They closed the street down, and all the Muslims prayed on the street in front of the building and the president was there too. The Jewish kids prayed with us and the rabbi. The Jewish kids that prayed

with us also have a corps now, the Middle Eastern corps. It's a Jewish fraternity and Muslim kids. I guess it's to open up dialogue or something.

Across these scenes, we hear about contact with police as racial profiling; contact with another student as an experience of misrecognition; and contact with a security guard, Jewish students, and even a rabbi, as allies.

Although our readers might not agree with these responses, we ask only to notice all the social psychological material that floods at the moment of contact. Multigenerational histories of loss and exploitation are suddenly enlivened, and multiracial and religious coalitions can be sparked from flames of shared outrage. Collective memories (Deaux 2006) may saturate the local scene. Tragedy can be imposed, averted, and/or protested. In the contact zone, in the intimate movements at the hyphen, walls are reinforced or may be torn down. We found ourselves moved by these stories and wanting to understand more about the micropolitics of engagement and retreat.

To study the intersubjectivities of contact, we held a series of sex-segregated focus groups with Muslim American young adults. These focus groups were designed to reveal how young people experience, embody, and enact their many identities in a space of social relations varying by nation, religiosity, politics, dress, social class, and community (see Wilkinson 1999; see also Wilkinson & Kitzinger 2000). We asked a series of simple questions about identity negotiation, experiences with surveillance and discrimination, and the degree to which they dealt with these issues in their everyday life (for the focus-group protocols, see appendix C).

Given the depth of what we term a *scaffolding of scrutiny*, on, by, and among Muslim American youth, we view these focus groups as social settings in which reactions to contact can be discussed and also enacted, even though all the participants were nominally Muslim. We sought to understand not only how they represented their experiences of the hyphen but also how they engaged with difference, how they dealt with discrimination, and how they survive in the contact zone called America (Pratt 1992).

Using the focus-group material as our data, we relied on two analytic methods to study how Muslim American youth and young adults talked about self and other in wildly diverse contact zones: airports, classrooms, train stations, television, the news, the street, and dorm rooms. First, we cataloged the kinds of contacts they experienced, in a straightforward content analysis. We coded for invited and imposed contact. Second, we traced their emotional responses to contact, and through these emotional cues we followed a discursive analysis of how young Muslim American women and men, in sex-segregated focus groups, created together a gendered, collective narrative of contact with the other, the people they consider "American."

We present next excerpts from two typical focus groups—one made up of five young Muslim women and the other made up of five young Muslim men—and undertake a discourse analysis to hear how self and other were negotiated individually and socially, in a conversation about what it means to be young and Muslim in America today.

Young Women's Focus Group: Engaging and Educating in the Contact Zone

Dara (Pakistani, twenty-two): I'm from Pakistan. My parents are from Pakistan, so even though we're not the minority there, you're still considered American, you're not so much Pakistani. Over here, most definitely people look at you as, like, "Where are you from? Why are you here?" Not everyone—*some people smile, which is great.* I remember one time we were in a Subway restaurant with this one guy, and we were just talking about a poster on the wall and this guy was shocked that I talk the way I talk 'cause he thought I would talk with an accent. Maybe like that you know [said with an accent]."

Interviewer: Was this a Caucasian man?

Dara: I think he was black. I mean he seemed happy about it he was, like, "*You go, girl!*" Or something like that. And one time I was on the subway, and a lady came up to me and asked me for directions and was like, "*Oh, never mind, you don't speak English,*" and I was like, Wow! Why would you do that to someone?! You ask them a question and then say hold on, let me insult you and say you really don't speak English, have no sense or thought or anything. But people definitely have their ideas on what a person who isn't American looks like and what a person who is an American looks like.

Interviewer: How did it make you feel?

Dara: I think it *made me feel angry.* It makes me feel angry. It makes me *feel frustrated* and a *little lost.* And actually I'll share that, too. Last semester in class we had a Friday cohort of education classes where it was just us juniors who have classes together and are all elementary education majors. We went to go to the Tolerance Museum and you know, it was pretty powerful and everyone was kind of moved. We were just having a free talk, and I started trying to share my thoughts but I wasn't so successful because we were talking about stereotypes and how we want people to see us. And I began to say how, you know, kind of what we were talking about right, the fact that I feel I am American but people around me don't necessarily think I am, and *I started bawling like crazy* and everyone was "Oh my god, she's a freak, what happened to her?" But they were supportive, and they were like "We hope you never feel like that again." But it definitely strikes me emotionally because, you know, it's your identity and you don't want to feel like that all the time.

These interactions are at once painful and profoundly human. Extensive histories of shared oppressions or colonialism lie dormant in bodies passing in the subway until someone says something offensive. Then suddenly these historic bonds break through, coming alive in the micropolitical discourses of human relations. For some, they say, "You go, girl." For others, it's "Never mind, you don't speak English."

Always fraught with power, collective memories spill over and into sites of contact, echoing what has been said to or about ancestors whose souls have been violated. At the contact moment, perhaps even in anticipation, each body fills with whispers from elders—dead and alive; wars fought and lost; subjectivities shaped in human contact. In between these souls we find psychological territory, occupied by traumas of the past and utopic and dystopic fantasies of what the future might be. Frosh argues that "social events are infused with fantasy—eroticized, exaggerated, full of fears and desires" (1999, 387). Each young woman negotiated the material of contact in her own psychological fashion:

Sabreeha: A lot of times *I don't get angry. This is really bad, but I think of myself as superior* to them. I'm like, "How are these people so stupid?!" That they think that, they don't *think.* I see them more as ignorant and I'm just like, how can I teach them? So instead of me being just like, "You know what? I speak English!" I'm just, "Actually I was born here." . . . When people ask me "Where are you from?" I *know* what they are asking me. I say, "Oh, I'm from Long Island." And they are like "Ohhh," and then they smile and they're quiet but then they ask me where I'm from originally, and I'm like, "Yeah, well, my parents were born in India."

But I think a lot of times when people say dumb things like that, they don't necessarily mean it. A lot of times people just don't know other cultures. They've never experienced, like us, we wear *jilbabs* and *hijābs*. No other ethnicity really wears their clothing . . . or even the Jewish women, they still wear their skirts and wear their, you know, their long stuff and I guess it's more foreign to them, so they assume that you are from a different place and I think that in the end, *this is my task.* You're trying to explain to them, to *make them not be so ignorant.* Sometimes I think people *deliberately mean to hurt* you, but a lot of times *they just don't know.* So I think a lot of times that's why I don't take it so offensively because I'm OK, they don't mean what they are saying. They just don't know what they are saying.

Interviewer: You don't think it is deliberate?

Sabreeha: *Not a lot of times.* Unless some people say it with like that harsh tone, like, "Go back to your country!" Then I'm just like, I'm not gonna even bother.

In all these varied responses young Muslim American women told us they were committed to working through these social relations with others and with peers. They are eager to educate and find common ground. The labor of educating others is a chance to grow the "we."

"They just don't know; they are ignorant." As long as "they"—non-Muslim Americans—are ignorant, lacking, without understanding, these young women take the responsibility of filling in the gaps. They educate and correct the misperceptions.

Interviewer: We talked a little bit about identity. So one thing that we wanted to touch on is, do you find it to your advantage to have a different identity? We talked a little bit about how hard it is to fit in, coming back home, we don't fit in there always, but do you think there are some positives?

Sabrina: Definitely a positive. I feel that the more people you meet that have the more different identities, the more open they are, the more culturally aware they are.

Relentlessly committed to educating others—even taking this on as a cultural and gendered responsibility, perhaps a burden—these young women launch personal campaigns to correct social stereotypes.

Within thirty minutes, the conversation moved from how non-Muslims stereotype Muslim students to how a particular group of young Muslim American women students commute to school with minimal extracurricular activity and avoid interacting with non-Muslims. Once the women in the focus group finished analyzing how "unknowing" and "ignorant" non-Muslims are, they shifted their criticism to "inward" young women in the Muslim community, who *refuse* to integrate into the broader American society. The following conversation reveals their yearning to educate others, which swells discursively and judgmentally into a patriotic duty:

Fatima (Pakistani, twenty-two): I know some girls who are Pakistani, who commute from Queens but *they don't talk to anybody* and they just go to class and they leave.

Interviewer: There's some girls who commute in and don't really interact that much. I was wondering what you guys thought about that.

Fatima: *I think it's wrong to do that.* I mean, how are the people that don't know anything going to learn anything about you and what you believe in? I mean, let's say the reason the girls don't hang out with non-Muslim people is because . . . maybe they have their own family-based community and they're comfortable in that, and they don't want to get involved and 'cause they commute, you know, and they don't have to be here or maybe they just don't want to associate. . . . I don't know what it is. I mean, they talk to me and stuff but . . . the non-Muslim people don't get a chance to interact with you and find out about you. I'm straight up: I tell them, "You can make fun of me, you can talk about me, but that's me —I don't drink." And a lot of people say that, you know, that's really abnormal. Anyone who says anything else, you know, that's your problem. You know I'm not gonna drink and you can't make me. . . . But I think the girls not associating with anyone . . . I think it's wrong. I don't think they should do that.

At this point, accepting the responsibility to educate non-Muslims rises to a civic, or even moral, obligation of the Muslim young women.

> *Dara: I think that [self-segregation] underscores the idea that we're not American. The ones that don't interact.* I don't want to be extremely judgmental of that because I'm not in that situation, but I mean, if you refuse to interact with others and decide that you can't interact with them, that it will be bad for you, that's just like . . . Fatima said, How are they going to learn about you, about who you are? *They are just going to continue on with their stereotypes about what a Muslim is like.*
> *Fatima:* They are not going to even know you're Muslim . . .

There are three discursive moves we want to note in this conversation. First, the group coalesces around their collective responsibility to "fill in" or teach non-Muslims about religion, politics, and the culture. They see it as their civic responsibility. Second, they characterize non-Muslims as relatively benign, if highly ignorant, beings in need of cultural remediation. And third, only after they have affirmed the ignorance of "Americans" does their conversation turn on their own sisters, the "inward" ones whom they blame for the proliferation of stereotypes. Because these "inward" women refuse to educate non-Muslims, "they are just going to continue on with their stereotypes about what a Muslim is like." Of course, it would be easy to dismiss young Muslim women's efforts to educate others as naive or hopeless. As Esses and Dovidio (2002) showed, educating people about immigrants in general is not nearly as effective as recategorizing them as part of an ingroup. National polling data, however, reveal strong evidence for the effectiveness of their efforts. For example, many of the public opinion polls show that those people who interact with at least one Muslim are less likely to endorse discriminatory policies against Muslims (Elias 2006).

The dominant discourse in this focus group, as in all the women's focus groups, was Muslim American women's duty to educate others about Islam. At one point in the focus group, the young women addressed how they responded when they heard racist comments in their classrooms or among friends, particularly directed toward African Americans. Here they stood firm about their desire to speak up but acknowledged that at moments it was awkward, especially if they were unsure whether people were being "deliberately mean" or were just "ignorant." But again we noted a pattern: once they collectively agreed on the need to remediate "Americans," they allowed themselves to recycle their critique back onto the Muslim community, this time onto their families, with parents who were often less acculturated than themselves. Grounded in both worlds, the young carried their criticisms across the border.

> *Dara*: Even [in] my social studies education class that I am taking this semester, my instructor is extremely, very focused on social justice and teaching kids in our classroom about social justice, and our whole curriculum has been about justice against African Americans . . . and just because of the demographics of New York City public schools and most of my classmates are white and a lot of our activities have been about race, a lot of times *I end up feeling like I'm taking their side.* . . . I don't want them [white Americans] to feel like [we are saying], "God, you people, look what you've done to others, the minorities." And I don't know it's weird. I tried to figure out why I feel that way and why.

It is easy to hear the ambivalence around *their* (other students') motivation, and therefore ambivalence about responding. The ambivalence then pivots back to their families:

> *Sabreeha*: A lot of *times I feel like they don't realize the stupid little comments that they make . . . and I get very offended* when people make racial jokes to the extent that when I was sitting with *my own family* and they're making racial jokes . . . they were just like, whatever, we can do it.
>
> *Interviewer*: And even minorities against minorities—they make racial jokes.
>
> *Sabreeha*: Yeah! And so then when my *white friends say something, I'm like, listen that's not cool, like, they don't realize. I think you have to make them realize* that you know you can't do these things. Like for me, I'll tell them every time, this happened to me. Because it happened to me, I feel like *I don't want them to throw a pity party* for me per se. But they don't understand how it makes me feel . . . it may have been something small and stupid, but it can hurt people and make people feel inferior and not part of society and stuff like that. And I think that when I am spending time with

someone, I will share my story with them just to let them know. They are surprised, they didn't realize that something like that can make you different.

When the focus groups' conversations got a bit tense about the decision to speak up versus the position that "I don't want a pity party," the conversation took a rapid dive into airport talk. That is, it's relatively safe, discursively, to return to a discussion of airports, where *everyone* has experienced moral exclusion:

Mariam (Pakistani, twenty-six): When I travel, I feel like I have to educate people more, especially when I cross the border. After 9/11, you know, you have interesting conversations with them. I remember once I was crossing the border, and I had my old Pakistani visa [from] when I went to Pakistan in like 1999. I had this twenty-minute conversation with this guy about my trip: "Who did you go to see? What were you doing there? How many family members do you have there? When was the last time you went? Why did you go?" It was like twenty questions and I was just like, what's wrong with you???!!!

Interviewer: And this happens every time?

Mariam: I went on a trip with a friend of mine once, my best friend, who is white, who is Christian, and she went to one border guard, and I went to the other and she was out like this [snapped her fingers]. And she was waiting for me, and he was just like, "Who are you going to San Francisco with? Why are you going? What is the purpose of your visit?" It was like the twenty questions again! I was like, well I'm with her over there . . . you know . . . why is she standing there and I'm not?

Interviewer: You have to play up that [American] self.

Mariam: That I'm more [American], to get through that cultural boundary.

Interviewer: It's about negotiating between those selves, again that is what we were talking about—the main different selves.

Sabreeha: On the street it's not that bad, but I travel a lot, so . . . I was going to Miami from New York, and from New York to Miami: no problem. In Miami we are waiting on that thing where you walk through and the guy in front of us beeps six times. Every time he walks through, it beeps . . . and they let him take stuff off and walk through again. . . . Finally it doesn't beep and they don't take him to a little room in the corner. Then *I* walk through, no beeping, and "Can we see you in the other room?" and it's like, "Why? Because it didn't beep!" and they're like, *"Oh, it's random, it's random profiling."* [Group chimes in agreement.]

My friend, random, walks through, no beeping, in the corner. So the lady's like patting me down—this is extensive—patting me down, doing this, swiping the luggage, all of that stuff, and she was like, "Oh, you're probably used to this by now," and I was like, "Actually, I am not; in New York, we don't racially profile," because in New York there are minorities working in the airport so they realize that not every brown person that is going to go through is going to be a threat. So then she was just taken back and I was like—*I am never rude, but I was just pissed off* because there was this white guy who beeped like twenty times and they let him take everything off, and I didn't beep and that was the first time I experienced that, because usually when you don't beep, they don't check you. That is how it's been for me in the past . . . so then I was just so angry and my friend was like, "I can't believe you said that!" I was like "What? She has to know!" Like it makes me really angry. And then this other time I was going from Chicago to Houston, and I was in Chicago's airport and the lady checked me off to go in this separate line, and I was like not a big deal, but the line was like a completely closed-off room and they scan everything. They scan me, they open my suitcase, and then they're opening everything within the suitcase and I was like, "Is there any reason?" And they're like, "No, we just have to do it."

Interviewer: Who were the other people on the line?

Sabreeha: They were brown, Hispanic. And I was just so angry, that's one time when I felt angry because *I'm not gonna educate these people—they do this every single day.* I was just like, how can they do that based on . . . ? *It made me so mad.*

Interviewer: I can tell by just the way you talk how angry it makes you, just remembering it. You guys feel anger? Or do you guys feel like you have to dilute it?

Sabreeha: That's different. I feel like [it's different for] the average Joe, but these guys, they're literally labeling me like a threat to society.

Fatima: I've been traveling a lot lately, like between L.A. and New York and nothing like that has happened to me yet, but *I mean I'd feel angry if something like that happened to me. I'd say something also, not just dilute it.*

And then the conversation returned to their solidarity with Latinos and African Americans:

> *Sabreeha*: Another thing I've noticed is when I was going from Philly to Chicago once and the guard was black, and I had pins in my hair and I was like, "Should I take them out?" and he was like, "You'll be fine." *I noticed that minorities are nicer to minorities and it's just very sad* that, that's the way it is. He said, "Don't worry about it, your scarf will fall apart a little bit." He was very understanding because he was like a minority. This happened a lot of times I have noticed, like *Hispanic guards, they are a lot nicer to me* they'll be like, "OK, let me get a female to help you out." Like there was one time in Chicago, the guy was just like gonna start patting me down right then and there and I was like, "No, you can't touch me!" and he was like, "Fine, I'm gonna get a woman." And some minority guy came from the back and was like, "Oh, actually you have to ask her if she wants her own room." And so he was like, "Oh." And so I felt, you know . . . maybe I'm totally stereotyping the white people when I'm saying this —I realize I am—but at the same time, *I realize that minorities are a little more sympathetic* [to us].
>
> *Interviewer*: What are your thoughts on that?
>
> *Dara*: I agree, and it's just . . . I don't know, I'm going off on another tangent, but I know people who are Muslim, who are *desi* [colloquial term for South Asians], who have a phobia of people who are not white. They're like, "Yeah, I wanna live in a totally white neighborhood." It's like, "You know, black people like us a lot more than white people, actually." You know, their intense fear of Harlem . . . gets me really angry. We're minorities too!

Now again we see that the web of "we" has expanded to include "black people . . . [who] like us a lot more than white people, actually." Once a firm discursive sense of grounding is established, the critique of racism can circle back into the Muslim community, targeting *desi* or parents. While a few of the young women spoke critically of family arrangements —"My brother has more freedoms than I do"—racism seemed to be the discursive site in which the young women could "safely" criticize their family life.

Suma: Yeah, my parents do that too.

Sabreeha: I told them like, "Do you think those white people want you to live in their neighborhood? You're brown, they don't want you there either."

Jana: It's true, they're not only discriminating against black people, they are discriminating against you.

Dara: It also goes into the idea of, you know, color in *desi* society and the whole of issue of like being darker and being lighter. Sometimes my parents talk about that . . . my parents aren't really big on that. but then my mom will be saying something about that and I'm like, "Mom, why are you saying that? Black is beautiful!" And I always highlight that.

Mariam: Even within our own society, the lighter skinned you are, the more favored you are, the more you are seen as beautiful.

[*Group*: That's true.]

Sabreeha: The more dark skinned you are, the more you are viewed as ugly. This one girl once asked me, "Why aren't you married, you are so light skinned?"

Interviewer: That's the criterion [for marriageability].

Sabreeha: She was like, "Oh, I'm so surprised you are not married yet!"

Mariam: That's the criterion among a lot of people when they get married, they're like, "I want a girl who is fair skinned, skinny, and tall."

Fatima: My mom does a lot of matchmaking, of course, all of you are single, I hope, you know [laughs]. So she always gets these requests, so recently this guy's mom called and was like, "Oh, you know my son is really good looking and he has green eyes, he's fair [skinned], and he is looking for a girl who is skinny, tall—you know, at least 5'6," whatever—and she needs to be good enough . . . she needs to be good looking enough, white enough to walk next to him so he looks good.

Interviewer: And do you ever hear, "She has to be a good Muslim" or "He has to be a good Muslim"?

Fatima: Yeah, I do hear it. They say, like, "She should wear a *hijāb*." I do hear that. I don't hear, toward faith or whatever as much, but I do hear, "Oh, *hijāb*."

Mariam: We have family friends . . . he [their son] got married a few years ago, and the one thing a lot of people said was like, "Oh my god, she's so much darker than him!"

Fatima: I know! *If my mom says that, I get really mad at her and say, "Mom that's not really nice to say."* And then she won't say it but it's ingrained in her. She knows . . . I mean, my mom came here when she was eighteen to the United States, you know? I mean she spent a lot of time here, but she still ends up saying some things that are really stereotypical or kind of condescending and I'm like, "Mom, why are you saying that?!" And she'll stop.

What is so interesting is that these young women, at least in this conversation, are very critical of white racism and yet are willing to educate white Americans. Ambivalent but committed, they know that if anything is going to change, it will be because they have spoken up. Because they are frustrated and angry when they can't create change, it is intriguing to notice that after they criticize white racism and confirm their solidarity with communities of color, the conversation shifts to expressed racism within the Muslim community. They ally with people of color and, over time in the group, were willing to critique their own families for color-based racism. By engaging across lines of race, ethnicity, nation, and context, these young women work and rework the hyphens that could, silently, simply weigh down their bodies and souls.

Young Men's Focus Group: Recoiling in the Contact Zone

Consider, for a moment, a comparable conversation about contact and identities in an all-male focus group:

Farid: I drew an Afghan flag and an American flag because they are two completely different things, and I drew a circle around them and I am outside the circle because I really feel like I don't fit in either group too well.

In this group we heard repeatedly that young men feel stuck outside, or caught between, two national circles; angry at and alienated from the most contentious aspects of the U.S. government, the media, and popular culture.

At the hyphen and in sites of contact, these young men psychologically defend their Muslim selves against intrusion, invasion, and what Pierre

Bourdieu (1991) calls symbolic violence. In the first focus group, the young women spoke of contact as an ambivalent but embodied invitation to engage and struggle. On the contrary, from the men we heard contact as contentious, as potentially dangerous, offensive, engulfing, or annihilating. They tell one another that they recoil silently and retreat. This is particularly interesting, given the literature of men's focus groups that suggest that young men tend to perform with hypermasculinity and bravado when speaking to and with other men (Frosh et al. 2003; Gough 2004; Stoudt 2006). Here there is almost an admission of politically induced retreat.

When asked about their identities, many of the young men spoke of tensions or conflict. Jamal, a nineteen-year-old college freshman, explained how he was struggling to reconcile the tensions that originated in global politics but live in his body:

I would identify myself as a Muslim, but I always had a problem identifying if I was Muslim American or anything to do with America because ever since I was about fifteen years old, I opposed anything that was American. When Palestine broke out and America was supporting Israel, as it does today, I am Palestinian, so it was difficult to consider myself a Muslim, a Palestinian, and an American because I felt they conflicted with each other. So when people asked me what I was, I would say I am Palestinian and they would say, "Oh, when did you move here?" and I would say, "Oh no, I was born here." And then they would like say, "Wait, that doesn't make sense," so then I picked up on the identity that I was American-born Palestinian Muslim. I still pretty much consider myself Muslim but American-born Palestinian because I don't want to say I am American because it's just, uh . . . 'cause . . . when you walk into my home, you're walking into a Palestinian home, when you step out, I feel like I'm an American, I was raised with like, Palestinian culture, Palestinian food, Palestinian way of mentality, and everything in my house is either Islamic or Palestinian. Of course we have MTV and VH1 and stuff, but the rules in the house are Muslim rules and Palestinian rules. Palestinian culture rules. What's accepted in America is definitely not always accepted in my home. So I don't really feel like I'm American sometimes. And although I may dress, speak, look like I fit as an American, but it's always been a difficult title for me to acquire.

Others engage in a cultural parsing in which they identify those elements of "American society" that they endorse and those that they reject, like government, the media, and social stereotyping.

> A lot of times when people discuss Islam in America, they consider them two mutually exclusive things, but I feel like you know what he was saying, you can't, how can you encompass everything that America itself is? You know, like an Orthodox Jew, his family might have been here for centuries now, but a lot of their values which, you know, their religion entails not watching the movies or music, how can you not consider that to be a part of the "American culture," and so if you want to call American culture "white culture" or "Protestant culture," then, yes, I would say we don't fit into that category. I lived in California, and if you go there, there are cities that are entirely Latino-speaking cities where you won't see a single sign in English or anything like that. And you know just the same, for me personally, I feel that the identities they don't clash per se, honestly I don't agree with the things the government does to a lot of people with other identities. They don't agree with that as well. I don't see why I can't call myself both American and Muslim, although I do understand where [others who claim the opposite are] coming from too. I can see why there would be a lot of anger, and it's easy at times to say you are not American. I can understand that too.

Amir, a first-generation Albanian immigrant, joined the conversation:

> *Amir*: Like I mentioned, I was at Switzerland for two years. [If you asked me,] do you feel if you would go live there for ten years, and you came back, do you feel you would be Swiss as well? I do acknowledge that I have a lot in my identity that's American, but at the same time a lot of people oppose the culture and politics but at the same time I see like lacking, you know, civility.
> *Calief*: Oh yeah [laughter]. . . .
> *Amir*: Yeah, and I can also see that because my roommate is Palestinian and he is also very passionate too because he has that personal experience, like his parents were born in a refugee camp and he was expelled from Palestine and lived in Jordan, and then he's not even an American citizen,

you know, he's like a green card holder and it's like I didn't experience so I can't, that's probably why I don't have these views.

It is interesting to note the number of times Jewish people are referred to as peers or cultural models. It also is significant that a cultural center and margin begin to be identified, with Palestinians seen as "passionate" and alienated, while Pakistanis, with more financial and cultural capital than most other Muslims in the United States, exhibiting more emotional and political privilege as they move across cultural borders.

Amir: Another thing I wanted to add is, well, I agree with the subculture idea, but I think there is this mainstream American culture that most of the subcultures take part in. And that's, you know, the night life, which even we take part in, 'cause I'm sure if you don't want to go to clubs, I'll find you in Astoria. I went to Palestine last year and everyone wasn't so much like that, you know people don't really go out that much, except maybe the guys but the girls, they stay in the house. But one thing that when I did go to Palestine that I want to mention I was a little worried that the Israelis would see me as an Arab, as a Palestinian, as their enemy, and the Arabs would see me as an American, as their enemy. *So I didn't know how I would fit in, and so then I realized that when I go there, yeah, they really did treat me like an Arab, like a Palestinian, when we went into the Palestinian territory, they treated me with great hospitality, and with so much love, and I was shocked because my tax dollars are the reason why one of them lost a limb, or one of them lost his sister or brother, and I realized that when I would walk into a room, they would all get up to shake my hand, and tell each other in Arabic "this is the American," and I'm like, wait a minute, what's going on here, and I realized that I don't really fit in there, or here, and I guess to them, I'm American, over here I may choose not to be.* Of course, if people see me as an American, then it's one of my identities.

While the young men struggle to claim their national identities and sample being "American," their parents insist that they (the children) are fundamentally American. "You are the reason we came here!"

Ali: For me, like I haven't been to Pakistan too many times, like once or twice, but I used to say that I was Pakistani, and *my dad would be like,*

"You're not Pakistani," I would be like, yeah, I am, both of you are Pakistani and he would be like, "No, you were born here. You have lived here your whole life. You may have been there for like, what, four weeks, how can you call yourself that?" I was like, I guess, but that's, like, my ancestors and my culture, and he'd be, like, yeah, but you lived here your whole life and you have this culture and the Pakistani-Islamic culture, and I said I guess that's true. When I went to Pakistan, I don't really look Pakistani, so when I go there, people like give me stares and stuff, 'cause people generally over there are one color, I guess, like a little bit darker, so when they would look at me, they would think I'm like white or American, *like they knew I was American from the way I talked, but like they would think I am white and they would stare at me, and I knew I didn't fit in there, I couldn't live there, I don't know, maybe if I went to Palestine, I would enjoy it more. But Pakistan, I didn't. I mean I enjoy[ed] some of it but some things, I just couldn't live there, I don't think.*

Kareem: Personally, I agree 100 percent with everything he said. But the one point *I guess where I make my differentiation, I differentiate between America as a society and America as a government.* I feel that these ideas which are being propelled by this conservative movement in the government are not the ideas that represent the overall mass, the overall public in the United States itself. You know, whenever I hear the president say all those words, I feel the same exact way but *rather than saying I am not American, I say I don't support this government.* That's I guess where I kind of differentiate.

These young men spent much time discussing the tensions of identification: To what extent am I American? Can I "go home?" Does being "American" require agreeing with culture and politics? And then they hear their parents asserting that they are indeed American, the reason for the immigration. Therefore the men speak explicitly about a conflict, a sense of alienation, and anger. The price of living in the United States is that "Muslims have to be apologists for everything."

Zayyad: In terms of there being a conflict, what bothers me the most is how Muslims have to be apologists for everything. You know we have to get on TV and say we are sorry because the people who are doing what they are doing are only a small proportion of us. So we are expected to, you know, be sorry for things that we are not doing. And on the other hand, when people come on TV and they can call other people violent when they themselves have bombed and killed three or four hundred thousand people, I just find it ludicrous that they have any moral position to, you know, tell anybody else that they are violent. And, *you know, this thing just really troubles me and you know it really pushes you and it looks as though you are being alienated. You don't want to be alienated, but it's like being pushed in a corner* when you stand and you just listen all day to Muslim bashing on every single channel—these people are violent, these people are this, these people are that you know.

Yaqup: I absolutely agree with that. I think that a part of that is due to media coverage, actually a large part of that is due to media coverage. But it's hard to understand especially when you are, let's say, a Palestinian living in the West Bank, Gaza Strip, and your family has just been bulldozed by the Israeli Mossad. I mean the rationale of the American people is, well, you know, the Palestinians are terrorists, but you know, just expanding upon what he was saying, what we have to realize and have to be cognizant of is that we have to take both parts into account. You know, I am not saying that what the Palestinian is doing is right, but Americans justly cannot say what the Israeli government or you know whatever is happening wherever in the world is right, just because Muslims are the proponents from the other side. I mean that does not qualify as a logistically satisfying argument.

Interviewer: How does it make you feel when you see such injustice happening everyday, the way you are describing and he is agreeing? How does it make you feel as a Muslim in the United States at this point?

Yaqup: Well, *I mean it gets me highly agitated.* Just from prior experiences, over the summer, I was interning at J. P. Morgan. And you know, while the whole Hezbollah situation was happening in the Middle East, you would have managing directors, and you would have certain people that are up on the corporate ladder, saying certain things that were just absolutely ridiculous.

Interviewer: Give me an example that really made you feel like . . .

Yaqup: They would say like, the Muslims didn't plan out this attack, did they? They are getting their asses kicked and so and so. And they would be like Hezbollah is completely wrong and . . .

Interviewer: And this was in your presence, they were saying all of this?

Yaqup: Yeah, Pretty much. When we were going to lunch, they would say certain things as such.

Interviewer: How did you deal with that?

Yaqup: I mean, I personally would not bring religion to the table. Because I feel like in the professional setting, that is not what one should do. But you know, I would express the opinion and say that, you know, it's not always like there is one right side, or that there is one completely wrong side. Obviously, both sides must be doing some wrong deeds; there must be something wrong on both sides that has led to a result of this.

It is interesting to note that the men in this focus group and the others were very reluctant to "bring up" religion or politics or to challenge colleagues or friends. Later in the conversation, Namir reinforced the need for self-silence:

Namir: Like I have views that I don't express because I feel that people don't want to hear them and won't accept them anyways. So, like, with the whole Israeli/Palestinian thing, I really don't like Israel, and a lot of people don't take that well so I just don't put it out there. *Like I try to avoid it . . .*

Interviewer: How many of you felt that way? That there are things you want to say but you couldn't?

Calief: That's why I say so much but still . . .

Kareem: You want to say more, you always want to say more.

Some suggest that instead of self-silencing, they are selective about language and audience:

Yaqup: I find myself using different vocabulary depending on which group I'm with. For example, if I'm with a Muslim community, I probably use a little more, more words like "God willing, I'm going to do this tomorrow," but if I'm with a non-Muslim group, I'm much more careful with the words I use . . . I'm very careful with the kind of company I'm with.

Among the young men we interviewed, only one suggested a third option, not silencing, not negotiating language according to the audience, but fantasizing about directly challenging the omnipotent gaze:

When I used to take the train home to Brooklyn, I would get random looks, and like, I would be in close proximity like on the other side and I would see people always be looking. And I would kind of be passionate at that point and be like, "I just wish somebody would say something." Kind of like charge at them. So I always have that crossing my head, especially after September 11. But one thing that's good: we were very overprotective over Muslim women, the Muslim sisters. I guess because I have two older sisters, I was raised to be overprotective of them. And I mean they feel safe around us, and at least we can give them that when they are not home. Maybe I can't be on the train with them or in other instances, but at least on campus if anything happens they know where to find us and most of the time we are around the same area 'cause we are around the same neighborhood.

Late in the conversation, the young men collectively acknowledged that not speaking took a toll:

"The hate, when it gets clogged up, it's just worse."
"Absolutely!"

Their caution about surveillance carried over into phone calls, relations with colleagues at work, and even their everyday language. Back to the airport:

Farah: When I came to the United States, I made the mistake of taking Saudi Airlines, and they made everybody, including the pilot, sit for three and a half hours, after [a] twelve-hour flight. After we checked in and showed our passports, everyone just sit down over here. And then they put everybody's passports in a bag and pulled out one passport, it doesn't matter if it was Saudi, Pakistani, American, whatever. And then they called that person and asked them a *bunch of fifty stupid questions*. Like, you know, "Where are you from? Where did you go? Where did you used to live? What did you do with your house? What did you do with your stuff?" They asked me, "How do you pay for school? What about your old apartment? Where's the furniture?" All kinds of crazy questions. And they have like such *a stern face, so that you're really scared*. Those marshals walking around and literally they look like, you know, they're going to throw you out if you say something. It's like no secret that they listen to people's phone calls; it's not like they try to hide it. They're tapping people's phone, and we all know whose phones they're tapping and what words they're looking for. So, I mean it's no mystery. They're not tapping John and Bob's phone call.

Interviewer: So what words are they looking for?

Farah: Sure, you say Islamic words, like you know, even if I say the word Allah, I'm scared. We Muslims, we use the word Allah in many different contexts. Like if we want to say something good, we say, "Mashallah"; if we want to say promise, we say, "Inshallah." And so, you know, that even [makes you] wonder. You know, hey, what if someone listens to your phone call and they pick up the wrong signal, you know? So there's been instance in the news that some person's saying something and it was construed as something else.

Again we hear from these young men a resignation and alienation from the government, a silencing of voice and a shrinkage of goals. These men live in an echo chamber of stereotypes and surveillance, in their bodies and in their social relations. With no expectation of legitimate state intervention on their behalf, they have little sense that anything can or will change. Instead, they adopt what one young man called "ingrained pessimism."

Interviewer: How do you cope with all this?

Ali: *I guess you try to be careful and you just keep short-term goals.* My goal is to complete my degree. Don't look to the long term because it's really depressing. And like I was saying before, what worries me is future policy. It looks like it's going downhill, it's not going uphill.

Interviewer: You're saying a lot of important things, and I want to make sure that I understand it right. How many of you feel that way? For the long-term future, it's going to get worse?

Saalem: *This is like ingrained pessimism.*

Ali: I lean that way. Unfortunately it's being Muslim and being American, it's almost like in a certain sense almost like being biracial because you have these both groups who are starting to, leaders are starting to detest one another. It's not as simple as, say, Bush and Bin Laden or anything like that, and I'm not either. OK? [laughter] But there are people in both groups that will label you as the other, and that doesn't make it fit well for a lot of Muslim Americans because you don't fit into either one there, but unfortunately the critics of both sides will label you with the other enemy name.

The emergence of a narrative of surveillance, alienation, and despair is clear. These young men spoke with a social-psychological sense of who they were, painfully aware of how others perceive them, tattooed with labels from Americans and Muslims. Whereas the men incorporate the social into their bodies, the young women interrupt the social with their bodies. When these men decide to speak back, it is through politics.

Sulah: Just from before what you were saying about having no faith in the law, I disagree with that. Especially in this nation when one strives to do something, anything is possible. But as a community, what we have to realize, especially *as Muslim Americans that we're on the forefront of the entire Muslim world. The entire Muslim world looks to us for advice, looks for us as a sense of inspiration, looks to us as a sense of direction. And what ends up happening is that when, you know, Keith Ellison is the first Muslim to be going to Congress for the first time,* you know; we have no representation within the political government and within the political movement. How can we expect that laws are made for us when we ourselves are not engaging, you know, within the American society, within the political dynamic? We can't expect that, quote unquote, Joe and Bob are going to make laws that favor Muslims, especially after seeing what they've seen on the media. That's a huge disconnect but, you know, it relates back to us as Muslims. *We have to engage ourselves within the society that we live in.* We have to, quote unquote, tough it out for the short term. We have to look at certain principles, and then we have to go on from there and really kind of connect each other amongst, we have to reconcile each other and we have to make a movement. In order to have representation, in order to have say, we have to have, we have to go toward Capitol Hill, we have to have representation there. And then that's when we're going to have laws that are going to be somewhat, you know, real . . .

Returning to the tension between speaking out and political punishment, Saalem responded:

Saalem: I know a lot of Muslims who got scared of saying a lot of things they used to say. People are becoming more politically correct, but it's not doing the job. We're doing what our parents were doing. We're just working like cows, and we're just, you know ingrained in our work. There's nothing else. And that's what I feel is the fuel of this pessimism. Because, you know, there's a sense of this powerlessness, that you know, what can we do? What can we do? How can we change society? I think what we really need to do is we really need to make a movement, a political organization, in which we go for, you know, political success. Fine, we're very economically satisfied. We're very, you know, affluent, but there's no political say. That's more prevalent now because of the Patriot Act and because of other acts, and yeah, we kind of have to move away from that idea like do your thing and the gain economic benefit of society. But we also have to, I think, really engage in the society we live in and the society that encompasses us and, you know, we have to make that movement towards politics.

These young men were painfully reluctant to talk to their peers, colleagues, students, or faculty about their politics. But they were much more eager to engage at a distance, through either an MTV video (as presented in chapter 3) or politics. Kareem enthusiastically explained:

Kareem: [Before 9/11, Muslim American youth] were talking about radical ideals, and these were influenced by certain Muslim groups such as the Muslim Brotherhood and Jamaat Ahmadiyya. Those are the two main Muslim groups, respectively, in Egypt and Pakistan that fueled this, you know, vision of an ideal Islamic society. Now, *you see the sentiment of trying to change society from within. You see Muslims getting more involved in civil rights movements,* you see Muslims joining ACLU, you see CAIR [Council on American Islamic Relations] taking more of a stand, too.
Interviewer: So there's more civic engagement.
Kareem: There's *more political engagement* and there's more American involvedness after 9/11 than there was before. And it's primarily due to the fact that *Muslims did not know what their identity was.* They were like, the parents' main . . . our parents, I think, you know, you and me can say this for sure, our parents, among many Muslim American parents, came here for opportunity, economic opportunity, because they weren't finding that

at home. And when you see that, they're going to try to cling to their culture as much as they can. And you know, when Islam is involved with that, *there's this disjoint.* And that's what happened before 9/11. As soon as 9/11 happened, people started questioning, "Yo, what am I doing?" And a lot of people left, a lot of people left.

Some find solace in the solitude of their mind and in reading critical histories and analyses of U.S. politics and orientalism:

Personally, I mean my experience of whenever I talk to my mother, she just tells me, "Stick with your own business. It's none of your business what's going on in the world. Focus on your studies and that's it." But personally, I read certain people like Chomsky, Edward Said, and they really helped me. First, I used to view it like, OK, this is an Islamic/West conflict, but it just puts things in such a larger perspective for me now that I realize that this is something that, you know, historically there's imperial power they have done this and used this, this is nothing new. And so it's really helped me.

Another young man challenged the isolation, explaining why civic engagement is necessary:

For example, Keith Ellison was the first Muslim to go to Congress. I think almost every Muslim I know has been very very supportive of this. In the past they may not have been. They said, "We don't want to get involved, we don't want to get in the muck of this." But now a lot of them are very supportive of this, now that he's in the Congress. And what I mean by in spite of, a lot of people campaigned against him just because he's solely Muslim, not because he's democratic, not because he's African American, but because he was Muslim only. Two days ago he was on TV and the reporter asked him, "Can you prove that you are not a dangerous thing?"

Most of the young Muslim American men, however, present a dark and ambiguous view of the future. Although they rally around Keith Ellison as a hope, they describe their collective emotional state as "ingrained pessimism." They see themselves caught in a global conflict that is likely only to get worse.

I mean like if American foreign policy stays its course, my main fear is that the American public, which I believe are the most tolerant people in the world, any people, you subject them twelve hours a day to this kind of propaganda and they would go crazy. I mean in India, when the religous riots happened, I mean it was just a few Hindus that died and those people went on a rampage. They killed a thousand Muslims. The American people didn't do that because they're civilized, much more civilized, much more educated, much more tolerant. But this media and this government are bombarding them twenty-four hours a day and true Muslims should act and I hope they do but, I mean, if that status quo continues, then I'm very fearful of the future.

Another joined in, "We're isolated, we're getting isolated from the mainstream America." And yet another explained:

What it seems like in the future, it seems like the American government is on a relentless crusade. They have to disarm Iran, they have to get rid of Hezbollah, they have to get rid of Syria. So it seems as if there is this unending, you know, and they ironically just all happen to be Muslim. It's just a big coincidence, you know, every single country that they go after just so happen to be Muslim. So yeah, it is really depressing in the future, I mean because, you know, all this is going to do is breed more hatred. It is going to breed more hatred in American society because basically the average American did not know too much about what Islam was pre-9/11 and post-9/11; all they are seeing is a war against Muslims because they are attacking Muslim countries and they are fighting against Muslims and that is all they are seeing. So what the average American if he is going to learn about Islam going to learn a really negative image. *And that is really troubling for our futures in this country; it is really troubling.*

Reflections on Gender, Self, and Other in the Contact Zone

In these two focus groups, and several others we conducted with young women and men, we heard poignant and sometimes humorous stories of contact gone bad; stories overheard on buses; "twenty questions" in airports that did not feel very "random"; and offensive comments from faculty, colleagues, or peers. At other moments, these young people recalled delightful vignettes about a security guard who offered help; Jewish students joining the Muslim protest; finding support in an unsolicited "You go, girl!" Yet *how* the young women and men responded to these forms of contact differed markedly.

To be clear: we are not arguing about "sex differences" and contact. That would be too easy. But the patterns are hard to miss. In each of our qualitative methodologies—the drawings and individual and focus-group interviews—the young women spoke of a strong desire to educate others, to connect, to challenge stereotypes, to educate for social justice. Conversely, the young men spoke with great ambivalence, conflict, and a sense of assault they often feel in contact situations. They described anxieties about speaking up, challenging or educating others. To complicate things further, we also found in our focus-group data that although the young women were more likely to fight back right away and "educate" (a more interpersonal form of action), the young men were more likely to talk about taking action and engaging with the American society politically and civically. In addition to their financial success, they argued that Muslims now should be more active in the political scene if they wanted representation. Hence the men were searching for power as well, but for a more long-term and collective engagement rather than the on-the-spot, face-to-face action described by the women. Because becoming involved in political organizations takes time and resources, especially for youth, and it is not as immediately empowering as the women's responses to exclusion, it is reasonable to assume that using Simon and Klandermans's model (2001), over time with the settlement of the "Muslim American" identity, there will be more effective ways for these young men to make a difference in their immediate contexts and in larger social spaces.

This observed gendered path is situated at a certain time and place in the post-9/11 United States. Young men and women seemed to operate in two quite different social psychological fields. The young Muslim men walked in the shadow of the label of *terrorists* and heard comments like "They hate women"; "They hate Christians"; and "They are really violent." Young Muslim women, in contrast, walked in the shadow of the label *oppressed*. In Gole's words, non-Muslims take "veiling . . . as a sign of the debasement of women's identity, as a sign of their inferiority to men" (1996, 4). Onto their bodies are projected adjectives like "uneducated," "submissive," and "unsophisticated." These young women are misread as waiting to be "rescued" from an oppressive culture.

It also seems important to notice with whom the young women and men engage when addressing these difficult misrepresentations. Our data suggest that when young women speak back, they are typically speaking with other young women and/or men of color. But when the young men describe contact situations, typically these are situations in which they are confronting men, often white men, in authority. These usually are not situations for negotiation. Walking in the guise of the terrorist, in conversation with a white male boss, may be more intimidating than walking in the guise of the oppressed woman, even in a law classroom.

In tension with these stereotypes and interpersonal relations of power, Americans report a far greater fear of Muslim men than women. According to a nationwide *USA Today*/Gallup Poll (Elias 2006), one in three respondents indicated they would be quite nervous flying on a plane with a Muslim male passenger, whereas fewer than one in five (18%) felt the same way about flying with a Muslim female passenger. Although young Muslim women, particularly the ones who wear *hijāb* and thus are visible minorities and emblems of Islam, experience contact as an opening for dialogue, for young Muslim men, dialogue does not seem like an option, not necessarily by choice, but simply because they are not asked many inviting questions.

Furthermore, we see that in the United States, the women may have indeed gained power and are "free to be as religious as my brother," "to be educated," and to "speak my mind." Many of the young women in our studies told us that they were thrilled to engage their newfound freedoms *within* religion, as well as within educational and political settings in the United States. But for young men, being raised in the United States may diminish their gendered and cultural status, both in the home and outside. While the women enjoy more public and private power compared with their mothers (with no illusions about gender equality in the United States), the young men may see themselves as *losing* power in comparison with their father's standing.

In her work with Muslim women in Europe and Turkey, Gole noted that "these [veiled] Muslim women [who] are no longer confined to a traditional role and to an enclosed space are now readopting this sign of passivity and seclusion within interior domestic spaces. They are crossing the frontiers of that interior space and gaining access to higher education, urban life, and public agency" (1996, 4). Similarly, Itzigsohn and Giorguli-Salcuedo (2002) and Jones-Correa (1998) showed that Latino/a immigrants also deal differently with threats to their group's status in the United States across gender lines. Immigrant Latinas seem to gain a relatively higher status in the United States, which makes their collective action more U.S. oriented. Latino men, however, experience a relative loss of status and thus focus more on their country of origin as a way to psychologically improve their position.

For many of the young Muslim women, the United States seems to offer a desirous, if fraught, freedom, a deep sense of power and an opportunity to engage in Islam without fear of repercussion. These young women spoke in a chorus about the liberties available in the United States, the "fluidity" of their hyphenated selves, the authority and power they carry, and the strength of education, religion, and peace. In contrast, in our discussions with the young men, hyphenated selves were splintered with the weight of the world. Many of the men's maps, including those in this book, showed that they view the United States government and military policies as an oppressive force in their lives.

Adamant about the split between the United States and "Muslim countries," a young boy, Hasim, wrote on his map, under U.S.A.: "People are accused of some terrorist attacks that did not even happen, and taken action against them. Muslims [in the U.S.A.] are hated and discriminated against because of something probably [sic] one person did and all have to pay back for it. [The U.S.A. is] Land of opportunity, rich, war, get drafted and die." On the other side of his map, the heading reads "Muslims in Other Countries" and under that is written: "People are accused but are not hurt or no action is taken against them. Muslims love each other and take care of each other. Land of peace." Ahmed, a fifteen-year-old boy, wrote on his map: "[In] Pakistan and other Muslim states, they teach us to pray and put our belief in god and follow the Islamic law. And teach us to prohibit fighting [sic]." Under "America," he wrote, "We get blamed and pushed around for something we didn't do." Torn between the land where they live and feel persecuted, and a strong imaginary about peace abroad, these young men carry global conflict in their bellies.

As Said wrote, for some young Muslims, mostly men, home countries become "the imaginative geography—the invention and construction of a geographical space called the Orient, for instance, with scant attention paid to the actuality of the geography and its inhabitants" (2000, 179). While Said was addressing the colonial/conquest version of the imaginative geography, we heard in our young men another imaginative geography, about a place far away where they had brothers and could find peace and a sense of personal integrity and power. Meanwhile, the women plant contentious seeds here.

Conclusions

This chapter described the complexity of the social-psychological life at the hyphen, in the contact zone. The focus-group material, from both young women and young men, reveals the psychodynamics of intergroup contact. This material confirms the intercultural and intergenerational traffic at the hyphen, carried and enacted differently by bodies of privilege and scrutiny, nation, class, social position, gender, skin color, and, surely, sexuality. We record how Muslim American women and men walk down the streets, into distinct social stereotypes, in their everyday lives at work, in school, on the streets, and even at home. Politics thus lie at the heart of this presumed gendered difference, that is, politics as they enter the social psychological life spaces of these young women and men (Lewin, 1951).

Meet Masood

Grounded in Islam,
Crossing Borders

I choose to only draw the symbol of my religion and not the symbol of my countries because I believe only one thing truly makes me who I am, and that is Islam. I believe culture only divides the Muslim *ummah*, therefore I do not draw the symbols of my countries.

Masood is a sixteen-year-old American teen growing up in Florida, the youngest son of a mother and father born in Pakistan. Attending public high school, he has earned a GPA of 3.8 and considers himself a very serious student—and a serious Muslim. He prays five times a day, goes to mosque twice a week, is reading the book the *Name of the Rose*, and identifies as a "Asian/Pacific Islander." He yearns to be an artist: "I would love to be an artist, a teacher. They don't make enough money . . . But basically in our culture . . . you're supposed to be a doctor or a lawyer. . . ." He already is all too aware of cultural pressures to conform to ideals of success.

Masood thrives in the tension of living in many worlds, "I actually like being Muslim in America, in a non-Muslim country, because we actually have [the chance] to show your religion to people and how great it is." Active in the Islam Club at his high school, he is excited and proud about showing his religious identity to others, particularly non-Muslims: "How great it is for us that we can wear our religious clothing on Friday and people know that we're Muslims." Grounded in his religion and the Islam Club, Masood dedicates himself and the club to a broad and inclusive sense of social change. "Oh yeah, last year, the Islam club held like a banquet for Katrina . . . and like a class auction, and we raised about $2,000 . . . which was spread throughout the community."

With a keen awareness of how gender works in his community and how distorted gendered stereotypes are projected onto his community, Masood offered a quite sophisticated analysis for an adolescent: "I just think guys have it luckier."

"Luckier?" asks the interviewer.

"Yeah, we are lucky in the sense that we don't have to wear a head scarf or anything which is . . . We do have our own, I guess, clothing thing. But it is not nearly as hard as what the girls have to go through." And then he reflected on the gender politics in his community:

> The thing is that it is actually the guys' fault that girls have to wear it . . . I mean I'm luckier in the sense that I don't have to wear it. But in the other sense women who do have to wear it in Islam and they actually wear it, they can be luckier too because in our religion after the day of judgment or in Heaven, or whatever, they will be rewarded so greatly, especially with all that they go through.

Not only is he well aware of what Muslim women go through in everyday life, but he also understands the challenges that come with being a Muslim man. "And I think that Muslim men are looked down upon because people think that they treat their wives or women with no respect."

Living between worlds, Masood appreciates the opportunity to educate non-Muslims, but he also must endure the stresses of social stigma when he wears Islamic clothing.

> Well, actually I was talking about the school uniform and how we got to wear the Islamic, well, not necessarily Islamic, but I think it's Islamic clothing. I do appreciate that, and I said I appreciate that earlier, but you know, the first day or like the second day of school, me and my brother wore that and we got written up and they starting talking to our parents, and I guess that the person who did talk to our parents was kind of rude and so that [was] really, really interesting. And they said that we could only wear it on Fridays, I do appreciate that, I really do, but like I don't find it kind of fair . . . it's a good thing, it's better than nothing.

A most thoughtful young man who lives at the hyphen between "mainstream American" life and "Islamic life," Masood also has experienced the unique position of balancing mainstream American education and religious education. He remembered the several years that he spent in the local Islamic school before deciding to transfer to public high school. "You learn about Islam and everything but at the same time, you are close minded to the American society and what the American people think. When I went to public school, I actually opened my mind a lot more, and you open other people's minds."

A delightful, reflective border crosser, he continued,

> I don't regret going to public school at all. People think that, and I would never regret it. I actually really appreciate it *and* Islamic school. But I wouldn't want to go to Islamic school forever because I think I would be so close minded . . . personally, not that people over there are, my really good friends are there, and they open their mind to other people. . . . [But] they're like in their own world with seventy people. And they have this thing against the world—I really don't want to judge anybody. . . . Since I did go to private school, I was one of the people who did judge people . . . [I judged] Muslims who went to public schools.

Masood lives on the hyphen, and he talked thoughtfully about the hyphen as a site for connecting with others and as a site for distancing from others. Eager to infuse the hyphen with diversity, Masood delights in his "diverse Islamic community . . . we have Arabs, we have Pakistanis, people from Russia and the Ukraine, people from all over the world, and I got to know them. I learn a lot from them." And yet he knows that he lives in a community under siege, where many retreat defensively from the diversity he so admires.

Committed to Islam as a diverse community, he views nation and culture as dividers. Refusing segregation, he fights against invitations to hang only with Pakistanis:

> It's bad . . . they're always segregating themselves. The Arabs stick with Arabs, the Pakistanis stick with Pakistanis . . . I would just say I am Pakistani, I'm not on their side, though . . . when my mom tells me there's a Pakistani dinner for Ramadan, I tell her I'm not going to go. . . . I think it's a bad thing that everyone segregates themselves, and I don't want to segregate myself.

Later in the interview he elaborated, "It seems like culture separates and divides Muslims. That's why I dislike it."

As he shuttles between worlds and consciousness, Masood observes with great precision the ways in which both non-Muslims and Muslims judge those who practice Islam. When classmates or friends who are not Muslim

> joke around . . . or say "Osama bin Laden!" it is kind of offensive. It is actually really offensive, but I try to take it very lightly. As long as they know that my

religion has nothing to do with those kinds of things, to do with terrorism and all that. It's about peace. As long as they know that, it's fine. They're teenagers and everybody does that—I've done my fair share.

Extremely sensitive to the position and perspectives of those around him, Masood tries not to be "too judgmental." Indeed, he even is concerned that he attributes negative comments too heavily to anti-Muslim discrimination, as he explained:

Just sometimes I feel discriminated against by my teachers, I know that's probably not true, but that's just what's running through my head. Maybe I'm just getting that feeling because I am Muslim and all this happening and someone's being mean to me. That's the first thing that comes to my mind. But that's what I feel, but like I don't think necessarily it's always true at all. . . . One day a teacher told me to shut up because I was just talking in class and everybody else was and it just came to mind that I knew she was telling me to shut up because I was talking loud but it just came in my head, that that's because I'm Muslim.

And yet he related extremely disturbing stories of racial profiling:

When I went to Boston with my dad . . . wow. We were like going through . . . we were going from New York to Japan and . . . we were going down to the 747 . . . All of a sudden these customs officers [popped through], and they took us into the room. And they opened my . . . you know, the wallet, and they're like, "How much money do you have?" But I kind of understand, but I don't appreciate all of it. I can't really blame them . . . I mean I might dislike it.

Ironically, Masood holds extremely high expectations for his country, the United States. When comparing "propaganda here and propaganda in the Middle East," he told us,

They are both being biased. The only difference I find is that the propaganda here is worst because apparently the United States is a free country. I do believe that and I am glad to be here. But the reason why I think propaganda here is worse is because we are a free country and we're not supposed to do that. . . . It's not necessarily the people, not from the people at all, but from the government. . . . I was watching CNN the other day before the ceasefire began about Lebanon and Israel. They seem to be like—maybe this is my biased opinion—but it seemed to me when CNN was saying the deaths, they really just tended to stay on the Israeli side. They named how many people died in Israel and everything, and for like one second they said like there are 382 Israelis dead and 800 . . . and some Lebanese. I was like, you should show both sides, not just one. I have nothing against. . . . I do have something against the Israeli government but not against Jews at all. A lot of Muslims tend to have things against Jews . . . but I don't.

A thoughtful, mature, and sophisticated sixteen-year-old, Masood yearns to be an artist in a community that expects him to be a doctor; he befriends Jews even as he criticizes the Israeli government; he believes in democracy and justice as the American way even as he and his father are searched in airports; and he adores his Islamic religion even as he worries that Islamic schooling creates narrowmindedness. He worries that "sometimes people say very rude and belittling things, but you just got to put that behind you."
Asked what he wants non-Muslims to know, he wrote,

I would want them to know that sometimes you may feel like you are being mistreated because you are Muslim, but it's not always true.
I would want them to know that being a Muslim truly betters your life! Islam makes our life easier, not harder, even though . . . it may be difficult to follow our religion completely at times.
I would also want non-Muslims to know that I practice my religion not because of what my parents told me to do but because I truly feel that the rules of Islam make my life easier.

And yet, always the border crosser, when Masood thinks about his future, he intends to marry a "person of the book." He went on to say,

We are allowed to marry Christians and Jews, I mean like, for some reason for example like one of my sisters said that she was really aggravated—I guess I'm not going to judge her on what she said, but—she just said you're not going to marry a non-Muslim. But that doesn't make sense! We are allowed to. Why would you say something like that when we are allowed it. I know I'm only sixteen but this is running through my head.

Perhaps as a result of being the youngest in a large, outspoken family, Masood tended to express his opinions in an almost apologetic manner, despite formulating insightful comments and arguments about his identity, his faith, and his space in the multiple communities he calls home.

7

■　■　■　■　■　■　■　■　■

Researching Hyphenated Selves
across Contexts

At the end of our studies, we recognize our intellectual debt to W. E. B. Du Bois. More than one hundred years ago, in 1903, Du Bois wrote *The Souls of Black Folks*, describing how dominant racist ideologies pierce the skin, soul, and consciousness of African Americans at the moment of contact with white Americans:

> Between me and the other world there is ever an unasked question: unasked by some through feelings of delicacy; by others through the difficulty of rightly framing it. All, nevertheless, flutter round it. They approach me in a half-hesitant sort of way, eye me curiously or compassionately, and then, instead of saying directly, How does it feel to be a problem? They say, I know an excellent colored man in my town; or, I fought at Mechanicsville; or, Do not these Southern outrages make your blood boil? At these I smile, or am interested, or reduce the boiling to a simmer, as the occasion may require. To the real question, How does it feel to be a problem? I answer seldom a word. . . .
>
> And yet, being a problem is a strange experience, — peculiar even for one who has never been anything else, save perhaps in babyhood and in Europe. . . .

The history of the American Negro is the history of this strife,—this longing to attain self-conscious manhood, *to merge his double self into a better and truer self.* In this merging *he wishes neither of the older selves to be lost.* He would not Africanize America, for America has too much to teach the world and Africa. He would not bleach his Negro soul in a flood of white Americanism, for he knows that Negro blood has a message for the world. *He simply wishes to make it possible for a man to be both a Negro and an American, without being cursed and spit upon by his fellows, without having the doors of Opportunity closed roughly in his face.* (1982, 1, 4, italics added)

Like Du Bois, we find ourselves interested in how young people situated at the nexus of a political cross fire regard "being a problem," how they "merge [their] double selves, wish[ing] neither of the older selves to be lost" (Du Bois 1982, 2,3).

Throughout this book we have presented findings from a number of mixed-method studies focusing on young Muslim Americans who have suddenly become "a problem" in the United States. We highlighted important patterns, themes, and even some explanations for how Muslim youth deal with these historical, cultural, and global challenges. From these young people, we learned that in spaces of comfort and contestation, they create and recreate their culture, in prayers, around the dining room table, in school and gym class, on the subway, in corporate boardrooms, in airports, and in the midst of family arguments. We also learned that the policies and practices of "Homeland Security"—very much alive in the United States today—may ironically be turning a generation of engaged teens into young adults at risk of becoming more alienated, more religious, and more marginal exiles in their homeland, the United States.

While all the youths experience the global conflict and the domestic war on terror, they respond differently, living at the hyphen with great variety and style. Sketching a theoretical and methodological program of research to interrogate what we call *hyphenated selves*, this chapter explores our research on and for those young people whose identities are publicly challenged, who are viewed as "a problem," and whose souls are filled with global and local politics.

Theorizing Hyphenated Selves

After reviewing hundreds of maps and surveys and listening to more than a dozen focus groups and individual interviews, we now consider the hyphen as the pivotal psychological hinge where identities cast "in tension" are at once joined and separated. The psychological texture of the hyphen is informed by history, the media, surveillance, politics, nation of origin, gender, biography, longings, imagination, and loss. *How* one experiences and narrates the hyphen may vary from a fence to a membrane, a point of collaboration to a checkpoint, a site of contamination and shame to a new "fusion" of selves. The hyphen may feel alive, like a vibrant, liminal zone for trying on new freedoms. Or it may choke, like a wall of constricted and scrutinized movement. This work builds on the scholarship on multiple selves and intersectionality (Deaux & Stewart 2001) but agitates for a thick understanding of *how* these selves coexist, how they make peace and struggle in the same body.

Our evidence suggests that all the Muslim American young people with whom we spoke feel intimately the pulls of global conflict, but they piece together the fragments of identity in highly divergent ways. Some felt alienated, and others felt compelled to educate. Some grew angry, and others sought to clarify. Some retreated, and others connected. With this evidence, we begin to look at what happens socially and psychologically when young people craft narratives of self from identities that hyphenate and then perforate, when they are separated from the larger body politic, and when they become exiles in their own nation (see Opotow 2004). With globalization, the widening gaps between rich and poor, anti-immigrant sentiment on the rise, and interethnic conflicts dotting the globe, we view this condition of hyphenating and perforating identities as increasingly normative, worrisome, and undertheorized as a political and a psychological project, relevant to youth well beyond the Muslim American community.

The psychological labors of the hyphen are at once individual and collective, conscious and unconscious, filled with pride and shame, politically shared, and wildly personal. In social settings, the hyphen thickens and effaces depending on context, with whom contact ensues, gender, biography, and the winds of politics at the moment. It is scrutinized, stretched, challenged, and threatened by larger social and political formations. The hyphen is a site of taboo and desire, fear and challenge, voice and silence, despair and possibility.

We know that young people can be born at the hyphen in political cracks between social identities, as W. E. B. Du Bois eloquently described the "double consciousness" of African Americans (1982). Or there may be a politically induced shift in the foundational plates of social arrangements that incites a tension between two previously compatible identities, as in the case of 9/11 and the subsequent "war on terror" and Patriot Act in the United States. Alternatively, a young person may decide to step into another social identity, taking up a version of self considered out of sync with prior identities, as Brendan Gough observed about gay athletes (2004). Across these means of acquiring hyphenated identities, young people experience the psychological and political jolt of "excluded citizenship" (Pinson 2008).

Working through the notion of hyphens complicates many basic assumptions of social science and enriches our understanding of the relations between the social and the psychological. In psychology, we are accustomed to studying fixed notions, things that stay the same and that can be measured and contrasted over time, across contexts. We know how to study individual processes of identity formation or coping, and we know how to study contexts, histories, and cultures. But we are not very comfortable studying constructs that vibrate and change, transforming across contexts and changing across time. Studying persons-across-contexts is different from studying persons and contexts, and so we must think carefully about our methods. Where does the skin of an individual end? How do political, social, and historical events move through the self, and how does the self affect the context? How do the deep connections of global and local become empirical evidence found in the body? Under what conditions do hyphenated selves move toward critical consciousness and activism? How can we join quantitative, discursive, and psychoanalytic methods? In response to these questions, we next consider the methods we did use, and might use, to interrogate the psychological dynamics at the hyphen.

Reflections on Methods and Design

Given our desire to research youth identities situated in a specific time and place and also affected by global politics, we take seriously Ella Shohat's call for a "relational approach to multicultural studies . . . [one that] does not segregate historical periods and geographical regions into neatly fenced-off areas of expertise, and . . . speaks of communities not in isolation but rather 'in relation' . . . stressing horizontal and vertical links that thread communities and histories together in a conflictual network" (2006, 207). We consider the tools of social inquiry for connecting young lives to both local and remote social and political formations, for documenting the range of life fields that youth occupy and create, and for acknowledging respectfully what it feels like to "become a problem."

As this book has shown, we lean toward a design that is at once participatory and framed by mixed methods. Those of us fortunate enough to engage in research with youth are obligated ethically and politically to recognize the knowledge they carry in their bodies and biographies. Our inquiries, then, have been grounded in participatory methods. As Anisur Rahman pointed out,

> Liberation, surely, must be opposed to all forms of domination over the masses. . . . But—and this is the distinctive viewpoint of PAR [Participatory Action Research]—domination of masses by elites is rooted not only in the polarization of control over the means of material production but also over the *means of knowledge production including, as in the former case, the social power to determine what is valid or useful knowledge.* (Rahman 2006, 119, italics added)

For the past decade, Michelle and her students and colleagues have been very involved with Participatory Action Research (PAR) designs in prisons, schools, communities, and global human rights struggles (see Fine et al. 2004; Fine, Tuck, & Zeller-Berkman 2007). In these projects, coalitions of young people and adults have theorized about and conducted research on their own experiences and politics. In sites as varied as a women's prison, the South Bronx Mothers on the Move, a community-based organization, and urban suburban public and private schools, we took up projects in which the youths themselves informed the research questions, and the products were harnessed to social movements. In these projects, youth crafted the questions, implemented the methods, collected the empirical material, and designed the reports, pamphlets, websites, and performances; that is, they owned the project.

Because of logistics, however, our Muslim American youth project was admittedly *PAR lite*. That is, this project was conceived and carved by us, Selcuk and Michelle, with a strongly opinionated advisory group of young people, who directed us toward the questions to ask, the nuances to understand, the points of "normalcy" to interrogate (What books have you been reading lately?), and the commitments that run deep in the souls of Muslim American youths. They helped us devise the methods to best capture and tell *another* story about Muslim American youth. From ethical and methodological perspectives and given the dangers lurking around these young people, we had to take seriously their vulnerabilities, that is, the dangers of their speaking aloud and even the pain of admitting their fragility to themselves. The challenge, therefore, was to develop methods that could reflect the complexity of their social and psychological dynamics.

We therefore found it interesting to consider a range of methods akin to what Fine and McClelland (2007) call "release methods," a hybrid of classic and innovative methods designed to invite the unspeakable to be voiced. Our design for this project brought together a variety of methods that often have conflicting epistemological groundings. We found this combination to provoke the release of the vast complexities of the hyphen: qualitative and quantitative information constructed by individuals and groups, about processes that are much on their minds and buried in their personal and collective unconscious. That is, work on hyphenated selves may indeed require working the methodological hyphen.

For instance, there may be good reason to include a survey, as we did, to learn, in the language of standardized items and scales, about the relative costs and pleasures of living between worlds while being pushed to the edge of both. Thus, for example, in our own project, we asked young people in two age groups, twelve to eighteen and eighteen to twenty-five, to complete quantitative surveys assessing commitments to "being Muslim" and "being American," their experiences of and responses to discrimination, and the health outcomes for their bodies.

In our work with varied groups of youth in schools, communities, and juvenile facilities, as well as with Muslim American teens, we also relied on an old social-psychological method—long buried and deserving of resuscitation—the personal "identity map." Variations of this projective method have their psychoanalytic roots with D. W. Winnicott (1989) and have been applied by environmental psychologists (Lynch 1960; Saarinen 1973), radical geographers (Hart 1981; Hart & Moore 1973; Harvey 2001; Katz 2001), and social psychologists, most notably Stanley Milgram and Denise Jodelet (1976). While the prompts may vary—draw the city, your selves, a conflict in your life, your journey into the future—young people accept the invitation to creativity. Researchers can then analyze the maps for content, form, and color and also for political representations and emotions and to determine how the mapmakers express the relationship among their many identities (for more details about the analysis, see Sirin & Fine 2007; Zaal, Salah, & Fine 2007).

Furthermore, we found it intriguing to consider the possibilities of studying young people's intersubjective relations by conducting focus groups of similarly, or even differently, situated peers. Sue Wilkinson (1999) and Sue Wilkinson and Celia Kitzinger (1995) argued persuasively for the empirical value of focus groups and conversational analysis. For our purposes, the focus groups enabled us to connect our understandings of (individual) *hyphenated selves* as a psychological rendering of self-in-relation to analyses of how young people (collectively and discursively) engage in *social settings*. By creating social spaces where "differences" were animated, we saw in our focus groups the varied intersubjective performances of self and relations with others.

The material produced in our mapping projects and in the focus-group transcripts enabled us to analyze hyphenated selves psychodynamically. That is, in the drawings and the transcripts we could code for *what was* but also for *what was not* present. As Ruthellen Josselson claims, and we would agree,

> Many experiences may be both known and not known simultaneously. That which is unconscious may nevertheless be apparent in symbolization processes. . . . Attention is directed then to the omissions, disjunctions, inconsistencies and contradictions in an account. It is what is latent, hidden in an account that is of interest rather than the manifest narrative of the teller. (2004, 14–15)

Josselson's essay offered a powerful theoretical and epistemological framework for our analysis of the qualitative material at face value and with a critical eye. In other words, maps and focus groups offered us interpretive material that could be analyzed psychodynamically, with great respect for the material presented as it is and also with an analytic eye for what is present and what is absent, and what emotions of excluded or engaged citizenship are expressed and buried. Explicit coding elements included representations of power and war, gender and nation of origin, emotion and politics, and who was portrayed and where the map was situated. More critical, we also coded how multiple selves were drawn: near, with, separate from, or opposing one another. What metaphors characterized the maps: Is the hyphen represented as a split, tear, flower, bridge, river, . . . ? To what extent were the drawings filled with tension, conflict, integration, or a new generative self (see color map 23)?

We realized that we needed techniques for coding the buried, the absent, the fleeting, the loss. How were these emotions portrayed at the hyphen? Ann Cheng (2001) and Brendan Gough (2004) helped us think about the emotional landscape at the hyphen, the melancholia that young people endure as they confront what is, for many, a *doubled loss*. That is, youth under siege typically find themselves disoriented by *both* sides of the hyphen (Cheng 2001). For immigrant or refugee youth, this may lead to the social and psychological tensions of transnational lives and imaginaries (Levitt & Waters 2002; Rumbaut 2002), which are exacerbated when home countries are divided by conflict *and* when their new country marks them as suspect (see D'Augelli, Hershberger, & Pilkington 2001; Rao & Walton 2004). Life at the hyphen deserves methods that can chronicle disruptions and innovations on multiple fronts as well as methods sufficiently robust to capture the intra- and intersubjectivities of young people whose fantasies of the past and desires for the future are shaken simultaneously.

Working the Methodological Hyphen

The studies we conducted with Muslim youth used mixed methods of standard research surveys, open-ended questions, identity maps, focus groups, and personal interviews. The empirical material derived from each method contributed in distinct ways to our understanding of these young women and men, boys and girls. In all these different methodologies, we concentrated on understanding how Muslim American youth negotiate their hyphenated identities. With each method we gathered a slightly more nuanced aspect of this larger question. Although working with mixed methods certainly has its own challenges, the intellectual traffic among methods increased our understanding of these young people immeasurably.

Although working with multiple methods is typically considered a strategy to *validate* findings across different methodologies, we also found it useful for identifying key nodes where the *different data sets diverged*. For example, in two survey studies with more than forty survey subscores, we found only a few meaningful variation by gender that could be sustained after correcting for those expected by chance (i.e., Type 1 error). This finding at first appeared in our initial survey study, and we simply explained it away with typical limitations, such as the small sample size of seventy participants, the low reliabilities of some of the items in the surveys,[1] and, of course, the lack of strong construct validity for the measures, given that they all were originally designed for populations other than the young people in our studies. Our second survey study, however, had almost twice the sample size, with 134 participants and much stronger evidence for the surveys' psychometric qualifications. Even so, we continued to find only a few areas where there were meaningful, statistically significant gender differences. This finding was puzzling, particularly because the qualitative data (i.e., focus groups, maps, open-ended questions) were full of gendered dynamics. In fact, we found statistically significant gender differences in the qualitative data when we found a way to quantify them on a few questions, such as the one about self-representation through an MTV video, as presented at the end of chapter 2.

What would account for these "inconsistencies" across methods in our findings? We could use the same explanations that we relied on before, such as the fact that statistical significance is a function of sample size and item reliability and validity and that our measures may not have been as finely tuned to the gendered dynamics of this group of youth. Perhaps we also should have considered other explanations that we had not considered before. For example, we wondered whether our desire to integrate

Muslim American youth into studies of youth resilience and "risk" may have kept us from hearing their significant differences from other populations in regard to how they handle stress. Perhaps the items and scales used in our studies systematically flattened evidence of gendered differences in the qualitative material. We also wondered whether the effect of 9/11 and its aftermath was so enormous that this particular generation of Muslim youth at this particular point in history responded in quite similar ways when presented with a standard set of questions about their identity, stress, coping, and overall psychological well-being. In other words, it is possible that because of the strong homogenizing weight of the current historical context, the Muslim young people, regardless of their gender, gave similar answers to questions about identity, discrimination, coping, and psychological well-being. Nonetheless, these concerns should be read as an inducement to pursue a combination of mixed methods, not a reason to retreat from quantitative or qualitative analyses.

It might be interesting, though, to reconsider what *triangulation means in a mixed-methods design*. That is, perhaps triangulation should not be thought of as simply a search for cross-method confirmation but instead as an opportunity to dig deeper into cross-method contradictions. Like cross-cultural travelers moving across the borders of methods, we found ourselves pursuing findings from different methodologies as pieces of a puzzle, stones on the journey toward more layered theorizing.

Future Research On, With, and For Muslim American Youth

Within Islam, there is thus an intense struggle between those who view Islam in terms of an "authenticity" and those who regard syncreticity as essential to the development of a modern view of an Islam committed to democracy and justice. If this is so, then educators in the West must embrace a more open view of Islam as not only diverse but also interdependent with other faiths and cultures, having certain shared values and aims, being affected by them and enriching them. (Rizvi 2005, 177)

In response to Rizvi's admonition, which we believe is directed to all of us living in the West, this book provides evidence of the diversity of identities woven through intricate interpenetrations of cultures and across generations, national boundaries and genders. Indeed, we have found great diversity, blended cultures, shifts in values and practices over time and place, a melding of traditions, and moves between more and less religious lives. Yet despite all the diversity in the United States at this moment in history, the designation "Muslim American" identity, under threat and surveillance, has acquired greater significance over the past decade. Popular culture and government policies continue to (mis)represent these youth and their communities, threatening their nations of origin and surveilling their families. Evidence from our studies confirms that U.S. policies abroad and at home may be unleashing a slow but toxic leak of political, social, and psychological isolation and alienation, as well as innovation and civic engagement. Ironically cast in the name of "homeland security," national policy may actually be exacerbating internal alienation in yet another segment of young people, rendering us all less secure at "home."

The evidence gathered in this book reveals just how faraway wars, U.S. government policies, social relationships with both intimates and strangers, and media representations affect youth development. Although the dotted lines that connect these faraway events may be difficult to measure empirically, and the paths may vary by gender, community, and context, the capillaries can be traced, especially with multiple methods differentially sensitive to distinct forms of evidence. Although attitudes toward Muslims have long been tinged with disparagement, there is ample evidence that the events on and after 9/11 have created a sea change in how Muslims are perceived both globally and in the United States. In this changed context, we do not know what the future holds for this particular group, but what is evident in our data is the urgent need to learn more. We hope that our study opens a dialogue about the vitality and the variability of Muslim youth in the United States, all trying to keep apathy and anger under wraps (see map 5).

One point that we hope we have made clear is that Muslims in the United States are a very diverse group but that despite its tenuous nature, the label Muslim American still contains some historical and cultural validity. We have presented this material to many audiences across the United States, Turkey, and in the Middle East. By now we can easily anticipate those readers or audience members who will challenge the categorical designation Muslim American. Like so many of our young respondents, we would agree. As scholars and politically engaged persons in the United States and abroad, our work reflects a strong commitment to intersectionality (Crenshaw 1995), as well as close attention to "difference" (Bhavnani 1994). So, too, many of the young people we interviewed told us that the category Muslim American has been involuntarily tattooed onto their bodies and subjectivities. The Pakistanis in our sample were not "supposed" to identify with the Indians, any more than Sunnis and Shi'as were "supposed" to see themselves as brothers and sisters.

Nonetheless, the contemporary politics of the United States and the globe, after 9/11 and after the war on terror, have amalgamated a set of extremely disparate groups under the generic, politically induced, category of "Muslim." It is still true, as Stuart Hall wrote more than a decade ago, that "power uses difference as a way of marking off who does and who does not belong" (Hall 1997, 298).

At this point we do not know much about the implications of race/ethnicity, social class, immigration status, and so on, for the way that Muslim American youth define themselves. However, given the racial, ethnic, and religious diversity of the Muslim population, we need studies of the different Muslim populations in the United States. While articles on South Asian, Lebanese, and Palestinian youth are beginning to appear, we certainly need more information about these and other groups. Further research on Iranian Americans, Turkish Americans, and those from central European and the former Soviet republics would certainly complicate and problematize the notion of a "Muslim American" identity. We also need studies of Muslim American youth living in the Midwest, South and on the West Coast; those living relatively secluded lives in religious communities and attending religious schools; gay and lesbian Muslim youth; and the poor and undocumented. We also have much to learn from U.S.-born African American youth whose families are Muslim and their relations with Arab and Middle Eastern families who share their religion but not necessarily their political biography.

Concluding Thoughts . . . For Now

Children exiled psychologically (and sometimes physically) from a place they call home, Muslim American youth in the United States today are not alone in American history. In fact, they are simply today's embodiment of a long line of excluded youth who have populated the history and geography of the United States. As we study the identities of young people who negotiate treacherous boundaries, we bear witness to the ways in which youths' bodies are routinely and often harshly volunteered by the culture as a canvas for global economic, racial, gendered, and sexual conflicts. At the same time we take delight in the complex ways that young people respond, performing new hybridities of resistance and innovation through personal style and popular culture.

Before we finish, we need to comment on those who believe they live nowhere near the hyphen, those of us who cannot imagine the toxicity of living amid feuding identities. Caitlin Dean was such a young woman. In February 2007, more than one hundred years after W. E. B. Du Bois wrote his searing and prophetic essay, fifteen-year-old Caitlin Dean decided to go undercover, in a burqa, at a Colchester, Connecticut, high school.

The 15-year old freshman volunteered with a few other students to wear traditional Muslim clothing to school for an entire day in February after a Middle Eastern Studies teacher at Bacon Academy announced that she was looking for students to promote her class by wearing the garb. Caitlin covered her slender frame and short brown hair with a periwinkle burqa, which concealed her face.

The hateful and abusive comments she endured that day horrified teachers, the teen and many of her classmates. The remarks underscored a persistent animosity toward American Muslims that is driven largely by the terrorist attacks of 9/11 and the wars in Afghanistan and Iraq. But they also opened up an important dialogue that could help teenagers in Colchester and across the state view the Muslim culture differently.

"Hey, we rape your women!" one upperclassman said as he passed Caitlin in the hallway.

"I hope all of your people die," another sniped.

"You're probably going to kill us all" and "Why do they let people like this in the country?" were other remarks she heard on Feb. 1.

Caitlin's observations that day did not surprise those who work for the Connecticut chapter of the Council on American-Islamic Relations, which arrived in the state about three years ago in response to hate crimes and prejudice against Muslims.

Caitlin wrote down 50 comments and names she was called. She did not respond because "I am a freshman. I like to avoid making waves."

But when she saw a friend and a teacher who knew that Caitlin was the person under the burqa, she broke down in a classroom.

"I started crying," Caitlin said. "There is way too much prejudice."

The lack of understanding of Islam and of the many cultures that contribute to a worldwide population of more than 1 billion Muslims is something Rabia Chaudry, a spokeswoman for CAIR, planned to raise with the state Department of Education when she meets with officials in a few weeks.

. . . [The teacher,] Parkinson, who has traveled to the Middle East and wants to participate in a teacher exchange with Saudi Arabia, said she is on a mission to have other cultures, particularly those in the Middle East, better represented in school curriculums.

"That happens to be my personal crusade," she said. "And I think we should start it sooner. It should be taught in elementary school."

"My fear of this hatred of Islam is that it will become synonymous with patriotism," Parkinson said. "We are a nation of immigrants. Some of the most disturbing comments were, 'This is America. Go home.'" (Fox 2007)

The stories, maps, surveys, interviews, and conversations we have gathered tell us much about how young Muslim Americans stand on a complex hyphen. With humor and pain, they narrate lives of meaning, dreams and loss. We have been overwhelmed by the generosity with which they trusted us with their stories, especially stunning when they discovered that Michelle was a Jewish scholar interested in their lives.

Our obligation, in return, is to develop deep theory and dynamic methods worthy of them. These young women and men remind us that none of us is outside; none is immune to the toxic impact of Islamophobia and other forms of racism that saturate the culture. They ask us simply to remember that fear of Islam is not patriotism and that many actions engaged in the name of homeland security render us all the more vulnerable to threats from both the outside and within.

In short, we offer "hyphenated selves" simply as a means for speaking about the ways in which contentious politics move through the membranes of young bodies and souls. As a tool of theory and method and an invitation to action, the idea of hyphenated selves insists that social researchers take responsibility to document a history of the present and to stand with youth under siege.

Appendix A

Survey Measures

Summary of Research Questions and Methodology

Topic/Question	Instruments	Data Sources
Discrimination and Surveillance	Discrimination Scale	$N = 70$ (younger cohort surveys)
What is the prevalence of discrimination among immigrant Muslim youth?	SAFE	$N = 134$ (older cohort surveys)
What is the degree of stress they experience owing to discrimination and surveillance?	Coping	137 maps (19 younger cohort, 118 older cohort)
How do they cope with discrimination and surveillance?	Interviews	11 focus groups
Identity Negotiation	CSE Scale	3 younger cohorts
How do they negotiate their identities?	AHIMSA	8 older cohorts
What is the role of discrimination for the identity negotiation process?	Identity maps	6 interviews (ages 12–17)
How does gender shape the identity negotiation process?	Identity maps	Focus groups

Experience of "self" and "other" in zones of contact?

What kinds of discourses do young women and young men use when discussing their "contact" with non-Muslim society?

How are identities and social relations engaged in collective conversation?

Survey Summary

Variable	Scale
Demographic Questionnaire	Age, grade, gender, school context, generational status, racial/ethnic background, religiosity, socioeconomic status
Muslim and American Collective Identities (older group)	Modified versions of *Collective Self-Esteem* (CSE; Luthanen & Crocker 1992)
Identity negotiation (Younger and Older Groups)	Identity Maps
Preferences for Social-Cultural activities (younger and older groups)	Acculturation practices: *Acculturation, Habits, and Interests Multicultural Scale for Adolescents* (AHIMSA: Unger et al. 2002)
Perceived frequency of discrimination (younger and older groups)	Adapted from Krieger & Sidney 1996
Discrimination-related stress (older group)	A modified version of *Societal, Attitudinal, Familial, and Environmental-Revised-Short Form* (SAFE: Mena, Padilla, & Maldonado 1987)
Coping strategies (younger and older groups)	A component of the *COPE* (Carver, Scheier, & Weintraub 1989)
Psychological well-being (older group)	A component of *Youth Self-Report* (YSR: Achenbach 1991)
Positive identity (older group)	A component of *Developmental Assets Profile* (DAP, Search Institute 2004)
Academic achievement (younger and older groups)	School grades, educational expectations, course participation (part of the *Demographic Questionnaire*)

Appendix B

Individual Interview Protocol

1. Introduction: We have been speaking to young Muslim Americans, middle and high school students, as well as college students, about their experiences in the United States since 9/11. Like all teens, these young people care about friends, family, school, and also about world politics and local issues. We have heard wonderful stories about how young Muslim Americans are working to integrate the many parts of your identities. So we would like to interview you to get a sense of your full life as a Muslim American teen. We also would like you to imagine that this story will be read by other teens, maybe educators, undergraduates, and people who don't know much about Muslim American teens but want to. We want them to understand all the variations within the group of Muslim Americans and the wonderful distinct things about you that they may not know from media, movies, etc. We will begin with some broad questions about identities and then move into different levels of experience, with friends, family, community, the media, police, etc. If there is something you want us to be sure *not* to record, please tell us. If there is something you want to make *sure* people know about you, please emphasize that! Thanks again for your time!

1. Survey administration: Start with the survey (8 pages).
2. Discuss identity maps: Based on the map, ask them to describe who they are in an open format.
3. Identity questions: Now what about identities—how does being Muslim and American fit together?
   a. "Tell me a story about being Muslim American, a story of pride, a time when you felt most comfortable with your Muslim-American identities."
   b. "What about a story of difficulty? Tell me a story about a time when you felt most uncomfortable about being a Muslim American."
   c. New question: Who are your friends? What do you do with friends? Where do you hang out?
   d. Follow-up: What do you enjoy doing alone, and what do you enjoy doing with your friends?
4. How do you think being a girl or boy affects your development or people's expectations of you?
5. What particular experiences/struggles/knowledge do you have in different places like
   a. At home as a second-generation Muslim in the U.S.?
   b. At school as a Muslim?
   c. With your Muslim friends?
   d. With your non-Muslim friends?
6. Experiences of discrimination?
   a. Respondents will be asked, "Many of the young Muslim Americans we spoke with talked about experiences of stress in school, family, discrimination, personal issues, etc. Can you tell us about the kinds of stresses you encounter in your daily life?"
   b. Follow-up: Whom do you talk to about these issues?
      i. What helps you resolve them?
      ii. Do parents/children/families talk about the discrimination, the media representations, etc.?
   c. Do you ever feel that people see you in ways that are different from how you really feel?
   d. Do you sometimes feel that you should educate people about these misrepresentations?
      i. If yes, how do you feel about that?

    e. What are some of the things you hear about Muslims in the media that really bother youth the most?

7. Given all that you know about American teens and Muslim teens, what is truly unique about you?

8. If you were writing an advice column, what advice would you give to a young Muslim American girl or boy, five years younger than you, concerned about life in the U.S.?

9. School question: What kind of school do you go to?
   Note: Depending on the kind of school the person goes to, ask a follow-up question about how it feels to be a student in that school.

10. Community question: What kind of neighborhood do you live in?
    Note: Depending on the kind of neighborhood the person lives, ask a series of questions about how it feels to be living in that setting.

11. Person-specific questions: This is when the interviewer should ask questions specific to the person. For example, if the teenager is wearing *hijab* or any other religious attire, ask about how he or she came to dress like that. Who was the inspiration? When did he or she start wearing it?

Appendix C

Focus-Group Protocols

Focus-Group Protocol (Female version)

We are interested in revealing how Muslim American girls and women live in the U.S. at this moment in history: the joys, the pressures, the secrets, the silences, the dreams, and desires. We have done some work that shows us the incredible strength that Muslim American girls and women bring to current political conditions. Many of the girls said they dislike being seen as oppressed, but they spend a lot of time educating others about Muslim beliefs and politics. But we also know that the pressures of discrimination, and being watched or being under surveillance can take a toll as well.

So we wanted to create a "safe" conversation. We will tape this but not use anyone's names or any other identifiers, and you may decide you don't want to answer any of the questions (and you'll still get paid!). We are hoping to write an article (we'll show it to you before we publish it!) so that the larger society can begin to understand your lives and cultures for the strengths you carry and the burdens imposed on you.

We expect to hear a wide variety of opinions and ideas. There are no right or wrong answers, and people do not have to agree with one another but simply respect others. We want to begin with a drawing exercise:

I. Draw an identity map.

Draw a map of your many selves as a student, a female, a Muslim American, a daughter, an immigrant, etc. that tells us a story about the joys and challenges you experience.

[40 minutes]

II. Share/discuss identity maps.

[Use these questions during the discussion of the maps.]

Ask young women to share their maps.

Identities: All people have different "selves" they carry around in the same body. You may be a daughter, cousin, student, writer, athlete, or a friend.

a. What are the different identities that define who you are?

b. How are these multiple and often flexible identities an advantage?

c. Does it even seem like they conflict, or there is a disadvantage to having so many identities and responsibilities?

d. How do you develop or find the strength to negotiate the identities that define who you are?

[30 minutes]

III. Confronting politics/discrimination: We negotiate all these worlds as Muslim American women.

a. In light of the current political climate and government policies, such as the Patriot Act, do you (as young Muslim American women) feel policed by society, the government, and/or your community? How?

b. Have you heard about the two Muslim high school girls who were detained last March, one Guyanese, one Bangladeshi, both Muslim? What have you heard about their cases? How did you hear about them?

c. Have these events and other stories of detention and increased surveillance changed how you go about your day-to-day activities?

d. How are you coping with the harassment and discrimination you may be experiencing?

*e. Whom do you turn to when these incidents occur? Do you tell your parents or family members about these incidents? Why or why not?

[30 minutes]

IV. Social representations:
    a. Do you ever feel that people see you in ways that are different from how you really feel?
  *b. Do you think there are stereotypes of Muslim women, and do you sometimes feel that you should educate people about these misrepresentations? If yes, how do you feel about it?
  *c. What one piece of advice would you give to young women about how to negotiate all of this with integrity and in healthy ways?

Focus-Group Protocol (Male version)

We are interested in revealing how Muslim American men live in the U.S. at this moment in history: the joys, the pressures, the challenges, and the dreams. We have done some work that shows us the incredible strength that Muslim American men bring to current political conditions. Many of them said that they dislike being seen as "terrorists." They also told us that nobody really cares enough to ask them how they think/feel about their experiences.

So we wanted to create a "safe" conversation. We will tape this but not use anyone's names or any other identifiers, and you may decide you don't want to answer any of the questions (and you'll still get paid!). We are hoping to generate a working hypothesis about how Muslim American man construct their identity in this difficult historical period in the U.S. We want to present our findings to the larger society so that it begins to understand your lives and cultures for the strengths you carry and the burdens imposed on you.

We expect to hear a wide variety of opinions and ideas. There are no right or wrong answers, and people do not have to agree with one another but simply respect others. We also would like to make sure that the conversations in this room stay in this room and do not go beyond this group.

Although our conversation has a loose structure, feel free to bring up topics that you feel are important for us to hear.

I. Share/discuss identity maps.
  [40 minutes]
  Ask the young men to share their maps.

Identities: All people have different "selves" they carry around in the same body. You may be a son, cousin, student, writer, athlete, or a friend.

   a. What are the different identities that define who you are?

   b. How do you negotiate these sometimes conflicting identities? Does it ever seem that they conflict, or is there an advantage to having so many identities and responsibilities?

   c. How do you develop or find the strength to negotiate the identities that define who you are?

II. Confronting politics/discrimination

[30 minutes]

We negotiate all these worlds as Muslim American men.

   a. In light of the current political climate and government policies such as the Patriot Act, do you (as young Muslim American men) feel policed by society, the government, and/or your community? How?

   b. Have you heard about the two Muslim high school girls who were detained last March, one Guyanese, one Bangladeshi, both Muslim? What have you heard about their cases? How did you hear about them?

   c. Have these events and other stories of detention and increased surveillance changed how you go about your day-to-day activities?

   d. How are you coping with the harassment and discrimination you may be experiencing?

  *e. Whom do you turn to when these incidents occur? Do you tell your parents or family members about these incidents? Why or why not?

III. Social representations

[30 minutes]

   a. Do you ever feel that people see you in ways that are different from how you really feel?

  *b. Do you think there are stereotypes of Muslim men, and do you sometimes feel that you should educate people about these misrepresentations? If yes, how do you feel about it?

  *c. What one piece of advice would you give to young men about how to negotiate all of this with integrity and in healthy ways?

■　　■　　■　　■　　■　　■　　■　　■　　■

Appendix D

Identity Maps Coding Sheets

Please use this rating scale for the "Certainty" ratings: 1 (Quite uncertain), 2 (Uncertain), 3 (Certain), 4 (Quite certain).

Issues	Rater 1	Rater 2	Agreed Code
1. Metacategorization			
Certainty of categorization			
2. Location of			
Map of U.S./America			
Map of country of origin			
Family			
Friends/peers			
School/education			
3. Identity labels			
Religious (Sunni, Muslim)			
Ethnic identity/country of origin			
U.S./American			
Hyphenated			
Family/relation (son, daughter)			
4. Use of symbols (religious)			
Religious (Allah, Qur'an, Crescent, Hijab)			
National (flag, map, language)			
Secular (peace, ying-yang)			

Issues	Rater 1	Rater 2	Agreed Code
5. Discrimination/surveillance			
External to community			
Within community			
6. Emotions			
a. Frustration			
b. Stress			
c. Anger			
d. Sadness			
e. Contentment			
f. Pride			
7. Responses/reactions			
a. Struggle			
b. Resistance			
c. Education			
d. Political activism			
e. Prayer			

Notes

Note to Chapter 1

1. We do not agree with the premise of this question, as it creates a false dichotomy, so we use it only to illustrate a point that we take up further in chapter 5.

Notes to Chapter 4

1. $M = 1.54$, SD $= 0.59$ versus $M = 1.96$, SD $= 0.95$, $t = 2.26$, $p < .05$.

2. $M = 6.35$, SD $= 3.07$ versus $M = 4.10$, SD $= 1.81$, $t = 3.1$, $p < .01$.

3. With a possible range of 0 to 39, our respondents' mean score was 14.01 for males and 17.15 for females. This observed difference was more than what would be expected by chance.

4. Using a scale that ranges from 0 (never) to 4 (almost daily), the frequency of reported discriminatory acts rises from 0.72 to 1.64 for women who cover their hair, compared with their Muslim peers who do not cover their hair. The difference between these two groups of Muslim women was statistically significant at $p < .05$, meaning that it cannot be explained by chance alone.

Notes to Chapter 5

1. $r = .38$, $p < .005$.

2. The results showed that the participants had stronger bonds with their Muslim communities ($M = 5.80$, SD $= 0.93$) than with the mainstream U.S. community ($M = 5.05$, SD $= 1.15$).

3. $r = 0.33$ and $r = 0.44$, respectively.
4. $r = 0.22$ and $r = 0.20$, respectively.
5. $\chi^2 (2, 115) = 9.80, p < .01$.

Note to Chapter 7

1. Cronbach's Alphas for the measures ranged from 0.68 to 0.95.

References

Abdulhadi, R. (2003). Where is home? Fragmented lives, border crossing and the politics of exile. *Radical History Review, 83,* 89–101.

Abu-Ali, A., & Reisen, C. A. (1999). Gender role identity among adolescent Muslim girls living in the U.S. *Current Psychology, 18*(2), 185–192.

Abu El-Haj, T. R. (2005). Global politics, dissent, and Palestinian American identities: Engaging conflict to reinvigorate democratic education. In L. Weis & M. Fine (eds.), *Beyond silenced voices: Class, race, and gender in United States schools,* rev. ed., 199–215. Albany: State University of New York Press.

Achenbach, T. M. (1991). *Manual for the child behavior checklist.* Burlington, VT: Department of Psychiatry, University of Vermont.

Adams, D. (1995). *Education for extinction: American Indians and that boarding school experience, 1875–1928.* Lawrence: University of Kansas Press.

Ajrouch, K. J. (2000). Place, age, and culture: Community living and ethnic identity among Lebanese American adolescents. *Small Group Research, 31*(4), 447–469.

Ajrouch, K. J. (2004). Gender, race, and symbolic boundaries: Contested spaces of identity among Arab American adolescents. *Sociological Perspectives, 47*(4), 371–391.

Alghorani, M. A. (2004). Identity, acculturation, and adjustment of high school Muslim students in Islamic schools in the U.S.A. *Dissertation Abstracts International Section A: Humanities and Social Sciences, 64*(12-A), 4351.

Allport, G. W. (1954). *The nature of prejudice.* Reading, MA: Addison-Wesley.

Amer, M. M., & Hovey, J. D. (2005). Examination of the impact of acculturation, stress, and religiosity on mental health variables for 2nd generation Arab Americans. *Ethnicity and Disease, 15*(1), suppl. 1, 111–112.

Anzaldúa, G. (1987). *Borderlands/Lafrontera: The new mestiza.* San Francisco: Aunt Lute Books.

Apfelbaum, E. (2000). And now what, after such tribulations. Memory and dislocation in the era of uprooting. *American Psychologist, 55,* 1008–1013.

Appadurai, A. (2004). The capacity to aspire. In V. Rao & M. Walton (eds.), *Culture and public action,* 59–85. Stanford, CA: Stanford University Press.

Arnett, J. J. (2000). Emerging adulthood: A theory of development from the late teens through the twenties. *American Psychologist, 55,* 469–480.

Arnett, J. J. (2002). The psychology of globalization. *American Psychologist, 57*(10), 774–783.

Ashmore, R. D., Deaux, K., & McLaughlin-Volpe, T. (2004). An organizing framework for collective identity: Articulation and significance of multidimensionality. *Psychological Bulletin, 130*(1), 80–114.

Ayala, J. (1998). In whose voice shall I write? In M. Fine & L. Weis (eds.), *Caution speed bumps ahead: Reflections on the politics and methods of qualitative work,* 51–55). New York: SUNY Graduate School of Education Publications.

Ayers, W., Ayers, R., & Dohrn, B. (2001). *Zero tolerance: Resisting the drive for punishment.* New York: New Press.

Bayoumi, M. (2006). Arab America's September 11. www.thenation.com, September 25, 22.

Bell, D. A. Jr. (1973). *Race, racism, and American law.* 2nd ed. Boston: Little, Brown.

Benet-Martinez, V., Leu, J., Lee, F., & Morris, M. (2002). Negotiating biculturalism: Cultural priming in blended and alternating Chinese-Americans. *Journal of Cross-Cultural Psychology, 33*(5), 492–516.

Benjamin, J. (1998). *Shadow of the other.* New York: Routledge.

Bernstein, N. (2005). Teachers and classmates express outrage at arrest of girl, 16, as a terrorist threat. *New York Times,* April 9, B3.

Bernstein, N. (2006a). Judge rules that U.S. has broad powers to detain noncitizens indefinitely. *New York Times,* June 15, A1.

Bernstein, N. (2006b). Manhattan: Asylum hearing adjourned. *New York Times,* October 27.

Bernstein, N., & Lichtblau, E. (2005). Two girls held as U.S. fears suicide bomb. *New York Times,* April 7, B1.

Berry, J. W. (1990). Psychology of acculturation: Understanding individuals moving between cultures. In R. W. Brislin (ed.), *Applied Cross-Cultural Psychology,* 232–253. Newbury Park, CA: Sage.

Berry, J. W. (1997). Immigration, acculturation, and adaptation. *Applied Psychology: An International Review, 46*(1), 5–34.

Berry, J. W., Phinney, J. S., Sam, D. L., & Vedder, P. (eds.) (2006). *Immigrant youth in cultural transition: Acculturation, identity, and adaptation across national contexts.* Mahwah, NJ: Erlbaum.

Beveridge, A. (2001). Arab Americans in our midst. *Gotham Gazette,* September.

Beveridge, A. (2005). Can NYC "Profile" Young Muslim Males? *Gotham Gazette,* August.

Bhabha, H. K. (1994). *The location of culture.* London: Routledge.

Bhabha, H. K. (2005). "Race," time and the revision of modernity. In C. McCarthy et al. (eds.), *Race, identity and representation in education,* 13–26. New York: Routledge.

Bhatia, S. (2007). *American Karma: Race, culture, and identity in the Indian diaspora.* New York: New York University Press.

Bhatia, S., & Ram, A. (2001). Rethinking acculturation in relation to diasporic cultures and postcolonial identities. *Human Development, 44,* 1–18.

Bhavnani, K.-K. (1994). Tracing the contours: Feminist research and feminist objectivity. In H. Afshar & M. Maynard (eds.), *The dynamics of "race" and gender: Some feminist interventions,* 26–41. Bristol, PA: Taylor & Francis.

Bilge, B., & Aswad, B. C. (1996). *Family and gender among American Muslims: Issues facing Middle Eastern immigrants and their descendants.* Philadelphia: Temple University Press.

Birman, D., Trickett, E., & Buchanan, R. M. (2005). A tale of two cities: Replication of a study on the acculturation and adaptation of immigrant adolescents from the former Soviet Union in a different community context. *American Journal of Community Psychology, 35*(1/2), 83–101.

Bourdieu, P. (1991). *Language and symbolic power.* Trans. G. Raymond & M. Adamson. Cambridge, MA: Harvard University Press.

Boyd-Franklin, N., Franklin, A. J., & Touissant, P. (2003) *Boys into men: Raising our African teenage sons.* New York: Plume Books.

Bradford, William. (1967). *Of Plimouth Plantation: 1620–1647.* New York: Modern Library.

Branscombe, N. R., Schmitt, M. T., & Harvey, R. D. (1999). Perceiving pervasive discrimination among African-Americans: Implications for group identification and well-being. *Journal of Personality and Social Psychology, 77,* 135–149.

Brennen, B., & Duffy, M. (2003). "If a problem cannot be solved, enlarge it": An ideological critique of the "Other" in Pearl Harbor and September 11 *New York Times* coverage. *Journalism Studies, 4,* 1, 3–14.

Bronfenbrenner, U. (1979). *The ecology of human development.* Cambridge, MA: Harvard University Press.

Bryan, J. (2005). Constructing "the true Islam" in hostile times: The Impact of 9/11 on Arab Muslims in Jersey City. In N. Foner (ed.), *Wounded city: The social impact of 9/11,* 133–162. New York: Russell Sage.

Cahill, C. (2004). Defying gravity? Raising consciousness through collective research. *Children's Geographies, 2*(2), 273–286.

Cainkar, L. (2004). The impact of September 11 attacks and their aftermath on Arab and Muslim communities in the United States. *Global Security Quarterly, 13.* Accessed on May 13, 2007 from http://www.ssrc.org/programs/gsc/publications/quarterly13/cainkar.pdf.

Carver, C. S., Scheier, M. F., & Weintraub, J. K. (1989). Assessing coping strategies: A theoretically based approach. *Journal of Personality and Social Psychology, 56,* 267–283.

Chan, C. S. (1989). Issues of identity development among Asian-American lesbians and gay men. *Journal of Counseling & Development, 68*(1), 16–20.

Cheng, A. (2001). *The melancholy of race: Psychoanalysis, assimilation, and hidden grief.* New York: Oxford University Press.

CIA World Fact Book. Accessed April 5, 2007, from https://www.cia.gov/cia/publications/factbook/index.html.

Cohen, C. (1999).*The boundaries of blackness.* Chicago: University of Chicago Press.

Crenshaw, K. (1995). Mapping the margins: Intersectionality, identity politics, and violence against women of colour. In K. Crenshaw, N. Gotanda, G. Peller, & K. Thomas (eds.), *Critical race theory: The key writings that formed the movement,* 357–383. New York: New Press.

Crocker, J., Luhtanen, R., Blaine, B., & Broadnax, S. (1994). Collective self-esteem and psychological well-being among white, black, and Asian college students. *Personality and Social Psychology Bulletin, 20,* 503–513.

Cushman, P. (1995). *Constructing self, constructing America: A cultural history of psychology.* Reading, MA: Addison-Wesley.

Dasgupta, S. D. (1998). Gender roles and cultural continuity in the Asian Indian immigrant community in the U.S. *Sex Roles: A Journal of Research, 38*(11–12), 953–974.

D'Augelli, A., Hershberger, S., & Pilkington, N. (2001). Suicidality patterns and sexual orientation related factors among lesbian, gay and bisexual youth. *Suicide and Life Threatening Behavior, 31*(3), 250–264.

Deane, C., & Fears, D. (2006). Negative perception of Islam increasing. *Washington Post,* March 9, A01. Accessed on April 23, 2007, from http://www.washingtonpost.com/wp-dyn/content/article/2006/03/08/AR2006030802221.html.

Deaux, K. (2000). Surveying the landscape of immigration: Social psychological perspectives. *Journal of Community and Applied Social Psychology, 10,* 421–431.

Deaux, K. (2006). *To be an immigrant.* New York: Russell Sage.

Deaux, K., & Philogone, G. (eds.) (2001). *Representations of the social: Bridging theoretical traditions.* Oxford: Blackwell.

Deaux, K., & Stewart, A. (2001). Framing gender identity. In R. Unger (ed.), *Handbook of the psychology of women and gender.* New York: Wiley.

Dion, K. K., & Dion, K. L. (2001). Gender and cultural adaptation in immigrant families. *Journal of Social Issues, 57,* 511–521.

Du Bois, W. E. B. (1982). *The souls of black folk.* New York: Signet Classics.

El-Amine, R. (2005). The making of the Arab menace. *Left Turn Magazine, 16.* Accessed May 16, 2006, from http://www.leftturn.org/Articles/Viewer.aspx?id=615&type=M.

Elias, M. (2006). USA's Muslims under a cloud. *USA Today,* August 10. Retrieved on April 23, 2007, from http://www.usatoday.com/news/nation/2006-08-09-MuslimAmerican-cover_x.htm.

Erikson, E. (1980). *Identity and the life cycle.* New York: Norton.

Esses, V. M., & Dovidio, J. F. (2002). The role of emotions in determining willingness to engage in intergroup contact. *Personality and Social Psychology Bulletin, 28,* 1202–1214.

Ethier, K. A., & Deaux, K. (1994). Negotiating social identity when contexts change: Maintaining identification and responding to threat. *Journal of Personality Social Psychology, 67*(2), 243–251.

Faith Communities Today (2006). *FACT Survey.* Accessed on April 20, 2007, from http://fact.hartsem.edu/Press/mediaadvsry5.htm.

Fanon, F. (1967). *Black skin, white masks.* New York: Grove Press.

Federal Bureau of Investigation (FBI) (2002). *2001 hate crime report.* Washington DC: FBI. Accessed September 23, 2006, from http://www.fbi.gov/ucr/01hate.pdf.

Fine, M. (1994). Working the hyphens: Reinventing the self and other in qualitative research. In N. Denzin & Y. Lincoln (eds.), *Handbook of qualitative research,* 70–82. Newbury Park, CA: Sage.

Fine, M., & McClelland, S. I. (2007). The politics of teen women's sexuality: Public policy and the adolescent female body. Equality and Reproductive Rights Symposium, Center for Reproductive Rights. *Emory Law Journal, 56*(4).

Fine, M., Roberts, R., Torre, M., Bloom, J., Burns, A., Chajet, L., Guishard, M., & Payne, Y. (2004). *Echoes: Youth documenting and performing the legacy of* Brown v. Board of Education. New York: Teachers College Press.

Fine, M., Tuck, E., & Zeller-Berkman, S. (2007). Do you believe in Geneva? In N. Denizin, L. Smith, & Y. Lincoln (eds.), *Handbook of Critical and Indigenous Knowledges.* Beverly Hills, CA: Sage.

Fisher, C., Wallace, S. & Fenton, R. (2000). Discrimination distress during adolescence. *Journal of Youth and Adolescence, 29*(6), 679–695.

Foucault, M. (1995). *Discipline and punish: The birth of the prison.* Trans. A. Sheridan. New York: Vintage Books.

Fox, T. G. (2007). Behind burqa, students get an education in bigotry. *Hartford Courant,* March 12. Accessed on April 23, 2006, from http://www.courant.com/news/education/hc-burqa0312.artmar12,0,3126355.story?coll=hc-headlines-education.

Friedlander, B. P. Jr. (2004). Fear factor: 44 percent of Americans queried in Cornell national poll favor curtailing some liberties for Muslim Americans. *Cornell News,* December 17. Accessed May 16, 2006, from http://www.news.cornell.edu/releases/Dec04/Muslim.Poll.bpf.html.

Frosh, P., Phoenix, A., Frosh, S., & Pattman, R. (2003). Producing contradictory masculine subject positions: Producing narratives of threat, homophobia and bullying in 11–14 year old boys. *Journal of Social Issues, 59,* 179–195.

Frosh, S. (1999). What is outside discourse? *Psychoanalytic Studies, 1,* 381–391.

Fuligni, A. J., Witkow, M., & Garcia, C. (2005). Ethnic identity and the academic adjustment of adolescents from Mexican, Chinese, and European backgrounds. *Developmental Psychology, 41,* 799–811.

Gallup (2006). Gallup press release. Accessed on May 25, 2006, from http://www.gallup.com/poll/releasespro010914c.asp.

Genesis Research Associates (2006). American Muslim voters: A Demographic profile and survey of attitudes. Accessed April 23, 2007, from http://www.cair-net.org/pdf/American_Muslim_Voter_Survey_2006.pdf.

Gergen, K. J. (1994) *Realities and relationships.* Cambridge, MA: Harvard University Press.

Glick-Schiller, N., & Fouron, G. (1999). Terrains of blood and nation: Haitian transnational social fields. *Ethnic and Racial Studies: 22,* 340–366.

Gole, N. (1996). *The forbidden modern.* Ann Arbor: University of Michigan Press.

Gough, B. (2004). Psychoanalysis as a resource for understanding emotional ruptures in the text: The case of defensive masculinities. *British Journal of Social Psychology, 43,* 245–267.

Grewal, I. (2003). Transnational America: Race, gender and citizenship after 9/11. *Social Identities: Journal for the Study of Race, Nation & Culture, 9*(4), 535–561.

Gualtieri, S. (2004). Strange fruit? Syrian immigrants, extralegal violence, and racial formation in the Jim Crow South. *Arab Studies Quarterly, 26*(3), 63–84.

Guidano, V. F. (1987). *The complexity of self.* New York: Guilford Press.

Haddad, Y., Smith, J., & Moore, K. (2006) *Muslim women in America: The challenge of Islamic identity today.* Oxford: Oxford University Press.

Hall, S. (1997). Subjects in history: Making diasporic identities. In L. Wahneema (ed.), *The house that race built,* 289–299. New York: Pantheon Books.

Hallak, M., & Quina, K. (2004). In the shadows of the twin towers: Muslim immigrant women's voices emerge. *Sex Roles, 51*(5/6), 329–338.

Hart, R. A. (1981). Children's spatial representations of the landscape: Lessons and questions from a field study. In L. S. Liben, A. H. Patterson, & N. Newcombe (eds.), *Spatial representation and behavior across the life span,* 195–233. San Diego: Academic Press.

Hart, R. A., & Moore, G. (1973). The development of spatial cognition: A review. In R. M. Downs & D. Stea (eds.), *Image and environment,* 246–288. Chicago: Aldine.

Harvey, D. (2001). Capitalism: The factory of fragmentation. In D. Harvey, *Spaces of capital,* 121–127. New York: Routledge.

Helms, J. E. (1994). The conceptualization of ethnic identity and other "racial" constructs. In E. J. Thicket, R. J. Watts, & D. Birman (eds.), *Human diversity: Perspectives on people in context.* San Francisco: Jossey-Bass.

Hofstadter, R. (1964). The paranoid style in American politics. *Harpers,* November.

Hogue, M. C., Hargraves, & Collins, K. (2000). *Minority health in America: Findings and policy implications from the commonwealth fund minority health survey.* Baltimore: John Hopkins University Press.

Howe, S. (2001). A nation challenged: Civil liberties; Americans give in to race profiling. *New York Times,* September 23, A1.

Hoxie, F. E. (2001). *The final promise: The campaign to assimilate the Indians, 1880–1920.* Lincoln: University of Nebraska Press.

Hughes, D., & Chen, L. (1997). When and what parents tell children about race: An examination of race-related socialization in African American families. *Applied Developmental Science, 1*(4), 200–214.

Hughes, D., Rodriguez, J., Smith, E. P., Johnson, D. J., Stevenson, H. C., & Spicer, P. (2006). Parents' ethnic-racial socialization practices: A review of research and directions for future study. *Developmental Psychology, 42*(5), 747–770.

Huntington, S. P. (1993). The clash of civilizations? *Foreign Affairs, 72*(3), 22–49.

Huntington, S. P. (2004). *Who are we: The challenges to America's national identity.* New York: Simon & Schuster.

Itzigsohn, J.,& Giorguli-Salcuedo, S. (2002). Immigrant incorporation and sociocultural transnationalism. *International Migration Review 36*(3), 766–798.

Jetten, J., Spears, R., & Postmes, T. (2004). Intergroup distinctiveness and differentiation: A meta analytic integration. *Journal of Personality and Social Psychology, 86*(6), 862–879.

Jones-Correa, M. (1998). Different paths: Gender, immigration and political participation. *International Migration Review, 32*(2), 326–349.

Josephson, J. P. (2003). *Growing up in World War II, 1941–1945.* Minneapolis: Lerner Publications.

Josselson, R. (2004). The hermeneutics of faith and the hermeneutics of suspicion. *Narrative Inquiry, 14*(1), 1–29.

Karim, H. K. (2002). Making sense of the "Islamic peril." In B. Zelizer & S. Allan (eds.), *Journalism after September 11,* 101–116. London: Routledge.

Katz, C. (2001). On the grounds of globalization: A topography for feminist political engagement. *Signs, 26*(4), 1213–1234.

Khan, S. (2002). *Aversion and desire: Negotiating Muslim female identity in the diaspora.* Toronto: Women's Press.

Kitzinger, C., & Wilkinson, S. (2003). Constructing identities: A feminist conversation analytic approach to positioning in action. In C. Kitzinger & S. Wilkinson (eds.), *The self and others: Positioning individuals and groups in personal, political and cultural contexts,* 157–180. New York: Praeger/Greenwood.

Kosmin, B. A., Mayer, E., & Keysar, A. (2001). *American religious identification survey.* New York: City University of New York Press.

Krieger, N., & Sidney, S. (1996). Racial discrimination and blood pressure: The CARDIA study of young black and white adults. *American Journal of Public Health, 86*(10), 1370–1378.

LaFramboise, T., Coleman, H. L. K., & Gerton, J. (1993). Psychological impact of biculturalism: Evidence and theory. *Psychological Bulletin, 114*(3), 395–412.

Langer, E. J. (1997). *The power of mindful learning*. Reading, MA: Addison-Wesley.

Leonard, K. I. (2003). *Muslims in the United States: The state of the research*. New York: Russell Sage.

Lerner, R. M. (1991). Changing organism-context relations as the basic process of development: A developmental contextual perspective. *Developmental Psychology, 27*, 27–32.

Lerner, R. M. (2002). *Concepts and theories of human development*. 3rd ed. Mahwah, NJ: LEA.

Levitt, P. (2000). Migrants participate across borders: Toward an understanding of forms and consequences. In N. Foner, R. Rumbaut, & S. Gold (eds.), *Immigration research for a new century*, 459–480. New York: Russell Sage.

Levitt, P., & Waters, M. C. (2002). *The changing face of home: The transnational lives of the second generation*. New York: Russell Sage.

Lewin, K. (1951). *Field theory in social science: Selected theoretical papers*. New York: Harper.

Lomawaima, K. T. (1994). *They called it prairie light: The story of Chilocco Indian School*. Lincoln: University of Nebraska Press.

Low, S. (2003). *Behind the gates: Life, community and security in fortress America*. New York: Routledge.

Luhtanen, R., & Crocker, J. (1992). A collective self-esteem scale: Self-evaluation of one's social identity. *Personality and Social Psychology Bulletin, 18*, 302–318.

Lykes, M. B. (2001). Activist participatory research and the arts with rural Maya women: Interculturality and situated meaning making. In D. L. Tolman & M. Brydon-Miller (eds.), *From subjects to subjectivities: A handbook of interpretive and participatory methods*, 183–199. New York: New York University Press.

Lykes, M. B., & Coquillon, E. (2006). Participatory and action research and feminisms: Towards transformative praxis. In S. Hesse-Biber (ed.), *Handbook of feminist research*. Beverly Hills, CA: Sage.

Lynch, K. (1960). *The image of the city*. Cambridge, MA: MIT Press.

Mahmood, S. (2005). *Politics of piety: The Islamic revival and the feminist subject*. Princeton, NJ: Princeton University Press.

Maira, S. (2004). Youth culture, citizenship, and globalization: South Asian Muslim youth in the United States after September 11th. *Comparative Studies of South Asia, Africa, and the Middle East, 24*(1), 219–231.

Markstrom, C. A. (1999). Religious involvement and adolescent psychosocial development. *Journal of Adolescence, 22*, 205–221.

Marr, C. J. (2006). Assimilation through education: Indian boarding schools in the Pacific northwest. Accessed on April 25, 2007, from http://content.lib.washington.edu/aipnw/marr.html.

Mass, A. I. (1986). Psychological effects of the camps on Japanese Americans. In R. Daniels, S. C. Taylor, & H. H. L. Kitano (eds.), *Japanese Americans from relocation to redress*, 159–162. Salt Lake City: University of Utah Press.

Mena, F. J., Padilla, A. M., & Maldonado, M. (1987). Acculturative stress and specific coping strategies among immigrant and later generation college students. *Hispanic Journal of Behavioral Sciences, 9*(2), 207–225.

Meyer, I. H. (2003). Prejudice, social stress and mental health in lesbian, gay, and bisexual populations: Conceptual issues and research evidence. *Psychological Bulletin, 129,* 674–697.

Milgram, S., & Jodelet, D. (1976). Psychological maps of Paris. In H. M. Proshansky, W. H. Ittelson, & L. G. Rivlin (eds.). *Environmental psychology: People and their physical settings.* 2nd ed., 104–124. New York: Holt, Rinehart & Winston.

Nagata, D. K. (1993). *Legacy of injustice: Exploring the cross generational impact of the Japanese American internment.* New York: Plenum Press.

Nesdale, D., Rooney, R., & Smith, L. (1997). Migrant ethnic identity and psychological distress. *Journal of Cross-Cultural Psychology, 28,* 569–588.

Newsweek poll. (2007). Available at http://www.pollingreport.com/terror.htm.

New York Times. (1942). Urges alien board for resettlement. March 20, 6.

Nguyen, T. (2005). *We are all suspects now: Untold stories from immigrant communities after 9/11.* Boston: Beacon Press.

Opotow, S. (1990). Moral exclusion and injustice: An overview. *Journal of Social Issues, 46*(1), 1–20.

Opotow, S. (1995). Drawing the line: Social categorization, moral exclusion, and the scope of justice. In B. B. Bunker & J. Z. Rubin (eds.), *Conflict, cooperation, and justice,* 347–369. San Francisco: Jossey-Bass.

Opotow, S. (2001). Social injustice. In D. J. Christie, R. V. Wagner, & D. D. Winter (eds.), *Peace, conflict and violence: Peace psychology for the 21st century,* 102–109. Upper Saddle River, NJ: Prentice-Hall.

Opotow, S. (2004). Conflict and morals. In T. A. Thorkildsen & H. J. Walberg (eds.), *Nurturing morality,* 99–118. New York: Kluwer Academic.

Opotow, S. (2005). Hate, conflict, and moral exclusion. In R. J. Sternberg (ed), *The psychology of hate.* Washington, DC: American Psychological Association.

Peek, L. A. (2003). Reactions and response: Muslim students' experiences on New York City campuses post-9/11. *Journal of Muslim Minority Affairs, 23*(2), 271–283.

Pew Research Center (2007). Muslim Americans: Middle class and mostly mainstream. Available at http://pewresearch.org/pubs/483/MuslimAmericans. Accessed May 30, 2007.

Phinney, J. S., & Devich-Navarro, M. (1997). Variations in bicultural identification among African American and Mexican American adolescents. *Journal of Research on Adolescence, 7*(1), 3–32.

Phinney, J. S., Horenczyk, G., Liebkind, K., & Vedder, P. (2001). Ethnic identity, immigration, and well-being: An interactional perspective. *Journal of Social Issues, 57*(3), 493–510.

Piligian, E. (2004). A town divided. *Seventeen,* November.

Pinson, H. (2008). The excluded citizenship identity: Palestinian/Arab Israeli young people negotiating their political identities. *British Journal of Sociology of Education,* 29(2), 201–212.

Portes, A., & Rumbaut, R. G. (2001). *Legacies: The story of the second generation.* Berkeley: University of California Press.

Pratt, M. L. (1992). *Imperial eyes: Travel writing and transculturation.* London: Routledge.

Prelow, H., Danoff-Burg, S., Swenson, R. & Puplgiano, D. (2004). The impact of ecological risk and perceived discrimination on the psychology adjustment of African American and European American youth. *Journal of Community Psychology,* 32(4), 375–389.

Rahman, A. (2006). The praxis of participatory action research. In P. Reason & H. Bradbury (eds.), *Handbook of action research.* London: Sage.

Rao, V., & Walton, M. (2004). *Culture and public action.* Stanford, CA: Stanford University Press.

Rath, J., & Buijs, F. (2002). Muslims in Europe: The state of research. Essay prepared for the Russell Sage Foundation, New York. Accessed August 22, 2005, from http://news.scotsman.com/international.cfm=id+371342005&format=print.

Rizvi, F. (2005). Representations of Islam and education for justice. In C. McCarthy, W. Crichlow, G. Dimitriadis, & N. Dolby (eds.), *Race, identity and representation,* 167–178. New York: Routledge.

Robin, C. (2004). *FEAR: The history of a political idea.* Oxford: Oxford University Press.

Romero, A. J., & Roberts, R. E. (2003). Stress within a bicultural context for adolescents of Mexican descent. *Cultural Diversity & Ethnic Minority Psychology,* 9(2), 171–184.

Rose, J. (1996). *States of fantasy.* Oxford: Oxford University Press.

Rosenbloom, S., & Way, N. (2004). Experiences of discrimination among African American, Asian American and Latino adolescents in an urban high school. *Youth and Society, 35,* 4, 420–451.

Ruck, M., Smith, K., & Fine, M. (2004). Resisting at the border: Warnings from the U.S. about zero tolerance. In B. Kidd & J. Phillips (eds.), *From enforcement and prevention to civic engagement: Research on community safety.* Toronto: Centre of Criminology, University of Toronto.

Rumbaut, R. G. (1994). The crucible within: Ethnic identity, self esteem and segmented assimilation among children of immigrants. *International Migration Review, 28*(4), 748–794.

Rumbaut, R. G. (2002). Severed or sustained attachments? Language, identity, and imagined communities in the post-immigrant generation. In P. Levitt & M. Waters (eds.), *The changing face of home: The transnational lives of the second generation,* 43–95. New York: Russell Sage.

Saarinen, T. F. (1973). Student views of the world. In R. M. Downs & D. Stea (eds.), *Image and environment,* 148–161. Chicago: Aldine.

Sacks, K. B. (1994). How did Jews become white folks. In S. Gregory & R. Sanjek (eds.), *Race*. New Brunswick, NJ: Rutgers University Press.

Said, E. (1979). *Orientalism*. New York: Vintage Press.

Said, E. (2000). Invention, memory and place. *Critical Inquiry, 26*(12), 175–188.

Said, E. (2003). *Orientalism*, 25th anniversary edition. New York: Vintage Press.

Sarroub, L. K. (2005). *All American Yemeni girls: Being Muslim in a public school*. Philadelphia: University of Pennsylvania Press.

Scott, J. W. (2007). Veiled politics. *Chronicle of Higher Education*, November 23, B11.

Search Institute (2004). *Developmental assets profile*. Minneapolis: Search Institute.

Sen, A. (2004). How does culture matter? In V. Rao & M. Walton (eds.), *Culture and public action*, 37–58. Stanford, CA: Stanford University Press.

Shaheen, J. G. (2003). Reel bad Arabs: How Hollywood vilifies a people. *Annals of the American Academy, 588*, 171–193.

Sherif, M. (1966). *In common predicament: Social psychology of intergroup conflict and cooperation*. Boston: Houghton-Mifflin.

Shih, M. J., & Sanchez, D. T. (2005). Perspectives and research on the positive and negative implications of having multiple racial identities. *Psychological Bulletin, 131*, 569–591.

Shohat, E. (2006). *Taboo memories, diasporic voices*. Durham, NC: Duke University Press.

Simon, B., & Klandermans, B. (2001). Towards a social psychological analysis of politicized collective identity: Conceptualization, antecedents, and consequences. *American Psychologist, 56*, 319–331.

Simons, R., Murry, V., McLoyd, V., Lin, K. Cutrona, C., & Conger, R. (2002). Discrimination, crime, ethnic identity and parenting as correlates of depressive symptoms among African American children. *Development and Psychopathology, 14*, 371–393.

Sirin, S. R. (2005a). Muslim adolescents on U.S. college campuses: Exploring ethnic identity. Paper presented at the 2005 annual convention of the American Psychological Association, Washington, DC.

Sirin, S. R. (2005b). Socioeconomic status and academic achievement: A meta-analytic review of research. *Review of Educational Research, 75*(3), 417–453.

Sirin, S. R., Bikmen, N., Mir, M., Zaal, M., Fine, M., & Katciaficas, D. (In press). Negotiating Muslim and American identities in post 9/11 New York: A mixed methods study. *Journal of Adolescence*.

Sirin, S. R., Diemer, M. A., Jackson, L. R., Gonsalves, L, & Howell A. (2004). Future aspirations of urban adolescents: A person-in-context model. *International Journal of Qualitative Studies in Education, 17*(3), 437–459.

Sirin, S. R., & Fahy, S. (2006). What do Muslims want? A voice from Britain. *Analyses of Social Issues and Public Policy 6*(1), 285–288.

Sirin, S. R., & Fine, M. (2007). Hyphenated selves: Muslim American youth negotiating identities on the fault lines of global conflict. *Applied Developmental Science, 11*(3), 1–13.

Sirin, S. R., & Rogers-Sirin, L. (2004). Exploring school engagement of middle-class African American adolescents. *Youth & Society, 35*(3), 293–340.

Sirin, S. R., & Rogers-Sirin, L. (2005). Components of school engagement among African American adolescents. *Applied Developmental Science, 9*(1), 5–13.

Smith, T. W. (2002). The Muslim population of the United States: The methodology of estimates. *Public Opinion Quarterly, 66*, 404–417.

Solis, J. (2003). Rethinking illegality as violence against, not by, Mexican immigrant children and youth. *Journal of Social Issues, 59*(1), 15–32.

Sreberny, A. (2002). Trauma talk. In B. Zelizer & S. Allan (eds.), *Journalism after September 11,* 220–234. London: Routledge.

Stockton, R. (1994). Ethnic archetypes and the Arab image. In E. McCarus (ed.), *The development of Arab American identity,* 119–154. Ann Arbor: University of Michigan Press.

Stoudt, B. G. (2006). You're either in or you're out: School violence, peer discipline, and the (re)production of hegemonic masculinity. *Men and Masculinities, 8*(3), 273–287.

Suad, J. (1999). Against the grain of the nation—The Arab. In M. Suleiman (ed.), *Issues in Arab America,* 257–271. Philadelphia: Temple University Press.

Suárez-Orozco, C. (2000). Identities under siege: Immigration stress and social mirroring among the children of immigrants. In A. Robben & M. Suárez-Orozco (eds.), *Cultures under siege: Social violence and trauma,* 194–226. Cambridge: Cambridge University Press.

Suárez-Orozco, C. (2004). Formulating identity in a globalized world. In M. M. Suárez- Orozco & D. B. Oin-Hilliard (eds.), *Globalization: Culture and education in the new millennium.* Berkeley: University of California Press.

Suárez-Orozco, C., & Oin-Hilliard, D. B. (eds.) (2004). *Globalization: Culture and education in the new millennium.* Berkeley: University of California Press.

Suárez-Orozco, C., & Qin, B. (2006). Gendered perspectives in psychology: Immigrant origin youth. *IMR, 40*(1), 165–198.

Suárez-Orozco, C., & Suárez-Orozco, M. M. (2001). *Children of immigration.* Cambridge, MA: Harvard University Press.

Swiney, C. F. (2006). Racial profiling of Arabs and Muslims in the US: Historical, empirical, and legal analysis applied to the war on terrorism. *Muslim World Journal of Human Rights, 3*(1), article 3. Available at http://www.bepress.com/mwjhr/vol3/iss1/art3.

Tatum, B. (1997). *Why are all the black kids sitting together in the cafeteria?* New York: Basic Books.

Tong, B. (2004). Race, culture and citizenship among Japanese American children and adolescents during the internment era. *Journal of American Ethnic History, 23*(2), 3–38.

Torre, M. E. (2005). The alchemy of integrated spaces: Youth participation in research collectives of difference. In L. Weis & M. Fine (eds.), *Beyond silenced voices,* 251–266. Albany: State University of New York Press.

Unger, J. B., Gallaher, P., Shakib, S., Ritt-Olson, A., Palmer, P. H., & Johnson, C. A. (2002). The AHIMSA acculturation scale: A new measure of acculturation for adolescents in a multicultural society. *Journal of Early Adolescence, 22*(3), 225–251.

U.S. Bureau of the Census. (2002). *March 2000 Current Population Survey*. Washington, DC: U.S. Bureau of the Census.

U.S. Bureau of the Census. (2003). *The Arab population 2000*. Washington, DC: U.S. Bureau of the Census.

Verkuyten, M. (2005). *The social psychology of ethnic identity*. Hove, UK: Psychology Press.

Verkuyten, M., & de Wolf, A. (2002). Being, feeling and doing: Discourses and ethnic self-definitions among minority group members. *Culture and Psychology, 8*(4), 371–399.

Volpp, L. (2002). The citizen and the terrorist. *UCLA Law Review, 49*, 1575–1600.

Waltzer, M. (1983). *Spheres of justice: A defense of pluralism and equality*. New York: Perseus Books.

Waters, M. (1990). *Ethnic options: Choosing identities in America*. Berkeley: University of California Press.

Waters, M. (1999). *Black identities: West Indian immigrant dreams and American realities*. Cambridge, MA: Harvard University Press.

Weis, L., & Fine, M. (2000). *Speed bumps: A student-friendly guide to qualitative research*. New York: Teachers College Press.

Wiley, S., Perkins, K., & Deaux, K. (2006). Through the looking glass: Ethnic and generational patterns of immigrant identity. Unpublished manuscript, City University of New York.

Wilkins, K., & Downing, J. (2002). Mediating terrorism: Text and protest in interpretations of The Siege. *Critical Studies in Media Communication, 19*(4), 419–437.

Wilkinson, S. (1999) Focus groups: A feminist method. *Psychology of Women Quarterly, 23*(2), 221–244.

Wilkinson, S., & Kitzinger, C. (eds.) (1995). *Representing the other*. London: Sage.

Wilkinson, S., & Kitzinger, C. (2000). Thinking differently about "thinking positive": A discursive approach to cancer patients' talk. *Social Science & Medicine, 50*(6), 797–811.

Williams, P. (1991). *The alchemy of race and rights*. Cambridge, MA: Harvard University Press.

Willis, P. (2002). Foot soldiers of modernity: The dialectics of cultural consumption and the 21st century school. In C. McCarthy et al. (eds.), *Race, representation and identity*, 461–479. New York: Routledge.

Wimmer, A., & Glick-Schiller, N. (2003). Methodological nationalism, the social sciences and the study of migration: An essay in historical epistemology. *International Migration Review, 37*(3), 576–610.

Wingfield, M., & Karaman, B. (1995). Arab stereotypes and American educators. *Social Studies and the Young Learner, 7*(4), 7–10.

Winnicott, D. W. (1989). The squiggle game and delayed reactions to loss. In D. W. Winnicott, *Psychoanalytic Explorations*. London: Karmac Press.

World Almanac and Book of Facts (2001). Mahwah, NJ: World Almanac Books.

Yuval-Davis, N. (1997). *Gender and nation*. London: Sage.

Yuval-Davis, N. (1999) The multi-layered citizen: Citizenship in the age of globalization. *International Feminist Journal of Politics, 1,* 119–136.

Zaal, M., Salah, T., & Fine, M. (2007). Weight of the hyphen. *Applied Developmental Science*.

Zhou, M. (1997). Growing up American: The challenge confronting immigrant children and children of immigrants. *Annual Review of Sociology, 23,* 63–95.

Zogby, J. (2004). Muslims in the American public square: Shifting political winds and fallout from 9/11, Afghanistan, and Iraq. News release and full report available online at http://www.projectmaps.com/AMP2004report.pdf.

Index

About the Authors

Selcuk Sirin is an assistant professor in the Department of Applied Psychology at New York University. He is the recipient of "Young Scholar Award" from the Foundation for Child Development for his research on immigrant children and Review of Research Award from the American Educational Research Association.

Michelle Fine is Distinguished Professor of Social Psychology, Women's Studies, and Urban Education at the CUNY Graduate Center. She also is the author of a long list of award-winning books in the fields of education and psychology, including *Framing Dropouts*, *Becoming Gentlemen* (with Lani Guinier and Jane Balin), and *Speedbumps: A Student Friendly Guide to Qualitative Research* and *The Unknown City*, both with Lois Weiss.

CPSIA information can be obtained
at www.ICGtesting.com
Printed in the USA
LVOW12s1456251117
557531LV00005B/488/P

9 780814 740408